Audio-Visual Education

AUDIO-VISUAL EDUCATION

Teaching Innovative Techniques

Janardan Prasad

M.A. (Philo., Socio), M.Ed., ND (Art), Dip. in Wd. Working
Former, Lecturer in Education (Art)
Central Institute of Education, Department of Education,
University of Delhi, Delhi.

KANISHKA PUBLISHERS, DISTRIBUTORS

NEW DELHI-110 002

KANISHKA PUBLISHERS, DISTRIBUTORS
4697/5-21A, Ansari Road, Daryaganj
New Delhi -110 002
Phones : 2327 0497, 2328 8285
Fax : 011-2328 8285
E-mail : kanishka_publishing@yahoo.co.in

Audio-Visual Education: Teaching Innovative Techniques
First Published 2005
Edition 2020

ISBN: 978-81-7391-771-X

PRINTED IN INDIA

Published by Madan Sachdeva for Kanishka Publishers, Distributors, 4697/5-21A, Ansari Road, Daryaganj, New Delhi-110 002, Typeset by Sunshine Graphics, Delhi, and Printed at Rajdhani Printers, Delhi.

Dedicated

to

Late Professor, J.R. Bimbrawh

Former Professor and Head of the Department of Mechanical Enginering, Delhi College of Engineering, Kashmiri Gate, Delhi, who very kindly inspired me to take up this innovative work.

Foreword

Audio-visual education had been recognised as an important input in the process of teaching-learning. Many a times children memorise without understanding the concepts. The reasons could be many, but are important reason documented is mere verbalisation on the part of teachers without proper use of a relevant teaching aid. Sometimes the teaching aids are used so indifferently that they don't help in concept clarification. Therefore, Audio-visual education as a separate paper or as a part of educational Technology is being taught in Teacher Education Departments and in Teachers training institutions.

This book "Audio-Visual Education: Teaching Innovative Techniques" which has a vide coverage of various aspects of the area will be an additional input for pre-service as well as in-service teachers in facilitating the learning process. I congratulate Shri Janardan Prasad, Former Lecturer, Department of Education, University of Delhi, who has been associated with the field of Audio-visual Education for a very long time for writing this book.

Professor Najma Siddiqui
Former Head and Dean
Department of Education,
Central Institute of Education
University of Delhi, Delhi

Preface

Sensory experiences are key to learning. This book has specially been prepared to meet the requirements of the school teachers and also trainee teachers of teachers' training institutes, pertaining to providing contrived sensory experiences to pupils through audio-visual aids during teaching.

Due to wide spread of formal education, teaching in schools is a dominant common feature these days. Parents send their children to schools with a hope that their children would learn and successfully pass out examinations conducted by the respective Education Boards, with a hope that they would further continue their further studies at the Universities for qualifying degrees required for employment.

Majority of the schools in the country are run by the state. A few schools are either run by private social organisations or by religious organisations. These schools also come virtually under the state control, as these are governed under state laws. In all these schools teacher-student ratio is unproportionate due to our demographic conditions. The school curriculum is loaded with many subjects. All students are required to study these subjects irrespective of their abilities and aptitudes towards all compulsory subjects. As such, individual differences among the students are ignored. All students are evaluated by the same yard-stick. The teachers are also required to teach the subjects and specific content to the students within a prescribed time limit without taking into consideration the acceptance by the students. The teacher has to take at least six periods a day out of eight periods in school timetable. In addition to this the teacher is required to take arrangement periods and to attend a lot of administrative work. Moreover, the society also expects the teacher to do all other jobs pertaining to inculcation of character building and enculturation which should begin and perpetuate at home, but the parents, in most cases, fail to accomplish this because of their pre-occupation on jobs.

Under such a situation the teaching becomes an extremely challenging job for the teacher. If the teacher does not employ some innovative techniques and methods of teaching, he or she cannot perform successfully. These innovative techniques which are nothing but are the use of audio-visual aids and follow-up actions. And education educed through these is generally termed as Audio-Visual Education.

Audio-Visual Education involves the use of innovative instructional devices for providing useful sensory experiences in the class from itself for catching students attention and motivating them to learn. Such instructional devices require the use of (1) graphic materials like pictures, illustrations, charts, maps, flashcards, chalk boards, etc., (2) three dimensional materials like, models, dioramas, x-ray and relief models, concerts objects, tools and specimens etc., (3) some projected aids like films, film strips, slides and transparencies etc., and (4) tours, excursions and puppets etc. All these instructional materials are very useful and advantageous in teaching. These make learning easy, reduce verbalism and pave the way for true education. The students do not depend upon mere information. They try to explore and learn themselves. Moreover, the teaching becomes a cooperative venture of the teacher and the taughts.

As such, to meet the increasing demand for education, the teaching in our schools requires a thorough overhauling and needs reformation. Use of audio-visual aids can help in this respect. There should be a sufficient orientation of audio-visual aids in teacher preparation, and thereafter in-service extensive encouragement for their use when the teacher takes up teaching in school. So, there should be a good reading material on audio-visual aids in school libraries which may further enlighten and encourage the teacher to make his teaching innovative by the use of audio-visual aids. Therefore, there should be good books on Audio-Visual Education.

In the opinion of the author, a very significant, relevant and useful information should be available in written form giving the genesis, development and benefits of the use of audio-visual aids in teaching. Yet, there are very few books on Audio-Visual Education which may enlighten our teachers about our educational epistemic ends. The books so far available mostly are contribution of foreign authors which do not sufficiently enlighten our teachers about our ideological and epistemological interpretations of education, as well as guide them how to prepare the visual aids out of our available resources. In this book an attempt has been made to bridge these gaps. I do hope that this material in the form of book would perhaps be more useful for the school teachers. The material given in this book needs further enrichment.

Finally, I would like to take the opportunity to thank all of my previous colleagues who encouraged and helped me. Prof. (Mrs.) N. Siddiqui, Prof. V.K. Sabharwal, Prof. R.P. Sharma, Prof (Mrs.) N. Panchapakeshan, Mr. S.P. Tyagi and Mr. C.K. Saluja helped and encouraged me to complete this work. Above all Prof. J.R. Bimbraw, very kindly first of all suggested me and inspired me to do this job. For the actual materialisation of this work, it was my son Prof. (Dr.) Satish C. Sharma, Department of Mechanical and Industrial Engineering, Indian Institute of Technology, Roorkee, my daughter-in-law Smt. Bimlesh and grand children Aakanksha and Anubhav who encouraged me to take up this work against any other hard work after my retirement which would not suit me. My thanks are due to the library staff of the Central Institute of Education, University of Delhi, as well as to the library staff of the Central Library, Institute of Technology, Roorkee (U.A.).

It is hoped that teachers and teacher educators will find this book useful. Critical comments and suggestions for improvement are always welcome for further enhancing the utility of the book.

Last but least, I would like to thank my wife for her patience and forbearance during the course of this work.

Janardan Prasad

Contents

Contents

1

Introduction

Teaching and Education are two sides of pedagogic coin. They both go in hand and glove together throughout the educational process. Still they are distinctively different. Teaching is not education, and Education can never be teaching. But what we notice that they are being considered as one and the same. So their functional properties are being confused. With the result their main functions, though these overlap, are misunderstood. Teaching is a means or a way to achieve the 'end' that is 'education'. Also, the process of teaching is not the sole way to achieve the 'end' that is education. It is one of the way. Better we apply the teaching methods supplemented by teaching aids rewarding will be the results.

The English word teaching (n) is the product of the Word 'Teach' (v) which is a derivation from the Latin Word 'Taecon', which means 'to tell', 'to make aware of', 'to inform', 'to instruct' or 'to pass on certain useful information' by an experienced and knowledgeable person to a semi-experienced, sometimes inexperienced sometimes, ignorant and an unknowledgeable person. The English word 'Education' is a derivation from the Latin words 'educatum', meaning to dig out and 'educare' meaning to bring out. Thus education is a process through which the latent potentialities of a person are derived, or raised and developed.

In our schools the so-called educating has totally been confused with the teaching or for passing on of information to students in order to get through in examinations for securing good percentage of marks. It is not rightly perceived correct perspective. Neither teaching of 3 R's nor passing on information for getting through in examination with high percentage of marks or with distinction can be true education. It is the development of the potentialities of the individual and his preparation for life. Good teaching can lead to both, higher academic achievements as well as to a balanced personality development, if the teacher proceeds having these twin pedagogic aims in mind. In our schools the teaching is done in a mechanical way aiming to mould all students in the same cast. Gurudev R.N. Tagore has rightly described our educational system as a mechanical process. He says that in our schools the students are taught subjects compulsorily, irrespective of their taste and individual differences, for passing out examinations. As such, our future guardians are prepared and produced in the manner the nuts and bolts are produced in a mechanical engineering unit, ignoring their capacities, needs, tastes and desires.

Mostly the teacher training institutions try to make the pupil teachers aware about this fact. But there are institutions also which produce the teachers on mass scale on ritual basis for mere certification only. Therefore, largely our teachers still follow the traditional conflict teaching model. They use generally telling and using information method which provides little incentive to the students for participation. Our teacher thinks as if he is more informed and knows better. Thus, very often he finds himself in a magiomanious state of mind. He does not realise that the students might also know something. His clientele is not ignorant as that of a medical man or of a legal man. As such, he does not apply didactic approach in teaching in which students become more active and contributive. This method allows a lot of freedom of expression to the students and a lot of elicitations becomes possible in the classroom. In didactic approach the teacher tries to involve the students in knowledge development by using certain innovative techniques and teaching aids which motivate the students to participate in the process of education enabling them to think reason and comprehend and finally learn as was done in India during Vedic and Brahmanic age under the Upanishadic method of education under *Guru-Shishya Parampara.*

So, the method of teaching should be so designed that the students may be allowed to emerge as thinkers, rationalisers, creators, inventors and actors. They should know how to live in the society, cohesively. Fellow feeling, cooperation, social integration and spirit of sharing should be infused in them. And this should be the prime aim of education. Since, education is only possible through good teaching, an appropriate approach to teaching should be adopted.

Now-a-days, there is a wave of instantivity in every sphere of life, and man has become a cog-pin of this instantivity. So he is missing his necessary social contacts too. This is because of the advancement of science and technology and consequent industrialisation, urbanisation and modernisation. These all resulted in ugly materialism which resulted in hedonistic life. The educational process has also been affected by this rat race of materialism. The materialism has resulted in hedonistic way of life which channelised the educational process on class lines. The entire educational process has witnessed a sea-change. The main necessary aspects such as cultural, sociological, economical, political and axiological, which are necessary for life, have receded to the background due to competitive temper of education. And teaching in schools and universities generally so designed that the students may come out in flying colours in their examinations.

Up to early twenties of twentieth century, the education was imparted by the teacher to the students teaching verbally in a face to face situation. The verbal mode of communication was one-way . The teacher was considered a man of knowledge, a man of character, devoted to his disciples and to teaching profession. One reason may be that teacher in these days had specificity, sincerity and devotion to his work. Also, there was the absence or minimum presence of material aspirations in human society. The teacher used to pass on information to the students what he had acquired from his teachers, books and by his efforts and own experience. Though, there were chances of reactions, counter-reactions and dialogues between the teacher and taught in the classroom situation, but by and large the students were passive listeners. As such, there was little scope for thinking, reasoning and comprehending for the students. Being mere listeners and receivers, under the traditional conflict model of teaching, the students used to be mere listeners and passive receivers. As such, they used to be mere crammers of books and not contributors. This kind of one-way system of teaching used to make the students introverts and non-expressive. There was also chances of misinformation too by the teacher. If the teacher did not know something in detail and he used to pass on what he knew, the students had hesitation to question the teacher because of his authority being considered as a knowledgeable person. On the other hand the teacher with the help of rode had an authority to crush the voice of the students.

As such, the rule of memorisation and mugging up had the precedence against comprehension and learning under the conflict model of teaching.

It would not be incorrect to recall that the formal education which was the result of industrial revolution was limited to very few in the beginning to very rich, rich or middle class people in the society who could afford to send their children to schools. The population of the world was not high as we witness these days. The spread of diseases like plague and cholera used to check the demographic growth in the past. So the school going population was not so high as it is in the present times. The number of the trained teaches was also not high. The problem of teaching was not so gigantic as we witness now-a-days.

The institution of the school which provides formal education was in limited shape in the past. There were religions schools, epistemic schools, sports schools and schools for laity in which the contact between the teacher and taughts was very intimate. In Indian Upanishadic method of teaching it was leased on *Guru-Shishya Parampara*. So the present system of formal education is not a match to the old system of education which was innovative in nature and rich in content, related to life. The aim of these old educational institutions was to educate youngs for life. The educational institutions used to establish a close rapport between the teacher and taughts. It was a kinship like strong relationship. The education imparted was not competitive and commercialised. The relation between the teacher and taughts was not routed through bureaucratic framework. In olden days the teachers and taughts had to live away from their homes in jungles in Gurukula Ashramas. Some of the famous Gurukulas of India were like Taxila, Kaushami, Ujjaini, Patliputra. Like was in the West there were academies. Platonic Academy in Greece was one such institution. In Muslim world there were such institutions at Cario, Gondeshpur and at Deoband at India. Some such institution like Gurukul Kangri, Haridwar, Darualum Deoband and Darualum Cario (Egypt) still exist. In these institutions the teachers and students still live under the same roof non-inclinatively. And aim of education in these institutions is, preparation for life through enculturation, inculcating social values, integration and cohesion. There was no room for competition and commercialisation. These institutions provided ample room for observation from the nature and experimentation.

Now the institution of school which is a place for formal education of the young has totally drifted from the path adopted by our old educational institutions. The present day school is basically a place where information is passed on generally for competitive purposes that is preparing for examinations and nothing else. The examination results are measure of standard and quality of school. There are numbers of schools which run on commercialised patterns. They have little to enculturate and more to acculturate. Generally all schools adopt the teaching patterns which congenial for passing out examinations rather than preparation for life.

The money making publishers in collaboration with school and university teachers add to this problem. They prepare *'Kunjies'* and guide books for helping the students in passing out examinations. This tendency relieves the teachers from proper teaching and boosts the 'no work culture'. These help books are treated as saviours by the students and their parents. The examination fever induces to many parents for arranging tuitions so that their wards may come out in flying colours in their examinations. Therefore, tutoring has become a lucrative business in teaching community. The teachers resort to this work due to economic hardship. In the present materialistic world, amazed and attracted by hedonistic glitter and luxurious life many teachers resort to do tuitions and sometimes to other money making activities.

Generally trained teachers teach in schools. Very often they resort to teaching on traditional teaching methods. Another factor which forces the teacher to use traditional methods is that the teacher has to pass on certain marked information to the students in a stipulated period of time. He has to cover the course to enable the students to pass examinations. As such the students remain mere listeners and receivers. They hardly react in the classroom teaching, because the process of reaction which allows elicitation is a time consuming factor, and the teacher cannot afford because of the coverage of the course. Therefore, the students are prepared in a mechanical way as nails and screws are produced by push, press and punch method in a mechanical nails and screws producing units. In many cases the students come out blank from the classrooms, as they do not grasp what is taught by the teachers. Because of dominance of verbal communication, they do not get a chance to visualise, experience understand, comprehend and learn the content what is being taught in school. As such, the psychosis of inferiority sets in their personality. They do not dare to express in the class. They remain withdrawn in the process of knowledge development. As such they do not get a chance to think, rationalise and learn. And the purpose of education is totally defeated.

This is because, either our schools are devoid of innovative pedagogic techniques or the teachers do not use such techniques for reason better known to them. One of the reasons may be that our school are ill equipped in this regard, and stress is merely laid on transmitting more information because of examination fever. Another reason might be the disinterest of the teacher in pedagogic innovative techniques. Reason may be, he is poorly paid, he does not get any incentive for hard work, which breeds no work culture. Nepotism and favouritism in teacher's recruitment which erodes merit may be another reason. When a teacher finds others doing work not sincerely he also does not find any point to take an initiative and use innovative techniques in teaching. So overall position is that teaching without use of certain pedagogic innovative techniques cannot be effective.

These problems cannot be discussed at length here. Efforts are, here, to present the educational innovative techniques or so to say educational teaching aids. This has been termed here as 'Eduinnovtech' which is generally called Educational Audio-Visual Aids or Educational Technology. These help in educating pupils through teaching.

Use of Audio-Visual Aids is very old. Its history can be traced to caveman, hunting man, sailors, explorers, early food gatherers, sea pirates, army generals and to social reformers. Extensive use of Audio-Visual Aids came into existence after the First World War first in army and thereafter in schools. The global war required big armies. The raising of armies in a short period involved recruitment of fighting forces as well as supporting hands, which entailed training of new recruits who were largely illiterates. The army operations required trained combatant. The army general chalked out a programme to train the raw hands through Audio-Visual symbols as it was quite impossible to train them verbally. Many charts and maps were prepared and used along with verbal communication to instruct the soldiers and supporting hands. Visual symbols were prepared and used for military armaments and their use. This training programme through visual aids proved useful. When the war was over it was thought why not these aids be used in schools?

Prior to this many thinkers like Comenius had advocated didactic approach in teaching by using concrete things, and in absence of concrete things their pictures or illustrations, when it is impossible to bring the actual things in the classroom. Many other thinkers suggested the use of some graphic aids for communication for educating people about some vexed sociological or religious problem. For instance, Martin Luther was the first person to suggest the use of empty walls, by colouring these walls with some dark pigment and write on these with white clay, for the promotion of Protestant Movement in Europe. This idea lead to the invention of chalk board (black board) which provided to be an effective communication tool for classroom teaching. Though chart was used earlier in many forms, but Captain Cook was the first person to think of the present pedagogic chart. He got the idea when he was serving in British Army in Australia and Africa. He was amazed by seeing the flora and fauna of these two continents. In the past Plato had suggested sense perception followed by comprehension for epistemic purposes. Aristotle suggested the study of matter for learning. Rene' Descartes, French Philosopher, believed that human beings are destined with innate ideas at the time of birth. These innate ideas can only be educed through thinking and reasoning. This theory of rationalism was repudiated by British Empiricist philosopher John Locke. He said that when the child is born, his brain is like a *Tabula Rasa* (an empty slate) and the child writes on this tabula rasa with is senses getting primary and secondary impressions. After John Locke many other thinkers like Pestalozzi, Froebel; Madam Montessori suggested the use of sense perception in pedagogy.

So right from the beginning there existed a strong case for the use of teaching aids. With the advancement of science and technology many new things for communications like radio, TV, VCR films, film strips etc., were invented. With the result use of soft and hardwares could be possible in education. Now the old concept of verbal teaching has altogether changed. To cope up with advance knowledge in many fields the use of Audio-Visual Aids has become necessary as an innovative technique. Their use is necessary because education is recovery of hidden potentialities of a person for which we need certain tools. The teacher will have to help the students in this recovery. Moreover, the clientele of the teacher are not ignorant clients like that patients of doctor, clients of a lawyer. The man is born with some latent faculties and potentialities this is why the student always is very eager to express and contribute in the classroom. These potentialities of the students are to be suitably and fully recovered by the teacher. And this recovery is education. Plato called the teacher a regent and helper for such a recovery. For such a recovery the teacher needs certain tools for application of some new innovative strategies and teaching techniques which may lead to real education. These tools are nothing but Audio-Visual Aids. Their proper timely use may be termed as Educational Technology.

Education is not information, it is much more. If the teacher merely informs the students he does not educate them. It is an established fact that education is recovery of what the students already have. This recovery is only possible by activating the students to think, reason and comprehend, and finally synthesise and learn. The teacher should use both verbal and non-verbal communication for this end. As such, teaching is a creativity like art activity and teacher is an artist. He has to work, the way the artist works while he completes a work of art. He thinks of new form for his composition. He completes his composition applying suitable material and skills and finally creating a virtual element in the work of Art. Like that, the teacher has to apply his voice with a suitable rhythm first while introducing the topic. Thereafter he will have to use some innovative techniques to motivate the children to respond and finally illicit knowledge from the students. Doing so, the teacher really educate the students. But majority of the teachers do inform the students, they do not educate them. This is not pedagogically sound. Without creating an atmosphere wherein thinking and reasoning is not evoked the education is not possible. Therefore, the emphasis should be laid that, there does not remain no need of '*Kunjies*', 'guide books', 'guess books' and 'guess question papers'. The use of Audio-Visual Aids will minimise the presence of these. If the students learn to know themselves, in the long run they will be thinkers, creators and inventors and not passive followers.

Therefore, it is necessary that the education should be based on sense perception and experience. The use of Audio-Visual Aids at all levels, right from kindergarten and nursery to school and university level, is very beneficial, so is necessary.

2

Genesis of Education and Audio-Visual Education

If we go through the etymology of education we find that the English word 'Education' is a derivation from the Latin and Greek Words 'Educate' and 'Educatum' meaning 'out', 'to lead out', 'to dig out', 'the art of leading out', 'to help in coming up', 'to bring up', 'to raise'. Likewise, Sanskrit word 'Vidya' has come out from the root 'Vidh' which means raising (ubharna). Also, the Arabic word Tallim = Ta + ilim means raising for knowledge.

But the question arises, what is to be brought out, dig out, or raised and from where? There are mythological descriptions and interpretations in our Hindu scriptures and Greek literature. Aryans believed that the soul of the person is immortal. It does not die when the physical person dies. Lord Krishna gave sermons to Arjuna at the first day of battle Mahabharata at Kurukshetra. In Sankhya-yoga Darshan it is stated that every soul, which is embodied in a physical person is part of bigger Soul. The bigger Soul is what we call 'Paramatma' and the individual soul which is embodied in every physical man is called 'atma'. This theory of 'Duality of soul' presupposes that 'atma' is part of 'Paramatma'. Since 'Paramatma' is non-perishable, 'atma' being part of it, it also does not die. Atma or individual soul when finds the physical body, its house, or garb, unsuitable for its use it leaves the body—bodies dies and atma enters into another body. Likewise, in Naya-Veshiska, it has been stated that it is the soul which enables the man to learn. When the child is born, and the mother offers him/her, her breast to suck, the child already knows how to suck, from his/her previous experience of sucking. It means the soul accumulates the earlier acquired experiences and recieves the experiences at a later stage. So it can be inferred, what we remember, we remembers, because of soul's previously acquired experiences. As such, all acts of our learning and doing are done with monitoring of our soul. Similarly, all other Indian schools of thought, be theistic or atheistic except *carvac* (चारवाक) believed in this epistemic function of the soul.

Also Greeks, like Indians, believed that the soul of a person, while it is embodied, acquires and accumulates experiences and stores these experiences with it, till it remains in the physical body. According to these experiences the soul of the person directs the physical body – the house or apron of the soul, to act and function in particular way. The body follows the dictates or commands of the soul. The soul is immortal and physical body is mortal. When the body goes old and the soul finds it unworthy for living, the soul renounces it. It changes it in the manner we change our clothes on getting old and torn out. So the soul leaves the body and till it gets another body to reside, it goes to Hades (*Samsan*) and lives there without body till it transmigrates to another body. When the soul re-embody or so to say it comes to another body through the process of rebirth, it comes to the body with all of its earlier acquired and accumulated experiences and knowledge. According to Greek thinkers recovery of these souls acquired experiences and knowledge and subsequent supplementing these experiences is a process called 'Education'.

It is also believed that Greeks came to know about the immortality of the soul from Indians. A mythologist (exact name not known) may be it be a truth or a mere hunch or pure imagination, come to India during the rule of Greek King Perciles (543-500 BC). The Spartans used to create troubles for the Greeks, as these days we are witnessing troubles from across the border for us. Ultimately the war erupted between Greeks and the Spartans. This war continued for about 30 years. Perciles made military service compulsory for all able bodied Greek citizens. A decree was passed by the Perciles government in this regard. And under this conscription scheme all able bodied persons above the age of 18 up to 40 were required to go to war front. Even the ill persons like Theatetus (a mathematician like late Ramanujan) were not spared.

There existed individual differences in all times. Some Greeks willingly liked to fight, some did not. Those who did not dare to go war front tried to escape. There was one who evaded military duties, escaped and fled to Egypt. There is not certainty about his name, but it is sure, he was a speculative thinker. He stayed for few days in Egypt. He wanted to know about the soul of the person. Having got no satisfactory answer from Egyptians about the nature of the soul, he went to Mesopotamia (the present Iraq). He could not know anything there also. From Mesopotamia he crossed to Aryna (present Iran). Then Iran was an Aryan country which had close links with India. Then Greek Sophist came to know the duality of the soul. The Iranians advised him to go to India (Bharat) for further knowledge. From Iran he came to India via Gondeshpur, (present Kandhara) Gandhara present Afghanistan. Entering India, he came to know about Taxila (now in Pakistan) a renowned seat of learning of Hindu thought. There he stayed for 8 years. He studied all Hindu scriptures that is Vedas, Upanishads, Arynakas, Brahmas, Ramayana, Mahabharata and Shrimad Bhagwad Gita. He participated in all Gurukulas activities at Taxila and came to know about the universality of soul as the various Indian philosophical school adhere to. According to Indians, the soul is permanent, invisible, imperishable, undestroyable and is part of the Permanent Soul which we call 'Paramatma'. The individual souls are part of the bigger soul 'Paramatma' like parts of a whole. The Prime Soul is present in all bodies as representative of Paramatma that is God. The individual souls takes work from the individual bodies. If the body does some wrong things or acts, he/she has to bear the brunt according to his/her acts (Karmas).

After staying at Taxila for 8 years the Greek Sophist went back to his war torn country and spread the message that the soul is immortal and does not die. It cannot be killed, burnt or destroyed. Therefore, there is no need to fear the war. In case the Greeks die at war front only their bodies would die since soul never dies, it would not die. If they fight the enemy and die at war front they would be rewarded by the God. The Greeks fought bravely the Spartans, they could not only win but they did stopped the Spartans to control and govern them and eliminated them.

The message was picked up by other Greek thinkers. They started thinking why soul does not die and is immortal. Socrates was an original thinker and philosopher. He used to think, reason, speculate and discuss all ontological, axiological and sociological problems with his disciples in the street corners. He was not allowed to discuss such problems in his house as his wife

Xanthippe was a strict lady. She did like the presence of any outsider in her house. She used to pour cold water over the outsider and be angry on him if he dare to enter her house. Plato, Isocrates and Crito were his favourite disciples. Socrates was keen to know about the concept of 'Immortality of Soul' so be and his disciples discussed the ontological aspects related to soul in the street corners.

Indians merely said that the soul is immortal. It cannot be destroyed or buried. But no concrete proof about the immortality of soul is available in Indian scriptures. And no further concrete proof about it has been advanced by later Indian seers. The Greeks were eager to know why the soul does not die along with the human body? Socrates discussed the problem at length with his disciples and came to believe that the human soul actually is immortal. Later on his disciple Plato after the death of his teacher Socrates compiled his dialogues with his disciples. These dialogues covered all problem relating to truth, beauty, justice, teleology, ontology, epistemology and axiology. The dialogue which deals with concepts of immortality of soul and education are Phaedo, Meno and Republic. In Phaedo, the concept of immortality of soul was discussed at length and three proofs were advanced in favour of the immortality of the soul. These are (1) the law of contrariness, (2) the law of forms, and (3) the law of reminiscence.

1. LAW OF CONTRARINESS

Everything in this world comes and goes. One who was born and brought up will positively die. Likewise, daily we have a day which is taken over by night positively and night is surely followed by a day again. All living beings, plants and trees and, flora and fauna in this world come and go. The life of a person comes and goes. There is continuous life circle of such happenings. Therefore soul is immortal it comes, goes and comes back again in body.

2 LAW OF FORMS

Since everything in this world is perishable and temporary. This temporariness has a permanent image or form elsewhere. All things in this world are illusory. This Greek idea of illusoriness and permanentness is analogous to the Indian concept of maya or physical person and metaphysical person or *atma* or Paramatma. The physical things which exist in time and space all are temporary and the element which governs and keeps these things in existence is permanent. It is nothing but soul. This idea is very close and analogous to the Indian concept of duality of soul, as given in Sankhya-Yoga.

3. LAW OF REMINISCENCE

We remember many things. How do we remember? What is the power which makes us to remember. It is the soul, since it does not die, and remembers past events. This idea of Greeks is also analogous to the idea of Naya-Visheska regarding the reminiscence of child from the ex-ultra wail. Therefore, it is nothing but soul which enables man to remember. It is permanent and immortal.

In Indian thought, Naya-Visheska advanced a more convincing argument in this regard. It says that we only remember till we are alive. What we remember is what we have experienced through our sense perceptions. We perceive through our body parts that is sense organs – ear, nose, touch, taste and smell. But the moment the human body dies, the sense organism do not remember what was experienced. Then what is force behind remembering? It is nothing but human soul. Till the soul exists in the body, the physical person is alive and human body can remember. So the process of remembering is an act of the soul and not of body. And taking out the reminiscence is nothing but education. Thus the process of education starts with the existence of our soul. Therefore, human soul is the main source of education.

Various thinkers have opined about education on these lines, though they do not attribute creditability to the soul for all of our education. A few quotations are given below:

> "Education is a training which leads you to hate what you ought to hate" and "love what you ought to love". — *Plato*

> "Education is the creation of sound mind in a sound body". — *Aristotle*

> "Education is defined as a harmonious and progressive development of man's innate powers". — *Pestalozzi*

> "Education is defined as a process of development which consists of the passage of human being from infancy to maturity, the process by which he adapts himself gradually in various ways to his physical, social and spiritual environment".
>
> — *T. Raymont*

> "Education does not mean teaching people to know what they do not know, it means them to behave as they do not behave".
>
> — *John Ruskin*

> "Education is manifestation of perfection what is already in man".
>
> — *Swami Vivekananda*

> "By education I mean an all-round drawing out of the best in child and man—body, mind and spirit. Literacy itself is no education".
>
> — *M.K. Gandhi*

We can conclude that education is drawing out what is already in man—his potentialities, capacities, diligence and good behaviour. Similar meaning of education, these days, identifies it with the process formal instruction or training that goes on in an institution of learning that is a school or college. This statement is also partially true. But the education is a wider term. It starts from the birth when mother offers the child to suck her breasts. So home is the first institution of education. Secondly the community also plays a vital role in this regard. The process of education is a deliberate attempt to raise the capabilities of the child which are already with him. Through a planned and deliberate attempt, these capabilities are raised and fashioned by giving the children direction to visualise and experience things and learn himself. Since every child and adult have been endowed with special faculties and potentialities by the nature, the development of these facilities and potentialities is nothing but education. It is, therefore, necessary to adopt measures in teaching to develop these facilities. And use of innovative techniques, which are nothing but teaching aids, becomes necessary in this pursuit.

3

Audio-Visual Aids in Education

'What sculpture is to a block of marble, Education to the soul".
— *Addison*

Education is a recovery and reformation. It is necessary for the refinement of soul. While educating the children their hidden capabilities and capacities are to be raised. As such there should be complete freedom for the children during the course of their education, so as to enable them to prove their dedication and erudition. The students at school should be placed in such a situation which may help to prepare them to create situations themselves to enquire, find out and learn. For an enquiry, thinking is essential Thinking leads to reasoning. Reasoning leads to dialectics, which leads to analysis. For an analysis thesis, anti-thesis and synthesis are necessary. Such a situation can only create a learning atmosphere and climate. Therefore, it is essential that educative system at home, in school and in university needs to be improved. At home the parents should create a congenial atmosphere. This can only be possible if mother is educated. At school the educational system should be so devised that it is based on perception and activities which may revitalise thinking and reasoning. At university the students should be encouraged to self-learning and enquiry.

Teaching should be designed for education, so it should not be primarily informative. Rather it should be didactic. Five things are essential for such a teaching: (*a*) motivation of the students, (*b*) their active involvement through perception and activities relating to the subject the students are intending to learn, (*c*) the mode of presentation should be based on healthy teacher-students interaction and it should be elicitation orientated, (*d*) the students should not be passive listeners and they should also be contributors and helpers in the knowledge development and (*e*) and finally there should exist a healthy system of feedback. Therefore, it is essential that the mode of presentation in the classroom should always be based on bi-polar communication system. Care should be taken that system of presentation and communication should be so designed and executed that no deserving candidate is denied an opportunity to participate and contribute in the knowledge development. Such an education will provide opportunity to the students for learning and will provide an atmosphere for their ego satisfaction. When a child is given opportunity to speak and contribute something during the lesson development in the classroom during teaching he is satisfied. He/she is enthralled with a joy and is overwhelmed about his/her achievement.

Such an education which is deduced through elicitations is going to be a recovery and real education. For a recovery or digging out we use certain tools, skills and tactics. Since education is a recovery it becomes imperative to use certain tools and innovative teaching techniques for education too. What are these tools and techniques? These are nothing but audio-visual aids and their application for education. Etymologically audio-visual education means education we get with the help of hearing and seeing. In the present educational world application of these aids and thoughtful planning and educational strategies for their application are also termed as 'Educational Technology'. Audio-Visual media and material have to play a vivid and vital role in the classroom teaching. Audio-Visual material and techniques provide the fundamental means of organising and revitalising the curriculum. As such, audio-visual aids open the gates of learning, and learning opens the gates of achievement in life. Without hearing and seeing we cannot know. So, for education, in teaching both telling and showing are essential.

Education is a two-way process. It goes on throughout the life of a person. Teaching should take this fact into account. So, in schools teaching strategies should be so planned for proper education, that the teacher may create an atmosphere of active participation for the students, and congenial rapport between the teacher and taughts. Since teaching is done for educating younger generation, who are not aware about many things, one of the aims of good education should be to design teaching which could allow and help the students how to learn themselves. In other words teaching strategies should lead the students to self-learning. Such a teaching can only lead to education. Audio-Visual aids in teaching play an important role in achieving this end. So the teaching can really be improved by use of such material because these can help make the learning experiences memorable. Many teaching problems can be solved by use of Audio-Visual aids in teaching. Improved strategies and skills entailing the use of teaching aids and teaching machines offer great opportunities for improving learning capacities of the students. Use of Audio-Visual Aids helps the learners to experience and concretise certain facts and develop concepts of their own, thus ultimately helping the students to comprehend and learn. The process of building concepts begins the moment student starts experiencing and learning. As the child starts applying these experiences and thereby drawing conclusions he/she emerges to face the new situations. The necessity is the mother of invention. Activity centred education always leads to creative, thinking, reasoning and creative acting. This always enlarges the scope for comprehension and learning. And use of Audio-Visual Aids always entails activity for the teacher as well as for the students (taughts). This provides an ample opportunity for the teacher to establish rapport with the students.

In fact all kinds of teaching involves the communication of ideas through senses, either orally—through medium of speech or by showing or by use of written words or printed material or by concrete three dimensional objects. Because through vision or visibility we understand better. Our sense organs are our gateway of all knowledge. All our sense organs help in understanding the environment around us. Hearing and seeing are most important in this respect. We know, comprehend and learn by hearing and seeing quickly. There is a Chinese adage that "what we hear we forget and what we see we remember". Both hearing about many things and seeing are done in the classroom teaching. Hearing provides only information whereas showing provides an opportunity to visualise and comprehend, to pupils. To meet the shortcomings of hearing through telling we have to look to some alternatives. So we prepare and use Audio-Visual Aids to meet this situation. There are many things which cannot be brought physically in the classroom. Suppose we want to make aware our students about South Indian temples, we cannot bring the

Rameshwaram or Madurai temples or Tanjore temples in the classroom. We are not giants like Hanuman who had picked up a hill, which had 'Sanjeevini Booti' for the cure of Lakshmana, to Sri Lanka. We can show such things through their republicas or there dimensional models or pictures in the classroom. The children learn best when they are virtual visualisers and actors in the process of experience. In actual experience, they see things themselves directly in their actual form and learn about these things directly. No doubt, it is not possible to provide concrete things or their republicas in the real and actual form in the classroom situation to make learning easier, quicker, impressive and effective. But we can do so, by substituting the concrete things by Audio-Visual Aids and improve the learning situations, stimulating by posing or showing these aids as real as possible making them stimulating, innovative and interesting. These provide us knowledge through our sense organs of learning and seeing, smelling and touching. All these play an important role in the acquisition of knowledge.

Audio-Visual Aids and their devices, which present units of knowledge through auditory and visual stimuli help in learning. These are the devices to concretise the knowledge to be presented in the classroom. These help making learning experiences appear as real and true as it ought to be. They help to correlate and coordinate accurate concepts and, draw interpretations and appreciations and, conclusions by themselves. Students are encouraged to draw inferences themselves. The audio-visual aids enable the teacher to make learning more concrete, effective, integrated, interesting, interpretive, inspirational, meaningful and more vivid. These help in establishing and completing the triangular process of learning that is motivation, stimulation and comprehension. Use of audio-visual aids in teaching further helps clearing channel between the learner and the things that are worth learning. The basic assumption underlying the use of Audio-Visual aids in education is that the genesis of all learning are our senses supplemented by continuous acquisition of experiences. Therefore, the teacher should always show as well as tell the students simultaneously. Senses provide significant gains in informational learning too. It boosts retention, imagination, recall, thinking, reasoning, interest, imagination followed by creative activity. Audio-Visual aids lead to better assimilation, personal growth and development. The audio-visual aids are proper stimuli for comprehension and learning involving the questions, 'why', 'when', 'which', 'what', and 'where'.

Education is a debt from older generation to future generation. The teacher being a member of older generation should repay the debt nicely to future generation by using better teaching methods supplemented with better teaching aids in order to effect correct education. The use of audio-visual aids in teaching can help the teacher in repaying this debt to younger generation. The use of audio-visual aids can be beneficial to the teacher in other ways also. Because of the demographic explosion in the world, especially in the third world countries, the student population in schools has gone out of proportion. It is, believed that India's population in Ashoka's period was about one crore only. Then India's boundaries were spread in far-flung areas including Afghanistan. In Akbar's period India's population was nearly 21 crores. India's boundaries in his lines were spread to distant areas. At the time of partition, the population of Indian sub-continent was less than 40 crores. Indian population was about little over thirty crores. Now the population of India has touched 103 crores 62 lacs (April 2001) mark. We are increasing like fungus grass. In 1947, at the time of partition, the population of Delhi city was little over 5 lacs. Now, today it is more than 1 crore 53 lacs. In 1947, Delhi had only about a dozen High Schools. Out of these three or four were Government run High Schools. And now number of schools in Delhi runs into thousands, say to say unaccountable. Gone are the days when education was the privilege of only few and as such the classes in the schools were half empty. Now the schools are over crowded with pupils. In school there are many section of one class. And the teaching is carried on differentiation basis. The principal of the school allots certain topics to certain teacher according to their proficiency. This is done hoping better results in annual examinations. So the teaching is done on job basis on production lines, as it is done in factories. If a teacher is found to competent to teach a particular topic or topics, he or she will be assigned to teach the specified topic of the subject throughout the session, and most probably after the current in the ensuing session or in coming years too. Many schools have seven or eight sections of one class. Seven or eight teachers are not employed to teach these sections; less teachers are employed and teaching is done on 'solo-job performance basis'. In such a case the teachers are generally over-burdened. Because of the continuous repetition of the same content again and again the teachers get bored and their creative ability in teaching is generally got diminished. Teaching several sections again and again makes the presentation blurred and virtually raises the chances of something missing, as same kind of graphic work on chalk board is not possible. So, there is likelihood of discrimination to students during the course of teaching. This kind of situation can be avoided and improved by using teaching aids in teaching. If the teachers carry on their teaching as per lesson plan and use appropriate Audio-Visual Aids and use a deductive methodology, this can be moral booster to the teacher. He/she be able to facilitate the pupils to learn quickly as the students will be motivated to learn.

Our present teacher is required to teach six out of eight periods of the school timetable per day. In addition to, when some teachers go on leave, their teaching load is also divided amongst other teachers whether they have proficiency in the subject or not. As such, the average school teacher may be required to take seven periods out of eight periods per day. In such a situation the teachers in schools get extremely exhausted and tired. Mostly in schools, the verbal communication is a common feature. The teachers after communicating verbally in first two or three periods get tired. If the teacher does not contain his verbal communication right from the first period, he/she cannot carry on teaching up to the last period. There are chances of getting her/him tired and exhausted. To meet this situation the teacher should minimise rather replace telling by showing and, making the students speak themselves. Though total verbal avoidance is not possible. But showing in teaching should get more time. This will help the teacher in saving, rather conserving his energy. It will provide more initiatives for the teacher. This will establish a closer rapport between the teacher and taughts. This will give chance to the students to speak, express and interact with the teacher and other students. This will help in the personality development of the students. They will develop a capacity to express without hesitation which will help them in their later life to express without fear and hesitation. So-called public schools try to generate this kind of atmosphere, therefore, these schools are considered better than Government or aidded schools. In younger or adolescence age, if the children get a chance to contribute, they get immense pleasure out of their achievement. These help them in their development of personality. One of the most important advantages for the teacher is, that through the use of Audio-Visual aids in teaching he/she can prove his/her specificity and sincerity as well as develop deep rapport with the students which is necessary not only for good teaching and education but for healthy socialisation and sociability of students. Rapport can be established by involving the students in use as well as handling and making of Audio-Visual aids in teaching. The students take up new work willingly and enthusiastically. Their involvement in the use of Audio-Visual aids will generate working habits in them. If the student adopt working habits in life they shall be able to meet the challenges of life boldly. As a matter of development of work habits is the need of the day, as white collar culture has badly eroded it and no work culture in our society has taken deep roots.

One of the most important impact of the use of Audio-Visual aids in teaching is that, it helps in establishing normalcy and discipline in the classroom. Generally when teaching is done through telling the students gets bored. As many of them are bright and because of their family background, they have assess to knowledge when they do not get chance to contribute and express in the classroom, they get bored. They start whispering. Whispering is the main source of noise and indiscipline in the classroom. When the interests of the students are continuously ignored and overlooked by the teacher in the classroom it takes a rowdy shape creating indiscipline as teasing of shy students, clinching at the feet of student sitting on nearby seat, peeping through window while the teacher is teaching, nasty talking during course of lesson development and even hooting at the teacher. Many teachers use the rods to curb such an ugly situation, which does not give good results as coercion is no answer to indiscipline in the classroom. A teacher can only control the class if he is proficient in content and efficient in communication. Also, he/she has an urge to upsurge to his proficiency. Tagore rightly described, "a true teacher is one who is always burning like a lamp". Besides, a teacher should be sincere to his students. Only the use of rod cannot succeed in bringing the class under control. Only the timely use of Audio-Visual aids in teaching can be beneficial and helpful in establishing discipline in the classroom.

All kinds of teaching can be greatly improved by the use of Audio-Visual aids because they help in achieving multiple educational results. Main merits of use of Audio-Visual aids are:

MOTIVATION

While teaching it is necessary to motivate all students in the classroom. The present day classrooms are over crowded. In many cases, the number of the students go up to seventy. There can be many reason for this as over population, political pressure etc. The students have individual differences too. If they are represented graphically, they show a bell shaped curve. Many of them are exceptionally intelligent, a few are intelligent, and the rest are average or below average. Many of them remain themselves withdrawn during the course of lesson development. While a few are very enthusiastic and take keen interest in classroom teaching and are eager to contribute in the knowledge development. Even though they all are supposed to gain equally and pass the same examination. Therefore, there is a dire necessity to motivate the students to learn through participation. Audio-Visual aids are important to motivate the students.

REALITY

The students want to know the reality about which they are being taught. If the reality is not presented in the classroom there will not be true learning. The reality about the content which is going to be taught in the classroom can be presented in the classroom by using Audio-visual aids which are pictures, charts, maps and models etc. Linking teaching with these can bring reality in the classroom.

CONCEPT FORMATION

Thinking and reasoning are core of concept formation. The use of Audio-Visual aids by minimising verbalism and invoking thinking and reasoning through elicitations can lead to concept formation. This also helps in comprehending concepts.

INTEREST

The Audio-Visual Aids when systematically and timely used cater the high degree of interest in the students, as they are always interested in things which they can see, hear about, touch, taste and smell themselves. Interest always motivates the students to plan, make do and try to fabricate themselves.

DEVELOPMENTAL LEARNING

The learning process should always be developmental. The students cannot grasp everything at one time. They learn bit by bit. And sometimes they learn by their mistakes. The use of Audio-Visual aids in teaching provides the necessary basis for developmental learning and, hence make the learning more permanent.

REALITY OF EXPERIENCE

The use of Audio-Visual aids in teaching offers a reality of experience to the students in the classroom which stimulates self-activity on the part of students. Self-activity generates self-confidence in them.

CONTINUITY OF THOUGHT

Long long back Chinese philosopher Confucius said "Education without thinking is a labour lost". Rene' Descartes a French Philosopher said that he existed because of thinking (Cogito ergo sum). If the teaching does not invoke thinking in students it is not only a labour lost or waste but harmful. Because teaching is based on mere verbalism leaves the students mere listeners and passive acceptors. They do not learn and remain mere listeners and receivers. They can never be creators or inventors. Also the process of education is related to the process of reminiscence. Reminiscence is said to be the function of soul. Only the process of thinking can invoke and bring out reminiscence which is really the process of education. The use of Audio-Visual aids in teaching can achieve to this end. Their use develop a continuity of thought in students which is necessary for real education.

RETENTION

The use of Audio-Visual aids contributes to the permanent retention what has been communicated to the students in the classroom. Audio-visual aids add to the process of retentivity as they stimulate the maximum response of the whole organism of the students to the situation in which the teaching is done and learning takes place.

...ORMATION OF IMAGES

The Audio-Visual aids while properly used in teaching help in making and formation of right usages of things in minds of the students. So this process helps in comprehension and learning.

EXPERIENCE

The use of Audio-Visual Aids provides avenues of gaining experiences which are not easily gained by mere verbal communication and any sort of communication like heaping, crying and even gestures. The use of Audio-visual aids in teaching can give sensuous experience which can contribute to imaginative efficiency, depth, variety and virtual learning.

INTEREST AND ATTENTION

The use of Audio-Visual aids in teaching catches the attention of the students and generates interest in them for knowing more and, which is essential for learning. The audio-visual aids further add to information given by the teacher, motivate the students to think and act and stimulate their overall mental as well as physical activity.

ECONOMY OF TIME

A thing which can be explained in so many words can be easily communicated and grasped by a picture of a thing. There are various types of parrots in a Zoo. Suppose a teacher visits alone at Zoo at his own interest and sees the various parrots of various geographical regions and then he learn about various categories of the parrots. Next day if wants to let his students know about the variety of parrots, it would be very difficult for him to communicate. It would be very difficult for him to make the aware about the distinctive difference in the categories of the parrots. In case the teacher has camera and takes photographs of the parrots he will quickly communicate to his students about the variety of parrots. The children will also grasp about the parrots. Some one has correctly said that a pictures saves one thousand words. As such the use of Audio-Visual aids saves a lot of teacher's as well as students time. Now, there are many machines like overhead projector, film projector, film strip projector which economise the teaches time as well as energy. The use of Audio-Visual Aids is essential in a situation when the teacher is performing solo-proficiency job of teaching the same topic in many sections. For example, black board work executed on a transparency can be used again and again on overhead projector for each and every section. This will enable the teacher present the content equitably in all section within prescribed limited time.

OTHER ADVANTAGES

As such, the use of Audio-Visual aids has multiple advantages both for the teacher and taughts, as these aids give vividness to the learning situations by providing clarity, correctness of abstract ideas, reducing verbalism, providing variety and invoking thinking. The use of Audio-Visual aids in teaching gives a chance to the students to use their sense organs, particularly eyes, ears and often use of hands while learning. This makes the learning lasting.

NEED IN SCHOOLS

The basic necessity in Indian school is to provide such teaching methods which make possible 'per se' in the classroom. So that atmosphere of self-acquisition of knowledge could be possible for the students. Self-acquiring of knowledge will prepare them to be comprehenders and not mere listeners. The habit of self-acquiring of knowledge is also necessary in view of the fact that the education is self-recovery and not a crate of information. This objective can be achieved if teaching is basically done on 'per. se.' (perception) principles. Though, this fact cannot also denied that verbalism, which is one of best gifts to man by nature cannot be scrapped from the teaching process. Both telling and showing should go hand in hand together simultaneously.

Also, the present approach to teaching that is preparation for examination alone needs an examination. In the present world of science and technology examination system is also a must. But for the preparation of examination the teaching should be so designed that the students may not run after '*Kunjis*' and 'guess papers'.

They should be prepared for self-study, self-knowledge and learning. The students should be prepared to critically examine the information given by the teacher. This can only done, if teaching is done scientifically. The different subjects should be taught through different methodologies followed by appropriate use of teaching aids and machines. In teacher preparation this aspect should be given due weightage. Teacher preparation is being commercialised through correspondence courses. There should be a check on this tendency. And also the established teachers' institutions should be strengthened. Now the National Council for Teacher Education is looking to this aspect.

HISTORY

If we analyse the use of Audio-Visual aids in learning through out the ages, we find that the man has ever been learning through his sense perception from the beginning, so to say, from the dawn of the society. He has been passing on his acquired experiences to younger generation through Audio-Visual aids. When language was not developed and the man was on the spree of hunting for food to satisfy his appetite, he used to chase wild animals. For this feet, he had to proceed for the chase along his group members. They had to run in jungles. The man used to place stones or other symbols on the path of the chase so that the group members may reach the desired destination. Later on when man shifted from pasture age to agriculture, he depicted his experiences through crude, cave paintings. A few of such cave paintings are still in existence in the world. Hooting by man, like Chimpanzees, in early period was the sole source of human language development. From the beginning hearing, seeing and memorising have been the main sources of education. Learning through actual living, and its imitation, in the family have also been source of education. Immediate contacts with the environment outside the family, are also based on our body audio-visual organs which are own actual source of learning and education. Our other sources of learning are based on one personal contacts in the community with our own peer group and with elders, which is based on our senses. If we peep into the history the man has been using personal audio-visual equipment for learning since the dawn of the society. As man is a thinking animal he always been contemplating to harness the nature for his own benefit and has been thinking and acting to achieve this end. Heiroglyphysics, development of language, writing and writing material like papers, scroll writing, bhoj patra, (भोजपत्र) paper, slate, writing on sand and mud tablets, wall painting, statue making, idol making for temples, sculptures, miniature paintings, temple paintings and temples wall sculpture depicting particular social milieus, black board writing and finally printing are gifts of human mind. These helped in human communication and learning. With the development of science and technology, there has been a revolution in the field of audio-visual aids material. And with its use the man is nearer to he reality and is able to learn quickly and quite effectively.

Man has been effectively using such aids in search of new areas of his interest and benefit. Columbus, Vasco-De-Gama and many other travellers like Fian Shiang used maps, compass and charts for their journeys. Until the beginning of 20th century the use of Audio-Visual aids in western schools was minimum. Though in ancient India the source of education was based on senses. Under the Guru-Shishya Parampara the chatras (students) used to reside in the vicinity of Jungles in Gurukulas. There, in the Gurukulas, there was direct touch with the nature. The pupils had ample chance of interaction with the fellow pupils. They had vast spectrum of nature to observe. The Guru-Shishya had vad-vivad (discussion) on philosophical issues on certain days. Those who did not have opportunity to join Gurukulas and were required to learn and adopt family profession to learn through sense perception, observation, imitation and experience. A son of a carpenter used to visualise a large spectrum of raw-material, such as different kinds of woods and metal fixers and a large variety of tools from morning till evening. Likewise in many other vocations senses played a vital role and instructions were minimum content and were only as guiding steps for learning.

When the First World War broke out in 1914, majority of the masses were recruited by waring groups in their armed forces. The training of these illiterate youths in handling armaments and weaponry at the war front was a tedious job. Ultimately these illiterate personnel were trained through graphic visual symbols. Charts, maps and models were largely used. The same thing happened when second world war broke out in 1939 and continued up to 1945; and similar approach was adopted for training the illiterate armed personnel. Up to this time the use of Audio-Visual aids was minimal in school. Only the chalk board (so-called black board) was universally used. In other words the teaching was done by the teacher in monopole way. The verbal communication had a dominant place in teaching. The teacher was teller or rather informer and the students were listeners and passive receivers.

In educational world it was thought that if graphic symbols when used in the army to educate illiterate soldiers proved successful, why these cannot be used in teaching. So the use of Audio-Visual aids started by selected few schools in Europe and America first. Later on it spread in the third world also.

As the time passed on the use of Audio-Visual aids became popular and finally it became a common feature. With the passage of time and with development of science and technology there has been a tremendous progress in field of communication. Radio, TV, telephone were invented and consequently used for reinforcement of the spoken words with the concrete images. As such many audio-visual techniques were developed for the improvement of teaching methods. Apparatuses like, stereoscope, magic lantern, epidiascope, scroll box, tape record, gramophone, film strips, slides and film projector, radio, short circuit and close-circuit TV, illustrated materials, models and study kits became common. The use of transparencies on overhead project lessened the black board work. The advanced countries like, USA, Canada, Great Britain, France, Japan and Germany tried to popularise such material for use in educational institutions, through their missions like USAID, British Council and Canadian Consulate. The implicit aim of these countries might to create markets for their goods. In spite of all this, the attitude of schools teachers has changed little. Still a few teachers use these innovative methods of these aids. Majority of the teachers stick to verbal communication which is required to be changed.

4

Psychology of Audio-Visual Aid

The sense of sight is a better source of acquirement of experience than hearing. The learning process involves seeing, hearing and doing on the objective side, are thinking, and reasoning are on the subjective side. The eyes make the situation distinctively realistic and speech serves to give it meaning; both result in achieving delightfulness. What we see with our own eyes, gives us a real sense of pleasure than what we hear from others. We judge the merits and demerits, of the thing what we see, ourselves. There is an old saying "To see with one's own eyes is always better than to hear from others". So what we see is always true. Often rumours, misunderstandings and even conflicts and quarrels are spread due to the reason that the people believe in heard things. Psychological studies, consisting of careful analysis of experience-comparisons which led to the conclusions that the use of Audio-Visual aids should be a must in every educational system.

The essential contrast is not between the sense of vision and hearing. It is rather a direct experience which consists of the perception of the material objects one the one hand and indirect experiences, which consist of generalised or abstract thought or ideas, on the other hand. Direct perception (per. se.) is gained by means of various senses – not vision alone, while thought is transmitted by sense experience and language both. If properly viewed both are not opposed to each other. They rather supplement each other. In education, in which teaching is an instrument, both education and teaching should go hand in glove. Without experience verbalism is meaningless. And without verbalism experience is not concretised. Error is possible in their solo use. Doubtful education and rather no education is due to much mere verbalism. Therefore, verbalism, which is essential for introductory and for information purposes, needs a closer link and contact with the world of physical objects, world of thoughts and world of actions. Therefore, it is essential and psychologically sound, to use Audio-Visual aids in teaching for providing concrete experience of the physical world; the actual presence of which being too distant or too heavy or too small or because of non-availability is not possible in the classroom.

It is, therefore, true that the sense of vision is particularly a valuable source of educative experience. First because it furnishes distinctive qualities of its own, it serves to represent or suggest many qualities which are given directly by other sources such as hardness, softness, smoothness, tactileness and weight. Secondly, it is especially adapted to depict nature.

In modern pedagogy, it is assumed and emphasised that showing of things is always better than telling. It helps the learner very effectively. Since education is a recovery and this recovery is to be done imparting instructions on a planned curriculum, showing along with telling is always considered better. The teacher has also numerous problems with the students and he has to perform multiple duties. Along with the multiplicity of his duties, the prime purpose of the efforts of the teacher is to aid and help the learner in the acquisition of knowledge as well as to direct training towards the acquisition of skills. In this process of education, efforts should be made by the teacher to elicit as much as possible from the students, in order to make them self-learners. This would be psychologically sound because the ego of the students will be satisfied and educative process will proceed democratically and smoothly. The main problem of the teacher is how to convey his ideas by passing on information, which may impart and further generate knowledge, in accordance with pedagogic principles of learning. Psychologically, to achieve this end, the use of Audio-Visual aids becomes necessary, which actually does not replace teaching but helps it, and makes learning easier and permanent. According George Bernard Shaw "the number of people who can read is small, the number of those who can read to any purpose is much smaller and the number of those who are tired after days' work to read is enormous. But all except blind and deaf can see and hear". The teacher, therefore, should show as well as teach. So every teaching should entail the use of Audio-Visual aids positively.

No doubt, we are all convinced that use of Audio-Visual aids is very essential for better and proper teaching. But, the teacher should try to comprehend the psychological situation of the classroom judging the mood of the students before using these aids in teaching for achieving better results. Children learn best when they themselves are virtual actors and participants in the experience. In actual experience they see things themselves directly in their actual forms and hear about the things directly. Since it is not possible to provide all learning through direct experiences. Also, it is not possible to take children to far of places, such as greenlands, tourist resorts, places of national interest as dams and river projects, because of certain economic and social handicaps, for giving direct experiences. We can apply other means. What are these other means? It is a device of contrived experiences through Audio-Visual aids. This helps the teacher in giving correct ideas about the content he is planning to teach. On the other hand this method is going to satisfy the students psychologically and emotionally.

USE OF AUDIO-VISUAL AIDS IN TEACHING TECHNICAL SUBJECTS

Use of Audio-Visual aids is also equally very useful in teaching technical subjects, as well as physical and biological science subjects. Their use makes learning easier. For example, in wood working a lesson in joinery or upholstery or polishing cannot be accomplished without using orthographic drawings, model of joints and practical demonstration. Likewise in tin smithy developmental drawings for making things like buckets, boxes, hose pipe etc., are necessary. In fine art classes, the arrangement of flora and fauna, live models – male or female, and films and film strips are necessary for anatomy classes in order to make the students aware about the hidden intricacies of things. For example this is necessary in wood working to make the aware the secrete structure of joints, in upholstery the underneath supporting springs and tapes are to be shown. Likewise, in tin smithy without developmental drawing no structure could be possible. These are done with the help of audio-visual aids, which help in learning process and provide psychological satisfaction to the students. In engineering, teaching, mechanical, electrical, civil, electronics, metallurgy, paper technology etc., etc. is only possible if Audio-

Visual aids and machines are used. And especially charts, cut out x-ray models, finished objects and soft material like computer and films are used at every step. So also in biology samples, models, x-ray models, detailed chalk board work and demonstration are used.

Use of Audio-Visual aids is also essential for teaching various crafts like tailoring, leather work, costume designing, Batik work on leather and cloth, clay work like terracotta and teaching so many handicraft, like alpna, rangoli, mosaic, wall hangings, mobiles and cut paper work. In many homes where both parents are educated and want to contribute towards the early education of their child can make and utilise many teaching aids like, counting slates, role-up-black boards, dolls and replicas. Such aids not only facilitate the children in learning but provide immense of psychological satisfaction to them. Also these aids also help in generating aesthetic sense in the young children. These also provide energy outlet to the young children.

So use of audio-visual aids can be applied in many pre-arranged and well thought educational teaching programmes to satisfy the special needs of children. Many theories can be explained through the use of audio-visual aids. Many big construction projects can only be explained through orthographic drawings and models. Many mathematical, physical, chemical and biological principles and problems can be easily explained by the teachers to the students quite easily who can comprehend and learn these problems easily without out any difficulty. Many principles concerning the working of machines like, heat engines, automobiles, also principles concerning like, rainfall, hailstorm, snowfall, changing of seasons, heat and cold, solar eclipse and lunar eclipse can be explained to the students quite easily with the help of audio-visual aids. There are many things which cannot be explained to the students through words, say, the working of human eye, can be explained through a x-ray model of an eye. Likewise, many theorems in mathematics can only be explained through mathematical models. So, the use of audio-visual aids is psychologically well founded.

DEMERITS OF AUDIO-VISUAL AIDS

Attractiveness

Use of audio-visual aids in teaching has always been devised. The critiques argue that often audio-visual aids turn to be end in themselves. If these are attractive and aesthetic, these tend to serve recreational purpose alone. In such a situation these have good temptation in themselves and small children are fascinated by these and tend to overlook the educational content. No doubt the children are amused to see the attractiveness of the teaching aids but do not learn what is intended to be taught. As such, it is blamed that the process of learning can be neglected and ignored and the main purpose of education is defeated. Attractiveness of audio-visual aids may lead the students away from the desired path of learning. In this way these may happen to waste the precious time, money and energy.

Choice of Desirable Aids not Possible

Careful selection of audio-visual aids becomes important, as badly selected aids will not only fail to catch the students attention, motivate them and add to the store house of knowledge, but will become a source of distraction to students causing loss of concentration. Cinematography is the best example of such audio-visual aids. But it is only used, if only useful educational films are produced and provided to schools. It is hard to get good educational films. We have to depend upon whatever films are available. Unsuitable films may be harmful and generally they result in mere waste of time. Also, the projection of educational films needs meticulous planning, pre-projection orientation and post-projection students-teacher discussion that generally often does not follow. Likewise choice of other appropriate teaching aids becomes difficult. Suppose in teaching chronology in history used of a pictorial chart of the particular ruler will be waste of time, for which use of a time chart will be more useful. Similarly, making the students aware about cultural and social aspects of a society about particular period use of a map will not be useful. Instead charts costumes, artefacts and models on monuments will be more useful.

Undesirable Display of Audio-Visual Aids

There happens in many cases when the teacher either use, in many cases, too many undesirable aids in the classroom at one time, which confuse the students on wrong aids, which mislead the students.

Selection of Audio-Visual Aids

Selection of Audio-Visual aids is also a meticulous job. There are various age groups of the students. For young children pictorial compositions are more useful, whereas, for grown-up post-adolescent age students, who grasp more information and analyse it flow charts are more useful. Flash cards can only be used for introducing new words in language. Sometimes, the teacher fails to do a good and appropriate selection. In such a case wrong aids if used do more harm than help and will not help the students.

Explanation

Unexplained or wrongly explained audio-visual aids can have an extremely negative impact on students. Proper explanation of audio-visual aids is a must, otherwise their use is useless. If a diagram is incorrectly tabled then students will get wrong information and will learn incorrect data. Likewise, if in a map of a place is wrongly shown the students will be misinformed. The critiques argue that such things generally happen and audio-visual aids do more harm than benefit to the students.

Class Management

Class student should be managed properly while using audio-visual aids. But this rarely happens. When the audio aids are displayed in the classroom during the course of teaching, the students are very impatient, as they are very eager to see new things. If their enthusiasm is not controlled and reaped there may be disturbance and noise in the class. When the teacher is giving a demonstration or showing samples, say the leaves of a plant, and he does not control the class, which usually happens at various occasions, the whole effort on the part of the teacher goes waste and produces a counter effect. So the critics attack the use of audio-visual aids on this count also.

Undesirable Films and Radio Programmes

Sometimes we have to depend upon such radio-programmes, or films or audio-visual aids which tend to acculturate our students and create aggressiveness in them. As such, such audio-visual material may not give healthy moral impression to our young adolescents. As our youngs tend to incline adopt foreign habits and culture. Such a cultural diffusion may prove suicidal not only to our younger generation and also to the identity of nation as a whole. Sometimes, our radio songs and programmes and films stimulate to our adolescents to sexually motivated undesirable acts. Films violence generates and breeds violence in the veins of our future guardians. So the use of audio-visual aids is strongly objected by the critics on this count.

Dependence on Audio-Visual Aids

Sometimes the teacher tend to depend on audio-visual aids only while presenting the content in the classroom. But only with audio-visual ids the teacher cannot teach all. These are used to make the teaching interesting and vivid and should be employed as teaching aids only.

Supplementation of Audio-Visual Aids

Some critics argue that often teacher seldom supplement or explain the aids he uses. He also does not do the related black board work and encourage the students to know themselves. They applies in the conflict teaching model in which the teacher imposes his authority on the students. In such a situation the aids remain in name only and correlated knowledge could not emerge due to the non-integrative approach.

Too Much Use of Audio-Visual Aids

Some of the audio-visual aids are used too much. This way much of students' time is wasted. Also the teacher gets flittered from study. The teacher should continuously study and should keep himself like a burning lamp said Tagore. Sometimes these aids are used aimlessly. I saw a teacher having displayed ten charts in a class indiscriminately. If a teacher does not use the teaching aids when these are required such a situation leaves the students in uncertainty and confusion.

So, it is desirable for the teacher to make a proper choice of the aid, make proper arrangement for its use and ensure follow-up activities, then only the demerits of the audio-visual aids can be checked. Above all he should understand the psychology of the students.

5

Epistemology and its Implications in Education—Various Theories and Schools of Education

Epistemology is a derivation from the Greek words 'Epistem" and "logos" meaning 'knowledge' or 'discourse or science'. Or we can say "Epistemologos" which later on termed as "Epistemology" meaning science of knowledge. The "Epistemology" or theory of knowledge deals with the problem of knowledge, concerning its origin, nature, validity, limits and ways and conditions acquiring knowledge. All methods covering the acquisition of knowledge and enquiries concerning knowledge or knowing all the domain of Epistemology.

HISTORICAL BACKGROUND

'Epistemologos' or 'Epistemology' first appeared in Greece. Sophists speculated about the beliefs of their predecessors and conflicted there upon. Some of the Sophists were traveller teachers. They used to teach what they knew and in turn used to charge for that. Some of them were speculative thinkers. They did not teach but speculate and share their ideas with others. They conflicted upon what should be accepted as true knowledge. Important of these thinkers were Herodotus, Theatetus, Pythagaras, Parmendes, Xenophones, Hippocrates, Hereclitus, Socrates, Plato, Crito, Isocrates, Aristotle and many others, who contributed in the field of Epistemology. They discussed the epistemological, ontological, teleological, axiological, political and social problems at length. Plato, after the death of his teacher Socrates, recorded these discussion and gave these the form of dialogues. Important of these dialogues which embody such epistemological problems are 'Phaedo', 'Meno', 'Lichi, Symposium, Republic and Theatetus'. The Theatetus is the finest document on Epistemology or 'theory of knowledge'.

One of the best traditions of the Western philosophy, right from the Greek philosophy up to present day Empirist philosophy, has been scepticism. One school of philosophy propounded a theory and the other repudiated it. Thesis anti-thesis and synthesis followed. Though, in our schools of thought, there has been a fine traditions of *vad-vivad*. Discussion followed for many days. The discussions ended on disagreements but it lacked scepticism and consequent rejection of a particular discussion. This might be because of reverence aspect of Guru-Shishya Parampara.

What Socrates said, was questioned by his disciples and challenged by his grand disciple Aristotle. Not only individual point of views were rejected even schools of thought were questioned and rejected. French philosopher Rene' Descartes put forward the theory of Rationalism which was challenged and rejected by the British philosopher John Locke. He was a most influential post Renaissance philosopher of the West who made Epistemology the starting point and centre of philosophical discussions. He gave new directions to educational epistemology. To him epistemological problems are prior to other problems. His dictum of *Tabula Rasa* is the core of his epistemology of education, which subscribes to educational principle of 'hardening' against the principle of 'latent ideas' propounded by Rene' Descartes. His successors John Berkley, and David Hume and other later thinkers, who followed him, subscribed to Locke's principles of educational epistemology and the present pedagogic principles in the world which subserve to the idea that senses and experience are better source of education.

Rene' Descartes was influenced by the principle of reminiscence propounded by Plato in support of the immortality of soul. The dialogue 'Phaedo' explicate this as one of the proof of the immortality of the soul. Reminiscenting or educaring or taking out, what the soul had acquired in earlier life was education according to Plato. Rene' Descartes inferred from this and believed that innate ideas exist in human mind at the time of birth of a person. And taking out these innate ideas is a process of education. He prescribed 'thinking' or 'rationalisation' for taking out or educaring these innate ideas. He suggested to doubt for thinking.

As such, he prescribed 'doubt' as a tool for this educative purpose. He said for knowing a thing one must doubt about it. His famous dictum 'cogito ergo sum' which means 'I exist because I think' was basis for doubting. Descartes' belief in reasoning is very true for education. If the learner does not think and reason he cannot know. Without thinking and reasoning a person remains only receiver and rote memoriser. For thinking and reasoning there should be a situation or premise to contemplate thereby the students may be motivated and activated to think and reason, then there can only be true education. Mere information cannot motivate the children. Therefore, there should be concrete to be perceived by them. Audio-Visual aids can play an important role in this respect for achieving this end.

John Locke, the British empiricist philosopher repudiated the theory of Rationalism for, educational epistemology advanced by Rene' Descartes. He said there exists no such thing which may be called 'innate ideas' when the child is born. Child is the product of reproduction. His mind and brain are like Tabula Rasa (empty slate). As the child grows his body organs also grow. He starts perceiving things. As such, child starts writing on his empty slate, that is brain by seeing things himself. As he perceives things he gets primary and secondary ideas from the environment around him. So the perception plays an important role in acquiring knowledge. As such, perception is very important and, plays a vital role in acquiring knowledge and is important tool for educational epistemology. The teacher should provide an ample opportunity to the students to perceive, comprehend and learn through experience. According to Locke, an educational system should strictly adhere to the scheme of providing systemic experience through perception in educating the youngers. Young children may have a tendency to evade certain experiences. The teacher should force the children to have such experiences. If the children are to be made aware about snow falling or raining, they should be forced to come out from the house and have such experiences. He termed this process as 'Hardening' in education. He said that the exposure to the nature can only give real knowledge about the environment.

Immuel Kant who stood as a bridge between Rationalist and Empiricists exercised a great influence in the field of educational epistemology. Rationalists and Empiricist both did not treat epistemology as a prior subject. Kant believed that knowledge involves both seeing and thinking which are supplementary to each other

DIFFERENT EPISTEMOLOGICAL POINT OF VIEWS

Authoritarianism

An unsatisfactory epistemological doctrine was employed in the periods of religious authority, which was strictly applied in the field of education. Authoritarianism asserts that knowledge is guaranteed and validated by the authority. Since man is naturally suggestable and is not in a position to verify all of the so-called knowledge. Such an authority is competent through books of authority of Religion, to guide the man. Authority had come from the mouth of Almighty God, therefore, those enjoying authority are true in all cases. If someone dares to repudiate the knowledge propounded by religious authority, his fate hangs in the balance and his existence may be in danger. We often witness such happenings in the world. Metaphysics plays an important role in such an assertion. Authoritarianism tends to limit the advancement in the fields of knowledge. Often it opts for 'blind model of teaching'. It exercises its influence on school education too. It lays stress on religious education in theocratic states. On the contrary, in communistic countries which denounce religion a stress is laid on obedience of policy following. How can knowledge validated thousand years ago, and too based on dogmas can be true today in the period of science and technology, as change in the law of nature. But authoritarianism's opinions are held to rest with the authority and thus constitute true knowledge. No criticism is possible, thus no thinking, reasoning, debate and dissent follow. This is not the case alone with religious authoritarianism it is more vehemently true with political economic and even with individualistic authoritarianism. Authority always keeps his prestige and personal ego high while enforcing pedagogic epistemological methods in the field of education. Everything is done under the banner of authority's prestige and honour. There is no place for suggestions and criticisms. Authoritarian theory of epistemology of education is also based on the psychology of belief. It fails to invoke thinking reasoning curiosity and creativity, hence there is a limited scope of use of audio-visual aids for this purpose.

Scepticism

Scepticism is a doctrine which denies that there is any genuine knowledge. Solve the problem of epistemology by denying, is its echo. It is not doubt but rejection of verified knowledge and getting nowhere. The history of scepticism is long and its literature is rich. It is scepticism which led to the development of knowing for which it was advanced for rejecting any new epistemological approach. Arguments advanced in favour of scepticism are:

I. The Historical Argument

In historical argument, the Sceptics point out the helplessness of experts' disagreement on various fields and issues of knowledge leads to scepticism. The experts often seem incapable settling problems and concerning disputes thereof on right track. Certainty is beyond their reach. The argument takes its cogency or treachery, as it does not show that knowledge is unattainable. It can be concluded that argument advocates that certainty has not achieved.

II. The Dialectal Argument

The dialectal argument seems more persuasive that the historical argument. It tends to show, in its every nature of the case, and finds itself frustrated in attempting ultimate results or issues. The Sceptics say that in forces of knowing we are beset with contradictions or antimonies which generally defy solutions.

III. The Psychological Aspect

Simple can be disposed of briefly. It asserts that we are living in an eternal now. Future is our consequent anticipation of the present. The past is our present memory. Memory is uncertain. Future is speculative.

IV. The Physiological Argument

The physiological argument is probably the most powerful and forceful argument against the theory of knowledge. It assets that we cannot have true knowledge of the real world. It is impossible to achieve. The nature of experience is such that the real world of which we think, is truly represented in perceptions and is like distorted one in knowing. The sound we hear, the colour we see, the odours we smell and the taste we feel, all are our own creations and modifications. They do not really represent outer world. Our tinny physical make up in the world is such that true knowledge is impossible. The psychological argument, put forward by Sceptics, seriously questions the empirical knowledge.

Scepticism in general is not a defensible position, but it is a corrective form of stratified dogmatism.

Mysticism

Epistemological theory of mysticism is one which either denies or relegates to a position of relative insignificance of the order and source or avenue of knowledge namely sensation, disclosure and thought. But it affirms that true knowledge is 'insight' to be found in an unique experience, which has been the unity with God or Ultimate or Universe or Nature. It differs with the commercial experience of life. The mystical notions rests on certain metaphysical and religious notions which would deny that the world of senses is real. According to this theory knowledge in true sense is not commercial with the world of senses, which exists in space and time or with the world of concepts. It is insight into the self and mind and God or Substance or ultimate entity which transcends the phenomenal world. This insight is gained through identification of the knower with the God. This insight is mystical experience. But the critics say that mysticism leaves untouched more pressing problems of knowledge.

Intuition

Intuition is more closely associated with mysticism. French philosopher Heneri Burgson made it popular. In his view, it is contended that knowledge which is conceptual, essentially is inaccurate and unsound what we ordinarily take to be knowledge. It is discursive, abstract and false. The chief instruments of such knowledge are concepts which in their very nature falsify the reality. The only true and right way to know the reality is through intuition which reveals a living dynamic world of constant change and novelty. The essential creative nature of the world is lost in conceptual knowledge. Only intuitional experience gives a true report of it. The conceptual knowledge has lacunae of being defective. The intellect picks up and chooses in relation to its interest, experience, capacity, thus knowledge occurs is always relative of these factors. In intuition, the world as it is, not relatively and arbitrarily accepts incomplete knowledge. Intuition takes the gestalt view in epistemic process. Intellectual knowledge is fundamentally analysed in uncertain character. The real world cannot be understood by analysis in parts. It can only be understood as a whole. Intuition takes intellect as a necessary evil, but we cannot live without it. We may conclude then, that intellectual knowledge, which depends upon concepts, is secondary and instrumental to life. Through intuition we get true insight into nature of the world.

Different schools of thought right from the Greek period up to the present day have been influencing the educational structures of different countries setting up different epistemological norms. In Greece the whole emphasis was laid for knowing truth, beauty and goodness. In Europe, the feudalistic structure of society influenced the educational aims, which aimed at perpetuating the existing system, which prescribed epistemological norms accordingly. In many religious societies the knowledge of religious tenets and adherence thereto has been the source to educational epistemology. In our country the prime aim of education was to inculcate the knowledge about the 'Supreme' – the creator the 'Paramatma', that is Almighty God. He is the creator of all and His manifestations are present and evident everywhere. In other words He is present in all living beings in the form of 'soul'. The relationship between the Almighty God or 'Paramatma' or Supreme Soul and the individual soul or jivatma is of the nature of a 'whole' and parts. Duality of soul has been accepted in 'Sankhya yoga' Indian school of thought. This is why the Indian society has been homogeneous throughout the ages; based on equality, sharing cooperation, brotherhood and free from exploitation. As man is greedy and selfish, though not all, there happened to be some lacunas in our society too. Our contacts with the foreigners specially with the western people and consequent cultural diffusion made us materialistic too. And now we notice a tendency of human exploitation in our society also. By and large it can be said that Indian educational system in the part was laden with an epistemology which provided education for sane and good living.

All educational schools have emerged out of the respective epistemological theories. These are like, Idealism, Rationalism, Naturalism, Dogmatism and Pragmatism. The Rationalist, and

Empiricist schools of philosophy have influenced most the present day educational epistemology.

Rationalism

School of rationalistic thought came into being with a belief in thinking and reasoning put forward by French philosopher Rene' Descartes and adhered to by his followers Liebnuz, Spinoza and Christian Wolf (1679-1754). They maintained that most of the form of knowing in the sort which is found in mathematical demonstration. Such demonstration consists in starting with a premise which is self-evident, intuitional, certain, clear and distinct and deduceable from axioms of truth. The source of first premise is source of light of the reason. The first principles have primarily their source, some how, in reason of man and are derived also from empirical experience. The Classical Rationalism is well defined by Christian Wolf. He covered the theory of knowledge (Epistemology) in three segments as given below:

I. Rational Cosmology

The principles of Rational Cosmology are clear and distinct to reason. These produce and deduce the consequences from cosmos.

II. Rational Psychology

The rational psychology principles are related to soul. Soul is the source of reasoning. The principle, more or less coincides or resembles with the Platonic principle of Reminiscence and role of soul in action propounded by Indian school of philosophy Naya-Veshiska.

III. Rational Theology

The principle of rational theology is meta-physical in nature. God is producer and protector of all. Man deduces his existence from God. This principle is analogous to the Indian principle of metaphysical 'Supreme Soul' – Paramatma (God) and the duality of soul 'Atma'.

EMPIRICISM

Empiricism is not itself a theory of knowledge (epistemology). It is one of the schools of Western philosophy which do not accept metaphysics. There are many schools of epistemology which are empirical in character. But empiricism basically influenced educational epistemology in the West and most of the thinkers like J.J. Rousseau, Pestalozzi, Froebel, Madam Montessori, John Dewey in the West and even in the east thinkers like Mahatma Gandhi, Tagore were influenced by empiricist epistemology because of economic reasons. This is the school of philosophy which boosted capitalism first in the West and thereafter in the east.

In general empiricism affirms that the source and validity of knowledge are to be found in empirical aspects of experience. To empiricist, the knowledge is the result of sense perception and experience. To them true knowledge is that which can be experienced and verified. A.J. Ayer maintains that real and true is that which can be verified. They reject metaphysics, and as such the existence of God also. They reject rationalism too. To them, since rationalistic epistemological approach can never be verifiable and empirical thus it can never be true and epistemologically tenable. So the epistemological principles of rationalism, since these are based on wrong assumptions of innate ideas, are wrong. The genesis of reason basically resides in actual experience and not in innate ideas or a prior knowledge. In fact the mind of the man is a 'tabula rasa' upon which the sense perception are entailed by experience. Thus, whatever knowledge man attains is firmly rooted in and dependent upon sense perception (per. se.) and experience. Thus, sensation is the beginning of all knowledge and ideas are reducible to sensory experience. The process of knowledge is inductive rather deductive. Therefore, sound knowledge can only be acquired by generalisation on experiences.

Experience consists of two types of sensation – inner and outer. The former sensations are of subjective character such as, desire, feeling, and thinking. And later are our sensations of internal world, such as sight, smell, touch, taste and feeling.

LOGICAL POSITIVISM AND PRAGMATISM

Logical positivism and pragmatism are theories which stand midway between rationalism and empiricism. These generate epistemological conditions which fulfil human necessities. While contemplating a scheme of Basic education Mahatma Gandhi was influenced by John Dewey's concept of Pragmatism in education. According to Dewey experience has a characteristic of properties of relationship. It generates thinking and reasoning. It motivates for activity resulting in the welfare of the individual. The individual should carry on experiences and activities for his well being. The pragmatism lacks axiological intent, therefore, it is materialistic in nature. We find the principles of relationships in Basic education, which is termed as correlation. As such, the concept of Basic Education is laden with hand work and experience related to life of the individual in the society. As such the concept of Basic education is also laden with morality and axiological intent. This scheme of education was aimed to bring a social change – a change in Indian social structure on the pattern of old Indian society. So the epistemology of Basic education was so designed.

So many epistemological theories have been advanced right from olden days – the Vedic period, the Greek period, the middle ages and recent theories of educational epistemology. The use of senses in knowing things has been accepted by all. Plato said that "knowledge is possible through sensation plus comprehension". In contrast to this theory another theory of sensation was advanced by another Greek thinker Protagaras, who said "Man is the measure of all things", "What appears to me is to me", "what appears to you is to you". But this assertion was rejected by Plato.

Sense is always an apprehension of something, which exists and is something as certain and infallible. But when we look to the generality and, try to understand and generalise all theoretical and epistemological aspects, and also common sense about knowledge; and we try to analyse and know from where do we get our knowledge, we see that we acquire knowledge from many sources. These sources are world around us, our minds, our sensory organs, mathematical principles, logical principles, activities followed by the principle of trial and error, goodness, beauty and the principles of aesthetics involving individual's emotional equipment. In addition to all these past experiences and inferences also plays a vital role in knowing.

Epistemological philosophy says that knowledge is the result of (*i*) inborn tendencies and capacities, (*ii*) thinking, (*iii*) reasoning, (*iv*) senses – sight, hearing, touch, taste and smell, (*v*) temperature, light, stress and strain. The last two provide a field for thinking and reasoning. And finally intuition also plays a role in the epistemic process. Knowledge is not something which comes into package. Ideas are not entities which can be built. The ideas generate concepts. There should be some source for the generation of ideas. In each of us, there is a faculty of reason which generates and guarantees a kind of divine serenity to utterances. Since Locke's time few people believe in innate ideas. Though innate dispositions, tendencies, interests we have all in plenty. These all are interacting in human organism, but it is believed by modern epistemological theorists that these do not provide knowledge.

The way to a better understanding of the theory of knowledge is or may be through genetic study of the subject beginning with the attitude of simplest living organism towards its environment. After sensing it, it is the reason which leads us to comprehension, analysis and finally to learning and knowledge. Both sensing and reasoning are supplementary to each other and go hand in glove. If one is absent knowledge is not possible. As such, the teacher make sure that these go and remain together and work hand and glove. Then only the students may be motivated to think, reason and act. So the innovative techniques, the use of Audio-Visual aids in teaching for appropriate education is a must.

Knowledge is funded by experience. Also, we can say that true knowledge is rationalised knowledge. John Dewey enlightened us in this regard by endorsing this position. Gandhiji also kept this point in mind while thinking of Basic education. No doubt knowledge is funded by experience but mental powers and activities play a significant role in this funding. Memory, thought process, conceptual analysis, reflection, inference, selective organisation, creative thesis, antithesis and synthesis play an important role in epistemic process. This interpretation of knowledge is not new, and as such, the credit does not only go to analytic philosophers. Plato tried to present his thesis in dialogues Thetetus, Phaedo, Meno and Republic long long back. Before, Greek thinkers Hindu schools of philosophical thought tried to present that the epistemic process takes the course of sensation, inference and rationalisation of senses by the soul. Buddhist tried to signify sensation and nihilism for attaining knowledge. Jains related to the acquisition of knowledge to the function of soul through senses.

Knowledge is not something which comes in the form of ready made packet or frame in the form of impressions. The theory of impressions is as old as impressionist like Protagoras. Though it is not a distilled product of Rationalism. It is a product of interaction of the individual with the environment. In this process remarkable powers of the self are most important. If we look to theories of Sankhya-yaga and Naya-Veshiska the soul is the interpreter and analyser of all kinds of knowledge. The position taken by Naya-Veshiska which lay stress on Anvik Shakti and Smaran Shakti and inferences drawn out of these through sensation. We find in India schools of thought that stress has been laid on sensation and comprehension.

This epistemological genetic account is very useful and important for the teacher. Because without the knowledge of the educational epistemic processes a teacher cannot proceed. The teacher is considered as the knowledge giver. He should not lay too much stress neither on verbal communication nor on the instrumental character of the mind. He should provide ample opportunities for sensation in the classroom teaching which may lead to contemplation and comprehension, which may finally lead to understanding, learning and knowledge.

The use of senses in knowing is obvious. There are various theories of learning regarding the use of senses. If we take a common sense view of it, we find that for knowing a thing, we have to see the thing first. For example for knowing the colour of a cow or a goat, it is necessary to see the cow or a goat. Many philosophers have contemplated upon the aspects sense perception in knowing and held that the senses are basis of all empirical knowledge. The theories sense perception are listed below briefly.

REALISM

The objects of perception are what one perceives in the world of objects. These objects are external to their perceiver. These objects exist independently of their perception and perceiver. These exist in time and space. These objects have certain properties which can be seen or perceived or known. For example by seeing objects we can visualise their shapes, forms, textures, colour, motion, temperature, order and taste. The externality of the objects beyond perception is called realism. One of the tendency in realistic perception is that the objects we perceive have discursive qualities which generate reactive waves in the mind of the perceiver and inculcate a process of thinking. Such reaction is not possible through verbal communication. This is why non-verbal communication through realistic objects is always considered better in teaching. Some philosophers found this theory inadequate and, called it naïve realism. Argument advanced against it are:

- We do not perceive the things as they are,
- A straight stick when placed in water looks bent,
- Objects in perspective look are different. Height of a building above eye looks slanting,
- A coin looks different from different angles,
- There cannot be many things as one and the same thing. Only one thing exists independently, and
- Sense data result may give confusing results.

IDEALISM

Idealists say that objects are collection of ideas. Objects or physical things exist without our mind. We do not immediately perceive physical objects since they are collection of ideas. The objects we perceive are the result of our ideas. But H.E. Moor objects to this assertion. He says that objects exist independent of our mind.

NATURALISM

Naturalism as a philosophy originated in a historic context. When European middle class was struggling against the church on the one hand and, the monarch on the other; and when man was asserting and claiming himself to be placed at the Centre as an object of significance. According to Naturalism, Nature has to be substituted for God, and man as an integral part of the Nature and to be elevated to the position of significance along with other physical objects. The Naturalist movement grew from the tendencies against Idealist doctrines originating from the sinful nature of man. Also the movement of science and technology required a corresponding to fight with religious doctrines and metaphysics of supernaturalism. Naturalism, therefore, appeared on the historical scene when it was most needed to combat for the rule of divine and law that helped the monarch to suppress the masses. Although it appeared as a reaction against Idealism. It was a monistic philosophy in essence replacing God for Nature.

THE ONTOLOGICAL POSITION OF NATURALISM

The essential features about the ontological position of the Naturalism are:

1. Naturalism believes that matter, life and mind are combined in nature,
2. Nature is a self-sufficient system,
3. Nothing exists beyond nature. Everything can be explained on the basis of natural laws in terms casual relationship, energy, motion, and life etc.
4. Nature is intelligible source of life; and soul and mind are part of natural order,
5. The universe has no moral character. Plurality, if any, has a meaning for man in relation to its harmony with the natural order, and
6. Nature is permanent and enduring. Changes are real, but these take place in accordance with the permanence of nature. World's permanence is the background against which changes occurred and these changes can be assessed.

External form of naturalism differ little from realities. One point of difference is that while realists believe that world of reality exists independently of man, naturalists view this realist position that the real world is in harmony with man. The view that the separateness between man and real world is a relationship of part and whole as these continue to be one. As such, this assertion of naturalist is very much analogous to the Indian idea of 'Parmatman' which is omnipresent in all living beings and worldly things.

Realists use the matter as prime, original datum, while naturalists prefer to use 'energy' perhaps due to the indefiniteness of the word 'matter' and changing views about it.

ESSENTIAL FEATURES OF NATURALISM PERTAINING TO EDUCATIONAL EPISTEMOLOGY

Bruebacher puts naturalism as a 'six dimensional' philosophy. These dimensions are:

1. The naturalists assert that the education should be according to nature. J.J. Rousseau was so much fed up with the current authoritarianism, that he said "Reverse the usual practice and you will be always right. He was influenced by French thinker Voltaire, who being fed up with French feudalism had fled to Russia and lived there in self-exile for sometime. He was a window of vision to Rousseau and also to the French revolutionists. Rousseau further said, "Human institutions are mess of folly and are full of contradictions ... men are devoiced by our town. "God made all the things good, equal, man meddles with them, they become evil". "Child is born free but he finds himself in chains". Influenced by Rousseau, sometime later, Piagot said, "a child is morally sacred and pure, but his seniors make him corrupt". Rousseau further said "therefore you must make a choice between man and citizen. You can train both".

   Nature in the context of education, meant to Rousseau, which explicated in Emile, the instincts and emotions of the child. These must taken care of in education.
2. Thc naturalists asserts that the learning should take place through senses. Here naturalism repeats the principles of Realism. In its fundamentals naturalism is very close to realism.
3. Naturalistic (philosophy) epistemology attaches great importance to 'reason', although it shifts emphasis from mental faculty to emotions and interests. Reason is considered to be of importance.
4. Its romanticism for individual care and upliftment is evident by way its emphasis on emotions. It considers human nature to be the trustworthy key for human development.
5. It affirms that child's nature is basically good. Thus, it is a negation of pre-renaissance belief of Catholics that human nature's evil consequence of which is that child was also treated an evil. Naturalism finds child as pure as nature and recommends child's upbringing in an atmosphere free of any coercion. Coercion curbs the personality of the child and makes him abnormal. Naturalism in education finds its best exponent in J.J. Rousseau. Pestalozzi, Froebel and

Madam Montessori in Europe and Gandhi, Tagore and J. Krishnamurti in East (in India) with a difference of spiritual sentiment-that is seen in the schemes of pedagogy of these Indian thinkers. Such an axiological element is totally absent in John Dewey's pragmatist educational epistemology.

6. Freedom and discipline. Naturalists are credited bringing teaching out of the four closed walls of the classroom. They allow maximum freedom and independence to the child like pragmatists. The concept of discipline for the Naturalists is not an imposed one but of auto-discipline. They adhere to the belief that education is life and not preparation for future living.

Naturalists' epistemology asserts that since Nature is governed by permanent natural laws and man is a cog-pin in the larger scheme of nature or so to say universe, the education of the child should be according to Nature. Moreover, the naturalists believe that the nature has endowed the child with such potentialities, powers and faculties that he himself learns. As such, the child should be allowed to use these endowed faculties and learn. In case the child wants to learn about fire, he should be exposed to fire, then only he will learn. Likewise, if he wants to know about the river let him go to the river visualise it and if he wants to know about snow he should be exposed to snow. John Locke's principle of hardening is based on this assumption Naturalists' conception of 'natural endowment' goes with the belief of Indian belief of 'Anvik Shakti' put forward by the 'Naya-Veshiska' school of thought.

VIEWS ADVANCED AGAINST SENSATION

Some thinkers felt that knowledge derived from sense-perception (per. se.) is fallible and not true. It can deceive us. The senses are unreliable source of knowledge. Senses can tell about a cow or a particular thing but not about the cows or things. All cows and particular things cannot be seen and examined. We can only generalise. Therefore, sensory knowledge is truly general in nature.

Another limitation of senses is that they can tell us only "what is the case?" and not "What must be the case"? All bachelors happened to be unmarried, but it cannot be concluded that they will not marry or they are to be married.

True knowledge is that which is 'a priori". Truths can never be justified on the basis of sensory experience. Senses provide only contingent truth not real.

But, Mill (John Stewart Mill) said that there are few kinds of truths that are necessarily true. These are true:

- Mathematical truths are well confirmed,
- Empirical generalisations are always true,
- Moral education is always possible through observance,
- Human behaviour is always learnt through observance and imitation,
- Theology can only be learned through observance and faith,
- Likewise many skills are learned, and
- Through observance, imitation and continuous practice, as the artisans of India used to learn hereditically.

There are many for and against views about the futility of senses in knowing. But in general it can be concluded or said that the use of senses in knowing is a common feature in the animal world. A blind, though cannot see, therefore, he cannot know and generalise as a sighted person does. But his other organs as hearing, smelling and touch do the sensory job in quite perfection. A blind person when crossing a busy road can anticipate motor vehicles coming from both side hearing their sounds. So senses are used by all creatures in the animal world in all circumstances.

The main purpose of education is develop the latent potentialities and faculties of the child and draw out the best. We see that every child has come with some special faculties and potentialities. We notice at many occasions, many children know better than other children. And sometimes they act as mistake rectifiers in the classroom. The main purpose of teaching should be to exploit such situations. This can only be done, if these natural faculties of the child are fully developed and exploited for the good of other students.

As such, the whole epistemic strategies of the classroom teaching should be planned and chalked out in such a way that the students are educated and not merely taught. For this purpose there ought to be used some elicitative devices while teaching the students for proper education. Since every sensory experience in its real form is not possible in the classroom it becomes necessary to use some other means through contrived experiences. The use of Audio-Visual Aids can provide such contrived experiences. Their use, will bring an atmosphere of cordiality, discipline, ego and mental satisfactions to the students and relief to the teacher by limiting his verbal communication.

6

Communication

Etymologically, the word Communication is a derivation from the Greek word 'communicare' meaning, to share, to make common, to make public and to pass on recorded or acquired knowledge. As such the concept of communication has sociological bearings, economical stakes and political purposes in society. Without communication a living being is a most unpurposeful creature.

All types of communication is a source of education since it creates reactions. And also education is communication. Communication is not a mere public information. It is a genre of education; it is only through education men try to mould the future of their future guardians in such a way so as to enable them or to provide them a well structured form, thereby they (youngsters) could know what is good or bad for them as well as for the society. Their innate capacities, potentialities and capacities are to be developed to enable them to socialise themselves and know how to rationalise in their surroundings, environment and worldly atmosphere, physical things and learn how to adopt roles for themselves for proper adjustment. Communication plays an important role in this regard.

It is impossible for living human beings and even for animals, not to communicate. They cannot survive without communication. Right from the Ex-utrawail, that is from birth, up to the final breathing, that is, death, each of us communicates in a infinite variety of models. As soon as the child is born he cries for help. The small children laugh delightedly and try to catch things and toys. Just after birth a young baby cries for milk. After sucking the breast his mother his mood changes which indicates change in the form of his communication. With the passage of time he starts responding pleasurably to the communication of his mother and other members of the family with darting eyes and muscular movements and further continues to pick up communication signals.

Human beings as well as animals have been communicating for the last many thousand of years; and human beings have also long been aware of subtitles in non-verbal communication also. Greek Theatre was characterised by masks. Dancers of Kerala in India have been using masks in classical dances. They also have been using pantography for depicting different characters. Sir Francis Bacon described gestures as natural, hieroglyphic writing in air. Estinne a sixteenth century French linguist described gestures as a form of communication by strangers to persons unaware about their facial language. Likewise facial expressions and body movements have been a sort of communication from the days of Greeks. In the beginning when language was not developed, human beings used to communicate either by facial expressions or gestures or body movements or by showing concrete objects or developed symbols for concrete things.

By passage of time, man to man interaction increased. Their needs also increased. Sharing of acquired knowledge, needs for cooperation in the field of agriculture and cottage industries and common security were felt. Necessity is the mother of invention. All this gave birth to human language which emerged out of Chimpanzee like hooting and roaring. Consequently aural and verbal communication came into being for social interaction and socialisation. As such, sharing of acquired knowledge could be possible and security measures in the society could be beefed up. The age of science and technology brought the voices of the world nearer. Man could understand people of different places. Different innovations, experiments and inventions could be shared by the men in the world. With the result the nations could harness their natural resources. The men could harness their natural resources, like becoming of the world entailed coming closer. Though economic prosperity increased but equally the lust of greed of man also increased. The strong men ruthlessly and mercilessly exploited the weak. And what Socrates perceived two and half thousand years ago that "justice is nothing but the dictum of strong" came true. The inventions of printing press, ship, railways, motor vehicles, radio gramophones, TV, close circuit TV, VCP, VCR and effective use of art forms could revolutionise the arena of communication. Better forms of communication helped education. Communication is at the heart of all social intercourse. When man tries to establish regular relations with another man, a form of communication is established between these two. In the beginning a form of permanent communication was possible within family, circumscribed groups and small committees. Now-a-days, the information media universally operates. Now people living in unapproached areas are not isolated. We are now interdependent. Hot beds of tensions, natural mishappenings, social tensions and strife's are immediately located and taken care of, know-how are easily shared due to better means of communication.

Communication maintains and animates life. It is also motor and expression of all kinetics of social activities, culture, civilisation and education. It leads the people from instinct of inspiration to a spirit of enquiry, command and control of natural resources. It converts and creates common people, people of ideas and strengthens the feeling of togetherness, through exchanges of messages and ideas translating thoughts into actions. It enables human beings to survive. Its main contribution is liberation of mankind from want, oppression and fear in social milieu.

Man's innate qualities for communicating are because of his intelligibility, spirit of diligence, organisational skills, capacity to assimilate information and acquire knowledge through perception and comprehension, and to make aware of his fellow beings about his achievements. This enhanced communication system in the world. Starting with simplest vocal aural and gestural signals, rooted in his physical structure, human beings developed a whole range of non-verbal communication system such as music, dance, drum messages, signal fires, placing signal objects such as stones while going out for hunting, drawing and paintings sculptures and other forms of graphic symbols including pictograms, illustrations, cave paintings representing objects with abstract ideas and, thereby innovating and motivating his fellow beings to think, rationalise and act. The systematic language development by man in the animal world made communication powerful and important. All these means and ways of communication, since the dawn of society, have been indispensable till today and will continue to be the same in future.

Virtually, there is no limits to variety and ingenuity of modes of communication employed by human beings. The forms and contents of communication developed continuously are varied. Different languages arose because of lack of contact among people in different regions. Distinct societies having distinct geographical and climatic conditions, moral norms, culture and civilisation developed different languages. Millions of people speak different languages which are not understood by all. Words being symbols of physical things and human experience designated to identify different objects and situations. Words have limited scope for clear understanding. But non-verbal symbols have wide scope and appeal for comprehension.

So the communication can be defined as a source of sharing ideas, telling about certain facts or informing people and making them aware about certain important events; and finally to pass on acquired knowledge or recorded information.

So the communication can be defined as a source of sharing ideas, telling about certain facts or enforcing people and making them aware about certain important events; and finally to pass on acquired knowledge or recorded information to others.

Some thinkers have defined communication as follows:

> "Communication is the broad field of interchange of facts and opinions". — *Redfield*
>
> "Communication is the form of interaction which takes place through symbols. The symbols may be gestural, pictorial, plastic verbal or any other form which operates as stimuli to behaviour, which is not evoked by symbols itself in the absence of special conditions of the person who responds". — *Lundberg*
>
> "Communication exposes all forms of expression which serves the purpose of mutual understanding". — *Revesz*
>
> "Communication is the effective agent to affect others, it influences to effect them with intent". — *Berlo*

Furthermore historic functional dimensions of the communications are:

- It maintains and animates life,
- It provides avenues of expression and prepares the individual for social activity through the process enquiry, command and control,

- It creates common pool of ideas, concepts and strengthens the feelings of sharing, cooperation and togetherness, and
- It generates supreme manifestations of either creativity or destructivity.

Since the inception of human lie, man has been aspiring to lead a social lie and hence has been communicating; but the age of science and technology has also made the lease of communication difficult as it had entailed the message of fear coercion, oppression and criminality.

The foremost job of communication is to make man human and relieve him of greed, dogmatism, superstition, fundamentalism which all are enemies of mankind. God has created all of us equal. It is man himself who creates hatred. Throughout the history, human beings have always to improve their ability to receive and assimilate information about their surroundings and at the same time enhance the speed, clarity and variety of their own methods for transmission of information. This was necessary firstly to create awareness of dangers that might be lurking behind and, secondly to share the vision of social possibilities of meeting the challenges posed by these dangers.

The development of Semantics made the man's position pre-eminent in the animal world as the development of language was important for potential scope and depth it gave to the content of communication. Writing is a great achievement of man. It gives permanence to spoken words. Long ago, laws which were designed for, the observance of ceremonial rites, to ensure continuity of a community, were recorded on clay tablets, scrolls on stone carvings. The development of writing permitted the preservation of meaning of symbols laden with messages, thus ensuring the community's permanent existence. Books, both handwritten and in copied form have a history dating back to thirty centuries. In the long run the books became an invaluable repository of thoughts and knowledge and also acquired ontological and teleological importance. All books of authority of all religions fall in this category. China was the first country which initiated the process of recording, chiefly historic and scientific information.

COMMUNICATION A BIOLOGICAL NECESSITY

Communication is essential for the existence of animal world. Human beings, animals and also birds and insects learn to communicate just after their birth and continue to do so throughout their lives. Similarly when human beings and animals anticipate dangerous situations in life they transmit fear signals. Also they transmit social signals through gestures etc. As such, both human beings and animals have innate faculties for communication. Man has been gifted by nature more to communicate in comparison to other animals. Man has been gifted by nature by vocal capacity so he can speak, recite and sing. He has been gifted by the nature with other better body organs. He has an erect posture, flexible hands, bigger brain, attractive face and well developed sensory-motor system as compared to other animals. That is why he has developed skills for his sustenance. He can plan for future. So he always wants to pass on every accumulated experience and knowledge to his off springs for their well being. Man always tries to be hedonistic and he strives for this end. In this pursuit he always try to avail the cooperation of his fellow beings. So, for his social interaction communication is a biological necessity.

FUNCTIONS OF COMMUNICATION

Functional credentials of communication are varied and many. Communication in its broadest sense is considered as a system of exchanging views and message. But we look more precisely to its functions we can say it is a compound collective activity of humanism in totally. It is sharing of ideas, novelties, facts, creations and inventions and data pertaining to these among the members of the society. Following are areas covered by communication.

Information

A well informed person is said to be well aware about his environment which leads him to be well educated. It is the information which generates thinking, reasoning and understanding of the facts. The collection, storage, processing and dissemination of data about facts through messages, components, ideograms require understanding, reactions, knowledge of personal, national, social and international level for taking proper decisions. Information through personal and mass level serves this purpose. So information plays an important role for educating people. Without information no education is possible.

Socialisation

Without socialisation the sociability of an individual is not possible. The socialisation of the members of the society is done through effective communication. Proper socialisation of an individual is the first requirement for his good education. The socialisation of the individual is done at various levels. It is a process which starts at home, continues throughout at various stages. From home when the child enters the school he interacts socially within the four wall of the school. There, he interacts socially with his peer group teachers and other staff members. Likewise it continues at the university level. When the individual enters in life as an adult he interacts with so many people. Through socialisation there is a provision of common fund of knowledge, which enables people to operate as effective members of the society in which they live. This fosters social cohesion and awareness for active involvement in public life. Without communication this cannot possible.

Motivation

For accomplishment of any job there is need for encouragement, which requires motivation and stimulation. This is necessary to do the jobs. So, motivation and stimulation is necessary at very stage. Take, for example, learning to walk or talk by a young child. If the child is not motivated to walk and talk he will face difficulty in learning these activities. So, the parents, bring in some toys and aids as an innovative measures which appear to child as most fascinating. So, motivation for the individuals for doing social activities is necessary. This can help in solving some problems and attain ultimate aims in the society. Any kind of motivation is only possible through effective communication.

Debate and Discussions

Exchange of views of different view points on public issues is necessary. This is necessary for openness of the public issues. In an open society this is necessary for fostering greater interest and involvement at all levels, local, national, international and relating to matters of common interest. Effective skills in communication play a vital role in this respect.

Education

Education, though considered a self-recovery, but generally it is a transmission of knowledge so as to foster intellectual development, inculcation of values, formation of character, development of good behaviour and acquisition of skills and capacities at all stages of life. This process of education can only be initiated and affected through effective communication. All types of communication are generally used for the purpose. Without communication education of any sort is not possible.

Cultural Promotion

The culture is the soul of a society, as well as of the nation. It includes, art, artefacts, language, traditions, manners, ways of living and conserving all these. The dissemination of cultural traditions is done through enculturation. This is necessary for preserving cultural heritage of the past. For the preservation of the cultural heritage it is necessary that acculturation and cultural diffusion are systematically checked. For this end the knowledge about the past cultural happenings is transmitted to youngsters and imagination is widened. Activities for enhancing and inculcating spirit of creativity are arranged so as to generate aesthetic sense in the youngsters. For the purpose the communication of various hues are needed. Without communication human beings are mute like deaf and dumb. So the communication plays an important role in the cultural production, development and preservation.

Environmental Understanding

Man is a tiny part of the natural environment. Environment is like an organic whole of which man is a smallest part. It is necessary that man should know this reality and understand his own position. But he cannot do it alone. He is to be made aware about it, so that there can be a diffusion of the individual with the environment of which he is a part. This can be done through various forms of communication such as signs, symbols, sounds, images of drama, dance, art, literature, picnics, excursions, tours and sports at various places. This will add to the enjoyment of the individual and will help him identifying with the sublimity of Nature. This is only possible if effective means of communication are made available for the purpose.

Integration

Integration at national as well as at international level is the need of the day. Though clouds of cold war, have receded and started thinking for global peace. But another disintegrative force has started emerging. This force is dogmatic religious fundamentalist force. There has to be a movement to make the human beings aware about the versatility of human integration which could be achieved by infusing a spirit of humanity in the man. This can be only be done by effective ways of communication.

Economic Stimulation

Now the man has become a cog-pin of economic stimulation. During the present period of material rat-race, it is impossible for an individual to isolate himself from it. No doubt economic activities are must for every individual, without these one cannot survive. But the current economic stimulation is for something more. It is for comfort, luxury and hedonism. For that a constant flow of information for entrepreneurship and for necessary economic know-how are necessary for better economic life. Economics is a decisive force in the development of a country. Communication represents a growing segment of a country's gross national product and has direct repercussions on production, employment and general welfare of the people. In this communication, in various forms plays an important role. Telecommunication instantly transmits economic information. We see such transmission daily on our daily television national network and programme. It also telecasts information in many fields like agriculture, education, industry, trade and consumption. Our daily newspapers also do not lagging behind in this respect.

So the societies cannot survive until and unless they are informed about economic activities concerning growth and development, rise and decline in demographic figures, literacy, trends in work culture etc., etc. The dynamic planning rests on information about commodity, money, market, inflation, deflation, corruption in the society and consequent steps to be taken to check it.

Security

The communication system plays a vital role in the security of the nation. Army, Navy, Air Force and Police cannot function without communication network.

Public Transport

The public transport like Railways, Roadways, Waterways and Airways cannot function without a well knit communication system.

Political Stability

The communication is a vital need for the collectivity, that is society without proper communication links collective entities like family and community cannot exist. Societies cannot survive until they are well informed about political affairs of the nation. Therefore, a flow of communication is inevitable and necessary for strengthening of a democratic process.

Social Change

Change is a must according to Greek thinker Hereclitus. There ought to be instruments of change. One of the most important instrument of change is flow of information which is only possible through a communication network.

Social Need

The play of communication is a social need. It helps in maintaining the social structure through enforcing social control, social stratification, socialisation, perpetuation and protection of culture by way enculturation, perpetuation of national culture and heritage, assigning social roles, transmitting social and moral values and educating people. So communication system is a life line of a nation.

KINDS OF COMMUNICATION

Forms of Communication can be classified as under:

1. Biological or in-built system of communication in human beings and animals. The biological systems of communication may be classified as under:

(*i*) Aural Communication,
(*ii*) Oral or Verbal or Audio Communication,
(*iii*) Visual Communication,
(*iv*) Gesturatory Communication,
(*v*) Olfactory Communication,
(*vi*) Tactile Communication,
(*vii*) Kinesitics Communication, and
(*viii*) Proximal Communication

(i) Aural Communication

This is inbuilt sensibility in human beings and animals to recognise odours. When trained dog proceeds on the track on which a criminal had passed and escaped, the dog gives signals and communicates. Likewise we the human being when recognise the purity of liquids like edible oils and ghee, it is aural communication.

(ii) Audio Communication

Audio or oral or verbal communication is a major biological inbuilt system of communication in human beings and animals. Man has developed language and semantics pertaining to it, but the animals have not. A sense of listening and hearing is a major source of communication in the human world. As a result listening and hearing play a vital role in human communication. The animals also listen and hear but do not have language like sound symbol load equipment or mechanism to convey.

(iii) Visual Communication

The nature has provided to all human beings and to all animals excepting a few with double optical apparatus called eyes. This is a divine biological gift. As such, sensibility to see things and visualise them and also draw comprehension through visual sensibility is one of the greatest source of communication. The vision as a source of visualising and deducing information and knowledge is one of the important source of communication.

(iv) Gesturatory or Pantography

When proper human language was not developed as a science of semantics, the man used to convey hi feelings and impression through gestures. Still the gestures are used by man in social discussions, in dance, in drama profusely. In Kerala the dancers generally make use of gestures. They use masks and paint their faces and body parts to influence their audience. Such make ups and paintings of faces is called pantogarphy.

Gesturatory is only way to communicate for deaf and dumb who neither can speak nor hear. For such people Doordarshan relays news on TV through gestures. As a matter of fact gesturaoty is also an inbuilt system of communication in human beings and animals.

(v) Olfactory Communication

Like aural communication system olfactory communication is biologically inbuilt system of sensation through smell. We understand many things through smell. We recognise sour food through smell and discard it from eating. We recognise pure ghee and pure mustered oil only through smell. As a matter of facts the thing we want to know itself emits smell and release communication signals. Likewise for knowing many chemicals and chemical laden things, which release smell or smell sensibility of a thing is a major source of communication.

(vi) Tactile Communication

Sensibility to touch is also a biological system of communication. Everything which is the manifestation of the nature has a form tactile surface and colour. As such all biological creations are tactile laden. Our face has a texture our arms and legs have textures. Likewise all flora and fauna have textures which are different to each others. The bark of many trees is quite different to the bark of other trees. All surfaces of riverbeds, wide spectrum of landscapes, all animal world, all have textures. We perceive textures through and vision. As the communication we get from tactile surface is a source of communication. Therefore, sensibility to touch through we feel texture is a kind of communication.

(vii) Kinesitic Communication

At occasions human beings and animal express their feelings through bodily movements, facial expressions and postures. When a person is angry over the other, he becomes aggressive. Either he well below his arm or try to push the person on whom he is angry. Likewise, we generally notice the faces of two warring bulls become radiant and full of anger. On the other hand a dancer tries to establish 'tadamtya' full rapport with the theme he is performing. So kinesitic communication is also an effective source of communication.

(viii) Proximic Communication

Proximity is ingrained in human beings as well as in animal nature. Proximity is a precondition of existence of animal world. For the continuance of human race, the mankind arranges marriage of young males and females. The live in proximic conditions and reproduce and make social conditions stable. Likewise male and female animals came in proximity, mate and produce. So proximity also always entails communication. Some proximic communications are explicit, whereas some are implicit. Explicit proximic communication often becomes common, takes the shape of value, which in due course of time such forms of explicit communication becomes cultural patterns. And such patterns often show national as well as international cross cultural variations. A Japanese will smile when conveying tragic news. An Anglo-Indian would avoid such a situation. In the west kissing is common, whereas in India it is a profane activity. So, proximic communication employs various patterns such as kissing, embracing, eye contact, loud and low pitch of voice. The proximic signals of communication are used in various situations such as fear, conflict stress and stress, love and sex signals, etc.

2. Sociological Communication

Society is a collectivity of individuals. In other words it is composition or a whole of individual members who have heterogeneous interests and nature. It is social interaction which makes the members of the society integrated through certain values and social norms which are voluntarily followed by the members. This is only possible through social communication. Social communication makes social interaction, social cohesion, social roles, social order and social stratification becomes possible. It is only through social communication socialisation of the individual can be possible. Without socialisation no education and sociability of the individual is possible. And without these there cannot be any difference between man and animal. When effective social communication, for making the individual sociable and cultured lacks, crimes like rapes, abductions, thefts loots, increase. And the society becomes a barbarous society. So social communication is a must. It starts from the family and continues throughout the life of the individual through various agencies like home, school, community, peer circle and workplace. So social communication makes social existence possible. It also helps the man in the economic activities.

3. Mathematical or Mechanical Communication

When traditional means of communication that is transmitting of messages orally in face to face situation are changed or replaced by mechanical devices or boosted by equipments like loud speakers etc., such devices are termed as mechanical or mathematical devices of communication. In the present age of science and technological devices such as radio, telegraphy, teleprinters etc., are very important for transmitting information.

Because of the availability of these mechanical or technological devices of transmission, today, the international communication became very easy. The world has come nearer. Whereas this was an impossibility seventy or eight years ago. And only five hundred years ago when the messages wee sent by Kings through messengers on house back communication was a dream.

4. Mass Communication

Mass media, like radio, TV, newspapers have brought the world closer. And when we think of mass media communication in relation to national goals, we are looking at the mass media primarily as the instruments of achieving social, cultural and economic development within the value framework of democracy, secularism and equality. This way relationship between mass media and national goals are visualised. Mass media are independent variable and national goals are dependent variable. In other words mass communication is expected to subserve the purpose of achieving national goals.

Mass media helps in achieving national goals by performing certain functions for the society they serve. The UNESCO report on Communication and society, entitled 'Many Voices, One World' (p. 14) identifies eight different functions for Mass Media.

(*i*) The function of disseminating information to that the recipient of the message is able to understand and react knowledgeably to the world and to the complex of social, economic, technological and political conditions around him.

(*ii*) The function of socialism through the procession of common fund of knowledge which enables to operate as effective members of the society in which they live. Socialism also involves the communication and inculcation of an agreed set of values.

(*iii*) The function of motivation through of immediate and ultimate the promotion aims of each society and stimulation of personal choices and aspirations through the fostering of individual and community activities, geared up to the pursuit of agreed aims.

(*iv*) The function of education through the transmission of knowledge is to foster intellectual development, the formation of character and the acquisition of skills and capacities at all stages of life.

(*v*) The function of promoting debates and discussions through the provision and exchange of facts to facilitate or clarify differences on public issues.

(*vi*) The function of cultural promotion through the dissemination of cultural and artistic products.

(*vii*) The function of entertainment through the diffusion of drama, dance, art, literature, music, sports, etc., for personal and collective recreation and enjoyment.

(*viii*) The function of integration through the provision to all persons, groups and nations access to variety of message, which they need in order to understand each other and to appreciate others' living conditions, viewpoints and aspirations.

As such, mass communication is one of the important source of transmitting information to all. But it has demerits also. It tend to convert the mass of the people into receivers of messages and provide them little chance to be originators of the message. It might vitiate the truth also as totally free or unbiased communicator is a rarity. Physio-technical factors for mass communication can only be provided by the state, so there are chances of state influencing it. So it happens that the party-in-powers always tries to have full control over the mass media which make mass communication possible, but state interests oriented.

5. Educational Communication

This is the most important category of communication. The most important function of education is to prepare the individuals as worthy members of the society. It is education which provides to the members of the society the opportunity to learn and acquire knowledge and skills. Moreover, education is a process through which latent faculties, potentialities of the learner are raised with the help of the learner. So, there are two aspects of education, as two sides of a coin, one is the teacher who passes on information and the other is the learner himself, who by receiving information tries to visualise, understand, comprehend and learn. In addition to this he contributes also in the process of knowledge development. So the process of education is a process of educating or taking out what is within the learner. In doing so, the efforts are to be made to communicate in such a way that maximum elicitations could be possible, so that the mass of the students could be benefited. This can only be done if there occurs a healthy pedagogic reaction in the classroom. In addition to this education fosters growth of all elements in the individual necessary for sound personality development of the individual necessary for social integration, social cohesion and healthy social control. As such, the function of education is to prepare a person for a sound and sane life. It assimilates all elements necessary for enculturation. It generates suitable conditions which stimulates a person for better living. Education builds character. Thus, for a sound and balanced education, the suitable modes of communication are necessary.

All types of communication are used in sociological, economical and cultural context. Main thrust in these areas on information. As education is a special area for human development. The process of education is initiated with teaching and ends in self-knowing and development, therefore, it needs a special kind of communication or combination of forms of communication such as verbal and non-verbal. In verbal communication the individual is only informed. It does not, or rarely, invokes thinking and reasoning which are necessary for comprehension and learning.

Therefore, for pedagogic aims, the strategies are to be chalked out for didactic communication which may be helpful in educaring or eliciting information from students as much as possible. So, for teaching strategies which may be helpful in didactic function, verbal, non-verbal which include graphic material, mathematical or technological forms of communication are widely used. As a matter of fact teaching strategies, which are like art styles, require different approaches of communication—verbal, non-verbal, visual, kinesitic and proximic.

The communication symbols are of two types discursive and non-discursive and the teacher is required to use both. The students first confront, either the voice or the verbal communication transmitted by the teacher, or they see the object or objects or their republicas in the classroom, library, school museum or in the school as a whole. This transmits to them the first set of messages. This also includes objects like desks, chalk board, cupboard etc. This also includes class display like charts and pictures etc. The classroom proximises the individuals and their belongings too – as dress and school bags etc. The school territory is divided into zones: the teachers, students and administrative staff. This composition entails social reaction between them. There happens to be a close repertoire between the teachers and the taughts. There are some trouble shooters amongst students. Very often there happens that the schools arrange displays in the school. This display generally include photographs and portraits of renowned persons, certain quotations, charts, models, maps, ideograms and chalk boards which continuously emits communications to the students and force them to react. Therefore, educational communication media are varied and many. The teacher uses them as a systematic epistemic tools. Such an epistemic communication media are nothing but audio-visual aids and their systematic appropriate use in teaching, may be called innovative educational techniques, when this has been termed as 'Eduinnovtech'. The audio-visual aids are a kind of meta-language which are unable to speak (only visual aids) but still send signals to the viewer, to think rationalise, comprehend, learn and to respond. And thus, through this type of educational communication the process of interaction between teacher and taughts and between the taughts themselves starts. Actually this is real education. Mere passing on of information can never be education. As such, audio-visual aids play a vital major role in educational communication. And out of the audio-visual, visual communication is always considered better than verbal communication. All other sorts of communication other than verbal communication help in educational process. So efforts should be made to minimise the use of verbal communication in teaching. It should only be used for introductions and explanations to be given out of interactions.

MODELS OF COMMUNICATION

One-Way Communication

In one-way communication, a knowledgeable person transmits information to a person through words who does not know but not an ignorant. It would not be wrong to identify one-way communication with a strong blowing wind or so to say a storm which takes everything with it. A diagrammatic representation of one-way communication may be as under:

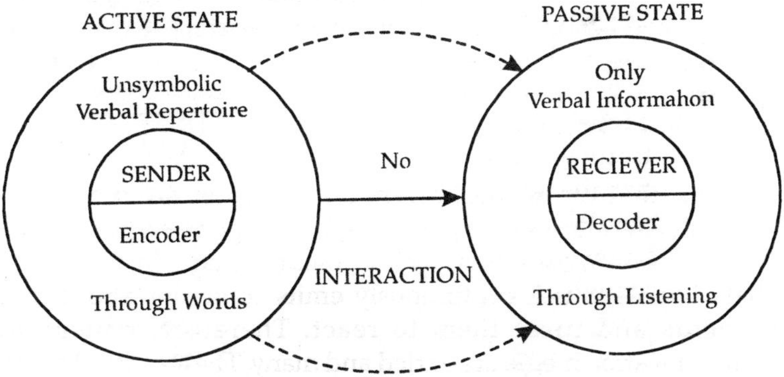

Fig. 1

In one-way communication there is a perennial flow of information from the one end that is sender, and the receiver accepts this information without questioning. Generally this happens when the teacher transmits information and the students accepts the information passively. This is done under the 'conflict model of teaching' wherein the teacher is dominant and the students are obedient followers. They are not able to react and respond as they are not motivated to do so. Hence, only the teacher who transmits information remains active whereas the students remains inactive and passive receivers. Their faculties of thinking, reasoning and comprehending remain undeveloped. In one-way communication the students cannot contribute, therefore, they can neither be creative and inventive. As such, in such a situation the main purpose of educating or educaring remains unachieved.

Two-Way Communication

In two-way communication a knowledgeable person transmits information to a less knowledgeable person through words plus through visual symbols, keeping in mind that the person who is being informed has some latent faculties and can contribute in the development of knowledge also. Many theorists view this type of human communication as looks similar to the figure given below:

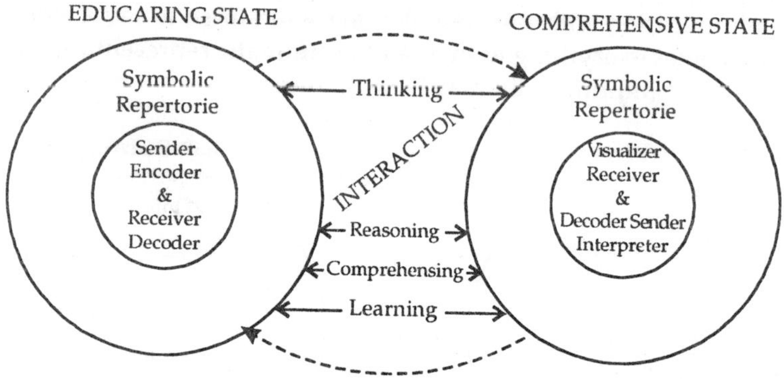

Fig. 2

In such a communication, each communication act involves a process in which a sender transmits a message through discursive and non-discursive symbols which he or she expects to be understood by the receiver easily. The unsymbolical information, for which the sender has no concrete things to show, is transmitted through words only. The symbolically loaded information, be it a verbal or non-verbal is first encoded by the sender and thereafter it is decoded by the receiver. Symbolic information does not mean graphic or concrete symbols. The words are also symbols for some concrete things. But when the words are arranged in semantic form, and their use becomes a regular routine feature they create a little reaction on the mind of the listener. So the process of thinking either do not take place or take place in a less amount. Since the transmission through words is a package transmission which comes out in the form of discussion or narration through the words are called non-discursive symbols, since such symbols do not emit any message which may force the receiver to think.

On the other hand silent or non-speaking symbols like pictures graphic materials, concrete things or their republica or models when shown without giving details ignites curiosity to know about these silent symbols. And getting no package information the visualiser is forced to think and reason about these symbols. Since such symbols unites. Communication symbols through their shape, form, structure, weight and size and texture give some hints which is not available to the students in verbal package form, such symbols are discursive symbols. These symbols compel the visualiser to think, reason comprehend and learn. And this is what we call response or reaction by the receiver. This leads to elicitation in the process of lesson development. During the process of encoding and decoding a symbolic repertoire is established which always entails thinking, reasoning, comprehending and finally learning. Therefore, too way communication is essential in teaching and education. This is also termed as interactive communication. The non-verbal symbols are generally interactive and are helpful in education.

INTERACTIVE NON-VERBAL COMMUNICATION BY ANIMALS

Communication has never been the monopoly of human beings alone. It has ever been the domain of the whole animal world. Animals, they do not have verbal non-discursive symbols which human beings have, have always been using non-interactive content or symbols along with sound symbols for their social interaction for their safety and existence. As such using sound along with other non-verbal symbols is not the sole prerogative of man.

It is also true that is not the only system of communication available. Another systems are also available. There is chemical communication of taste and smell like pheromone system generally used by many animals ranging from called organism – mesus found in monkeys and many other animals. Pheromone is a chemical substance released by animals to communicate with members of species. The queen bee prevents all other females of the hive from reaching sexual maturity by releasing pheromone. Both males and fema. es secretes pheromone to establish territories, warn of danger and attract males. Pheromones, it is said, have been detected in human beings, but the scientists do not accept it as yet, as if they affect human behaviour.

There is a tactile communication between two male and female monkeys taking part in mutual grooming. Also, there are usual signals like leg waving of spiders. Some male hunting spiders wave their legs an bodies in unusual courtship dance. The flashing of fire by flies (जुगनू) or spectacle of peacock tail are such visual symbols.

With 3,000 languages spoken in the world today, however, hardly one may try, and it is impossible to communicate with all peoples of human race. If you speak English you can communicate with 400 million other persons. If you learn Spanish you shall be able to speak to another 207 million people. Likewise every language has its own limited scope of communication. In our country (India) we have many languages and dialects spoken by the people. There is a contempt for our national language in few parts of the country. But when we use non-verbal symbols of communication it is understood by all because it is silent visual medium and is universal language.

Among animals, because of the lack of an adequate and elaborate verbal language, the use of body language plays a main role in communication. The honeybees from any part of the world would have the same method of communication amongst its members. A series of rituals performed by a bee would tell the others about the distance and direction of nectar. A worker bee performs a distance dance in the pattern of figure 8. The more rapidly the bee dances, the nearer is the flower. An imaginary between the loop of the figure 8 would indicate the direction in relation to the sun.

A visual signal available to mammals is erection of the hair shows hostility and fear. Cock fight is one of the examples which proceeds such signals. Vast arrays of expressions by non-human exhibit signals, which show that they communicate feelings of anger, displeasure, joy and gratitude. The dogs show such arrays of expression in relation with human beings. Dominant animals, be goats or be monkeys use a graded series of threat gestures to control their subordinates for sexual readiness.

An American anthropologist R.L. Bird Westell developed the science of kinetics. Scientists using kinetics study the movement gesture, facial expression, eye behaviour and body posture in relation to verbal communication. Body language or non-verbal behaviour, though too vague in term, is what kinetics is all about. Ray L. Bird Westell recognised that kinetics was only one of the many systems of communication, it is sufficiently important for him to have made a career of it.

No one knows how verbal language developed. The first real evidence of it is writing. The earliest known written records are Sumerian word pictures which are only as old as 3500 B.C. But scholars believe that did not appear until thousands of years after the origin of spoken language. In Indian context, though it has not been universally recognised as Indians were not very found of historical recording, it can be observed by the happenings of epics like Mahabharata and Ramayana that in India written language Sanskrit existed long-long before Sumerians could develop picture language. Therefore, knowledge or claim put forward by anthropologists about written language seems to be ambiguous. The question one feels and compelled to ask is whether, "before spoken language developed slowly", there existed sound signals such as grunts, barks, groaning out of which spoken language developed slowly". Before that non-verbal behaviour of body language would have been the means of communication with human beings too.

During the use era of silent movies Charlie Chaplin, a finniest man of the world played major role in non-verbal communication. Through, gestures, facial expression, postures and silent antics he managed to spread laughter—the world over and communicated stipulated social themes. Through the body language one can win friends crossing all barriers of race, colour or creed whereas spoken language fails to achieve it. So body language as a non-verbal communication is an Art.

Communication is essentially a social process for animal world too. It is important to all animals that live in organised way and form a cooperative relationship for food gathering, shelter and other relations and necessities. When social psychologists use the term communication they have in mind the way one mind affects another. Communication encompasses not just spoken or written words only, but it consists of all signals made by one organism that have meaning for another organism and affects their behaviour. It is not uniquely a human behaviour or process but occurs throughout the animal world. While human beings rely primarily on sounds and images, other animals communicate also by taste, touch, smell and body postures.

The animal kingdom has always intrigued man who has tried to study them, learn from them and exploit their means to his benefit. Investigations into animal world have revealed characteristics unique to different species. However, the man has still not been able decipher of the exact ways, animals communicate. Signals are there, but due uncertainty about their nature these cannot be detected or their patterns of communication be recognised. As Diana Reiss, an animal and human communicator expert puts it how does an observer finds that one species penetrate the communication system of another when we are deaf and blind to that system. Scientists all over the world are making continued efforts to study animals. Here are few fascinating examples of communication system found in animal species.

By their dance direction honey bees tell each other in what direction they should meet or nectar is to be found and far it is from the nest. Towne and Kirchne have shown that bees detect air born sounds produced by the vibration of the dancers wings by detecting the air particles movement occurring within few millimetres of the dancer's abdomen.

During the summer we notice the appearance of insects. They give signals to insects to follow in order to cooperate in taking grain to their hideouts. Cockroaches also have coordination in the collection of food. It is said that cockroaches predict natural calamities like earthquake by earth vibrations.

Elephants maintains a complex social order. A recent study by Katherine Payne suggests that elephants exchange greeting signals for their readiness for mating. They locate each other and organise groups to migrate by calling out in a based rumble that is below of human hearing. As a low frequency call an elephant may carry several miles to be heard by other elephants. These sounds may also explain the strange ability of elephants to migrate to distant parts of their territory soon after the main season has begun there.

Bats emits high frequency sounds beyond the range of human perception. These sounds are reflected of by objects and this helps bats to orient themselves. A blinded bat is also perfectly capable of finding its ways in the dark because it sees with ears. The reflected sound waves are 'distorted' depending upon the distance of the object and composition of the obstacles the sound bits. Bats have an excellent system not only to establish the location of the obstacle and its size, but also whether it is edible or not. Given an abundance of insects, a bat can catch 160 to 170 mosquitoes in an hour. It can feel and avoid a wire of the thickness of human hair stretched on its way. But it can intercept one another signals which could mean that they share perception about external world. Likewise, in human beings blind persons more depend on sound signals while they walk.

Other animals too are equipped with echo sounding devices. Some fishes, whales, and dolphins have sonar locators as well. The dolphins produce two general categories of sounds, chicks which they use to probe world around them, the way a submarine uses sonar. Dolphin whistle, which plays a central role in dolphin to dolphin communication. In the dolphins, the sonar or echo locating blasts are in the form of short bursts of sounds pulsing through fatty tissues of dolphins' forehead. Here they are focussed into a beam that travel through water four or five times faster than air.

The returning echo contains information on the surrounding environment. The dolphin hears through fat deposits in the jaws from which sound is transmitted in the inner ear, then to the brain. Thus, the dolphin is able to navigate in turbid waters, locate and identify objects up to 800 meters away, well out of the reach of the reach of visual range. With such a fine tuned sonar system of dolphin can detect a vitamin capsule from the end of a large pool.

The whistle produced by dolphins convey its identity and may also contain messages about the emotional state of dolphin. James Ralstone, a psychologist and Humphrey William a Computer Specialist compared the acoustic picture or sonograms of the dolphins' whistles during normal social activities and stressful situations, such as when they are removed from the tank for routine veterinary proceedings. They found that when animal is under stress each dolphin's signature whistle keeps its general configuration but differ in pitch and duration. This change may convey the information on their emotional state of anxiety to other members of the groups.

Whales sing songs. The songs mainly sung by males and during the breeding season serve as mating dominance displays. These are not merely noise but have intricate stylised composition. The songs of bumps back whales can change dramatically from year to year, yet each whale is an ocean wide population sing the same song as other.

How do they manage to do this? Biologists Linda Guinea and Katharina Payne have come with an intriguing possibility. Like humans, humpbacks seems to be using rhymes. To ascertain if the rhyme, served as an aid to memory. Guinea and Payne analysed 548 humpbacks' songs for number of themes and prevalence of rhyme. It turned out that rhymes were more prevalent in more complicated songs containing more material to be remembered.

The animals calls have more meaning than might be apparent. Eugene Morton says that gentle thrill of a bird is in fact an ongoing battle between singer and other birds that covet territory. Male birds sing to attract females, but other male birds listen to the song to judge how far away the singer is and whether he is encroaching on their territory. Among several species of birds male songs can actually accelerate the ovulation of females.

Sea gulls are even more subtle in their communication. They lie a gull that spots food will sometimes cry out a danger call causing the surrounding gulls to hesitate for a split, while the caller drives to grab it pray.

Birds like parrots, *mynahs* have been known to display vocal mimicry of human speech. Many species, from insects to mammals use buzzing or kissing sounds when threatened, perhaps such sounds make them seen larger and more formidable. When cornered burrowing owl utters his hiss that sounds remarkably like rattle of an angry rattle snake. Mathew Ross reports that experiments suggest that hisses are indeed a mimic of rattle snakes, and have not independently evolved as warning signals.

The inclinative speech displayed by parrots and *mynahs* does not demonstrate any understanding of the content of the utterance they produce. A lot of research projects have been set up in the last 15 years to see if it is possible to teach animals of another species some different from human language. The primates and dolphins have shown the ability to understand, respond to and initiate artificial language.

Primates and dolphins really depend upon a very complex network of social affiliations and interactions in order to make their living substantial in the world. The glue that holds together is communication says Lois Herman, a psychologist, engaged in research on dolphins.

Koko, a 16 year old gorilla communicates in American sign language which she has been learning since she was one year old. Koko can depict her emotions, for example, her wish to have a baby. She can utter words and rhymes in English like black, red and heads. She is also a maker of metaphors: a mask in an eyes hat, a cigarette lighter, a bottle match. She can write her own name and she is learning to read. She laughs and cut jokes. Penny Patterson, her teacher says that her humour is primitive.

Penny Patterson sees no dividing line between humorous and animals, their characteristics and our merge. He further says that there is only qualitative difference between the two.

Thus as the secretes of animals are unravelled, one can see that human beings are not alone and magnificent on a superior plane. Animals and humans are branches of an animal world tree. Both belong to animal world yet have different characteristics.

As such, it can be concluded that, in humans, information and ideas are mostly conversed through spoken words and visual symbols. Other members of the animal kingdom, that is animal and birds, have their own unspoken language that is non-verbal to communicate. For example croaking of frogs, singing of birds, speaking through music, colourful patterns of fish, distant scent of mask dance of bees, barking of dogs in case of danger and playful gestures to their masters. Like humans, the animals also express feelings through bodily gestures. The animals also do form social groups like humans in which they communicate amongst themselves. Animals also respond to visual symbols also. Of course the animals do not have a well developed language and well developed system of expression through visual symbols, but their power to smell and emit alarm signals is praiseworthy. Dogs are used to detect crime. Ants and cockroaches can very well predict the earthquake as they leave well in advance where it is going to occur.

On the whole it can be presumed that animals make use of non-verbal symbols of communication more effectively than human beings. Since it is observed that their communication is done always through non-spoken symbols, which is well coordinated, organised and interactive between them followed a remarkable comprehension and understanding. Whereas human beings largely depend more on spoken and written symbols which generally emit interaction and sharing between the members of the group to which communication is made. Therefore, pedagogically, it is desirable that verbal communication should be minimum and that too should always entail non-verbal communication in educational practices that is in teaching.

THEORIES OF COMMUNICATION

Theories in all disciplines are built after constant study, observation, experimentation enquiry and research. Many researchers working with relevant concerns of disciplines, have sought possible theories or laws of "cause and effect" to explain the way in which human dispositions are effected by certain trends, and try to put forward reasons for certain circumstances and reasons thereby which cause change or effect. According to Hereclitus, a Greek thinker, change is inevitable and human beings are also governed by this law of flux. They too desire change.

The communication became institutionalised in the society after a long journey. Looking to the development of communication some of its theoretical aspects can be traced. Words being symbol of human experience give information. And in these regard light of philosophical and metaphysical theories have limited epistemological relevance. Those who believe in metaphysics and in the existence of God rely on the authenticity of words from authority – like descriptions recorded in some religious scriptures like Vedas, Upanishads, Aryanakas and Shrimad Bhagwad Gita, Ramayana and Mahabharata of Hindus, Holy Koran and Hadish of Muslims, Old Testament and New Testament of Christians and Zeverta of Zews and likewise scriptures of other faiths. But on the contrary, who either are atheists or empiricists and do not believe in metaphysics and solely rely on natural development and experience believe in perception and experimentation. For them deductive logic has no meaning. They believe in inductive logic.

Nothing is true which cannot be verified, said A.J. Ayer. They adhere to this dictum.

As such epistemological meaning and relevance underlying words in the light of metaphysical sense, the old theories of knowledge have undergone change. And some thinkers started believing that words have no corps of learning but only serve as an instrument of awareness adapted to human purpose. The words symbols are always laden with information and less knowledge, whereas other symbols of communication which are generally non-verbal lead to person to knowledge.

George N. Gorden described Communication as a mind and body problem. He termed it as 'Logics of Communication' and 'Psychologies of Communication'. Logics of communication deals with problem concerning with mind and psychologies of communication deals with problem concerning with body. Von Bertahanfly noted as 'Public or Shared Communication' and 'Private or Mental Communication' which leads to perception and experience. The earlier leads to information. According to both of their communication constitutes two major classes of description of phenomena-common talk and specialised comprehended reporting. These two concepts – Public (or shared) perception or events and Private (or mental) perception followed by comprehension or understanding are two different categories of communication.

Philosophers, right from Plato up to Rene' Descartes maintained duality. Main source of knowledge according to Plato is sense perception followed by comprehension. Aristotle maintained that the study of matter followed by its analysis is the source of knowledge. Cartesian dualism rests between natural things which can be seen and comprehended by conscious ego. Knowledge is only possible when things can be seen and rationalised through brain. Rene' Descartes believes that every human being comes with innate ideas, until these innate ideas are educared, education of human being is not possible. Aristotle before Rene' Descartes had laid emphasis on deductive reasoning. On the Contrary Bacon stressed that inductive process can only be a source of knowledge. And on this premise the foundation of empiricism was laid which affirms that only experimentation can be the source of knowledge.

Main purpose of education is both (1) transmission of information leading to knowledge and (2) comprehension leading to learning and knowledge. The language of communication in education should reflect all aspects through dissemination of sound, actions, art forms and republicas or models of big or small concrete things which have common meaning to sender or receiver. In other words, this can be said, the logics of communication. This can also be aesthetics of communication. According to Aristotle, there are three ingredients to communication (1) "Process, the speaker" (2) "the speech – conveyer of ideas" and (3) "Audience – the receivers":

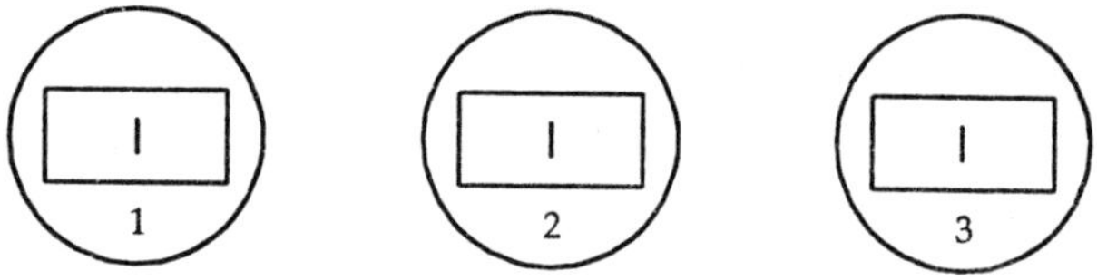

Man with an Idea (Speaker Process of Speech) | Conveyer of Ideas (Speech) | Audience (Receivers)

Fig. 3

These three elements are needed for communication. If one is missing, the communication is not possible. For the reinforcement of the communication by those three elements, there is a need to bring non-verbal symbols of communication including art forms. Thereafter, there is a need of deliberate and concentrated efforts to communicate.

Communication can be formal, non-formal and aformal. When a communicator deliberately and intensely communicates with a purpose and with a hope to achieve a desired end, such communication may be termed as formal. When something is communicated through actions, grace of beauty and love, fashion, make up, folk arts and socialisation through imitation, such a communication may be termed as non-formal. Many things are communicated by the peer group. New trends in fashions, some secretes of adolescents of life, and some cultural patterns are communicated through peer group and is termed as aformal or informal communication.

Psychologies and Logics of Communication

The word 'psycho' is described as the study of several mental states. Intellectuals like Rousseau, Swift, Samuel Johnson, John Stuart

Mill, Voltaire, Emerson even Rene' Descartes contributed much to the psychology of thinking. Lately in nineteenth century, Sigmund Freud, Chareot, Janet, Jung and other psychologists contributed in this field also. Logics and Psychologies can be presented graphically as under:

(deals with the problems concerning mind)

Fig. 4: Logics of Communication

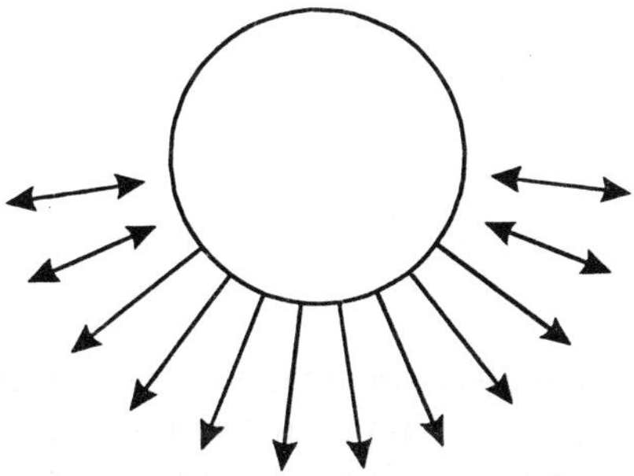

(deals with the problems of body)

Fig. 5: Psychologics of Communication

Education in any way has always a purpose. It is imparted with a body of stipulated goals in view that is to transmit a body of knowledge to enculturate the younger one, and to inculcate an urge in the pupils to think and rationalise about their surroundings. Communication plays a vital role in achieving these objectives. Furthermore, communication establishes S-R bonds, does conditioning by establishing conditioning bonds. Sometimes it is termed as operant learning. As such, communication helps in learning and gestalt learning. Therefore, while communicating, emphasis should be given on elicitations of operational responses which ensure learning. So the educational communication is to be, according to both logics and psychologies of communication, followed by persuasive and motivational approaches in teaching. In other words both techniques of communication that verbal and non-verbal should be used keeping in view that it should invite healthy interaction in the classroom. Success of educational communication can only be ensured through these principles. An educational communication cannot be like a telephonic communication where a communicator conveys his message in a concealed situation and disappearances. It has to be interactive two-way process where in the encoder and decoder of message face each other.

PRE-CONDITION FOR COMMUNICATION

Pre-disposition

Man is an occupant of niches – psychological and social. He adapts to his diverse environment. In this long environmental diversity he procured long gestation extended infancy, lengthy maturation. He is endowed by the nature big brain, flexible muscle movement of hands and feet, erect posture with a chance of longevity of life to comparison to another animals. In addition to his optical apparatus is also superior than other animals. In the society, man finds complex division of labour, task performance and accomplishment devices which entail coordination, cooperation and sharing amongst fellow human beings. According to G.H. Mead (1934) society depends upon flexibility, predictability and regularity. According to her man is composed of biological mechanism equipped with signified symbolisers. So communication plays a vital role in his survival.

Inter-Corporal Influence

The human organism is an integrated whole, stimulated to responses by his physical signals. It is not to be considered or thought to be a box carrying various independent pairs of terminals and tables. God has gifted man with mouth, eyes, ears, nose, etc., organs of perception (Cherry 1957 pp. 127-28) along with flexible body, bigger head, speech and intense sensibility. Besides, man has vocalic language and non-vocalic expression power such as creative impulses.

Timing and Structure

Human body organism is an integrated whole. It is regulated through coordination of heat and nutrition. "Complex organisms generally depend upon another organisms. Each organism has patterned partials for its survival which gains competition through coordination. By means of kinetics analysis we could know structured and patterned communication elements in visible aspects of human body system based on interconnectedness of human potentials etc. These directly or indirectly affected by the semantic system based on interconnectedness of human potentials.

The climatic, geographical and demographic conditions also affect human communication. Timing, readiness, readiness and motivation are essential for interactive action. So also, these are essential for communication as these are essential agents for interactive action. Timing coordination for readiness are essential for work, as part or whole work.

I.A. Richards defined communication "as a process of exchanging meanings between individuals through common system of symbols. A discrete aspect of human communication takes place when mind so acts upon its environment that another mind is influenced – and to the mind experience occurs".

Jurgen Rusech, an American scholar has advanced as much as forty definitions of communication, basing upon many theories that of art, architectural anthropological, sociological, political, formal, informal (sexual attraction) and a formal through play of behaviour and depending upon interpersonal communication and also on technological innovations like, telegraph, telephone, telex, wireless, radio, gramophone, telephoto, telestate, TV, VCR, VCP, broadcasting, advertising, newspapers and periodicals have apparent influences on human communication.

Social scientists have been theorising and identifying communication. Through various myths, styles of living, traditions, customs, manners, mores, cultural patterns and culture which are passed on from generation to generation one segment of society to another. Political scientists and economists have recognised that communication of many types which lie at the heart of regularities in social order.

In the 1960s a Canadian educator, Marshal Mehulian drew threads of interest in the field of education regarding communication. He associated many contemporary sociological and psychological phenomenon affecting education and culture. He associated many contemporary sociological and psychological phenomenon affecting education and culture. He asserted that "the modern society is moving from print to visual and the medium is message". He said that, this trend stimulated the film making photography, visual arts, mass media. He believed that now the following are centring up:

(*i*) Mass media communication concentrating on industries,
(*ii*) Persuasive communication is the need of the day,
(*iii*) Process of interpersonal communication is required at all levels including education,
(*iv*) Dynamics of verbal and non-verbal communication in education and other fields is the need of the day,
(*v*) Effective use of communication for socialisation, artistic and social living, including education in and out of school, and
(*vi*) Necessity to develop effective means of communication, its use and evaluation at all levels.

In short, it can be said that a communication expert including the teacher has to be well versed in the art of communication, as it moulds the human behaviour, about which the sociologists, economists, politicians, theologists, educationists and psychologists are concerned.

THEORIES OF TRANSMISSION OF MESSAGE IN COMMUNICATION

Dyadic Frame

It is a process of passage of information between two units through transmission of more or less meaningful symbols from one individual to another or more; or from a group of people or an organisation to another group of people or organisation. Thus the idea model of communication is based on Dyad, a knowledgeable person monadic as father or mother or teacher emits knowledge carrying symbols that enter into the head of a less knowledgeable or non-knowledgeable person – say a student on an ignorant but eager to know person is a Dyad. This model has strong bearing on our attitude towards teaching and learning process entailing the concepts of super-ordination, sub-ordination wisdom and ignorance. It is relied or supplemented by writing and reading process and derivation of literacy, represented by books, newspapers, motion pictures, radio and television. Dyadic model is part of cultural tradition and basically helps in enculturation. The dyadic communication view focuses research into photometric structure of communication behaviour. As such, the process of communication is defined as "that process whereby encapsulated particles of meaning are transmitted between individual organism by means of sending and receiving devices". The sender is termed in this process as 'coder' and the receiver as 'decoder'. In this process of communication symbols such as aural, verbal, non-verbal and gestures are generally used. Anthropocentric and ethnocentric predilections are also important in communication. Often it is suggested that tangibility takes preference over visibility. And visibility takes preference over audibility. And over above all self-view and comprehension are considered better for learning and knowledge. The epistemologists and pedagogists are of the view that knowledge acquired through books or words is misleading and incomplete. Therefore pedagogic communication should always entail non-verbal means of communication, so as to enable the decoder to understand, comprehend and learn about the matter or content which is being transmitted to him.

Finally, we can say that our daily life starts with communication. It is impossible for human beings and animals and birds insects not to communicate. It continues from ex-ultra-wail to the last most of life. It is essential for existence for all. Man is a communicating creature. He has been communicating before the language developed. Man has been cooperating, dealing, sharing with his fellow beings. This could not have been possible without communication. Throughout communication man shares information, experience knowledge and thus he understands, persuades, converts and controls his fellow beings.

Means of Communication

Means of communication are many:

(*i*) facial expressions and gestures, the possible way of attracting,

(*ii*) touch (especially for blinds),

(*iii*) smell (especially for animals like dogs),

(*iv*) visual and mathematical signs, and

(*v*) aesthetic symbols such as music, dance, drama, art, acting, mono-acting, solo-acting, and pantonomy.

All these communication symbols are old and pre-historic and are invocative. With the passage of time, man developed language which became a major tool of communication. But the language symbols, as they communicate explicitly, are non-invocative. They do not force decoder to think and rationalise. There is simple logic behind it, if a readymade pack of food is offered to any person what is the necessity for him to cook. And in education thinking and reasoning are must. So communication through spoken words and written words is considered by the educationists an non-invocative and ill-suited for educating young students. They say that such communication makes the students passive listeners and lethargic. The students do not tend to think and rationalise. So they cannot be active creative and innovative.

The communication is an essential social activity. As the education of the young children is also an essential activity, both communication and education go hand and glove and are inseparable. There are different theories of communication, which have been described under the heading kinds of communication briefly. Though it is a kind of repetition, since few points were missing all are elucidated again as below:

I. Mathematical Theory

This theory is attributed to Norman, Wiener and Claude Harmon. This applies electronic and Mechanical Engineering concepts to communication. It explains on lines of transmission, based on data, content from sender to receiver. Integer theory in terms of integers and quality scheme that the meaning of message or content is materially affected by the accuracy of efficiency of *modus operandi* of the technological transmission which called Mass Media is useful in distant communication. It has defects too. It tends to denigrate the legitimate semantic communication, that its integrity of the message is lost because it is done through one-way system of communication.

II. Sociological Theory

It is a process of making ideas common dealing with subjective states such as ideas', beliefs and customs, by way of (*a*) verbal and non-verbal means of communication, (*b*) social interactions in human beings in small or big groups through articulated speech, signs, signs and symbols through visual arts and folk arts, (*c*) through bodily forms of bodily gestures such as pantogany etc., (*d*) spoken language, visual graphic arts, higher forms of communication through recorded experiences and sentiments.

Education is a vehicle to promote and transport ideas, experience, customs, beliefs and culture through discursive and non-discursive systems that is invocative and non-invocative communication symbols. Communication keeps unity and continuity in this process of enculturation. So, it would not be wrong to say that communication is a vehicle of culture as well as of education. Education can be accomplished if twin action is ascertained, that is actions y the teacher and taughts both. So, in education there should be two-way communication that is verbal and non-verbal through recorded experiences and sentiments, then only the prime objective of education can be achieved.

III. Psychological Theory

Psychological theory of communication is based on S.R. Bond principle (stimulus-response) dealing with consciousness and cognitive level of the learner. Cognitive level of communication manifestation is to be related to environment stimuli. Behavioural approach is to be adopted to psychological communication, which should be followed by reward and punishment approach. A reductionist approach by combining psycho-linguistic theory and mathematical theory is to be adopted for making psychological communication a success.

IV. Semantic Theory

Consciousness with the continuity of thought is the basis of this theory.

V. Functional Process Theory

It is a process by which an individual transmits stimuli to the learner through verbal symbols to modify his behaviour in a communication culture which is no better than information. It cannot be tantamount or equal to non-verbal communication which is essential for education.

VI. Liner Theory of Communication

Finally it can be said that in education a communication method or many communication methods are useful, if they result in clarity through simplicity in transmission. Moreover, the communication should be attractive which may motivate the students. The coder and decoder both should proceed in harmony. They should proceed in liner method that is they should have close links. Negative entropy and redundancy like noise, disinterest and distraction should be avoided in the process of communication in teaching for education.

7

Communication Planning for Educational Teaching

Since the dawn of human civilisation, non-formal or formal planning has ever been on the human agenda for any human activity – be it hunting, or pasturing and tending of animals or capturing of fair sex for reproduction and raising family or attacking wild animals or doing agriculture or any handicraft. In all spheres of human activity planning was there implicitly or explicitly. It is believed that in the earlier periods informal planning used to be adopted by man. As the societies grew more complex the human activities demanded great care in execution and the concept of planning increasingly gained importance.

In the past all human endeavours for search of new lands, which entailed expeditions were undertaken after well thought and well prepared voyages. Necessary due planning was done before hand before proceeding on these expeditions. Equipments like boat diving, sticks, strong boats (mini-ships), compasses, maps, charts and food and drinking water weapons were taken by the person who undertook expeditions.

Likewise in military expeditions, when army generals thought of conquering particular countries first planned, prepared and than attacked the enemy. Not only army generals, the burglars, sea pirates and even dacoits used to plan before action. Also, the planning is needed in all walks of human life.

The modern science and technology has boosted planning. For economic activity, be it is carried on small scale or on advance scale the planning is must. Not only that in every sphere of human life the concept of planning is seen, be it a family, home budget planning and planning for human routine activities. Earlier it was done informally. Now it is done formally in every walks of human life and field of work.

So the concept of planning is as old as human existence. When man aspires to achieve something, he contemplates over the problem. He thinks over the pros and cons and prepares himself for the feat. Necessity is the mother of invention, he finds some via media for achieving the objectives. The planning for action is generally done by man in the animal world. Animals too do some kind of planning. The cat plans for her catch. Likewise other animals also plan for their catch. But in comparison to man their brain equipments are not so developed.

It is observed that by the end of the last century (19th century) planning for human action was, usually done informally. The law of 'cause and effect' also used to play, and still plays a vital role in planning in human actions. Human exploitation, that is exploitation of man by man also boosted the concept of planning. The rich always exploited the poor. The poor always thought of getting rid of exploitation by the stronger. The formal shape of planning was first given in Russia in 1917 after October Revolution, to get rid of the economic backwardness. It were the Russians who thought of Five Year plans at government level. Earlier the planning was not chalked out or detailed for a stipulated period.

In the earlier periods all educational activities in the societies were planned by the societies themselves informally. State had no or very limited control over educational activities. Mostly, the masses were educated informally either at home or at the guilds throughout the world. Only a few of the upper castes (in India) and upper class (in the rest of the world) used, to attend institutions like *Gurukulas*, academics and *madarsas*, where formal education was imparted to some extent. But by and large the education was based on informal system of instruction wherein meticulous planning was not needed.

With the development of science and technology and unprecedented development in human population necessitated planning for education too, along with other human activities.

1. OBJECTIVES OF EDUCATIONAL COMMUNICATION

For any human activity there has to be prescribed certain aims and objectives. So educational communication should also entail some specified aims and objectives which could help in the realisation of national educational goals, while deciding about the objectives of educational communication we should keep in mind that education and teaching are two different concepts. True education is only possible when the educator, who is generally identified as the teacher, sincerely tries to take out what is already within the so-called eudcand or student, because education is nothing but recovery of what is already there within the person who is being taught.

Teaching is a form of communication. The aim of good teaching should be how to communicate to the pupils to enable them to teach themselves. In other words, the teacher should communicate in such a way that the educational communication should help the pupils to learn themselves. Learner should be a guided for learning. It can only be possible when communication process is based on sharing, that it has to be two-way directional process, where in continual adjustments in responses, that a continued dialogues between the teacher and taughts are possible, whereby continued adjustments in responses are established between the teacher and the students in the classroom. For effective educational communication two situations are essential: (1) The idea must be clearly expressed first verbally and later it should follow reinforcement through non-verbal symbols, (2) There should be feeling tone of mutuality, that is, there should be sharing of experiences between the teacher and the students.

We learn through our sense organs. Senses are the gateway of our knowledge. The organs of seeing and hearing are most important, as all sense organs help us in understanding the environment around us. Most of the knowledge we acquire or learning takes place in the school we get through our eyes and years. Therefore, main objectives of educational communication should be to utilise properly both the body sense organs that is ears and eyes, and coordinating these with mind. Therefore, one of the objectives of educational communication should be to create an atmosphere of mutuality between the teacher and taughts. This can only be done and promoted if the individuality of the student is respected, which have characteristics like personal ego, eagerness to contribute creativity etc. Moreover, there are wide and varied individual differences in students.

Some of them are very extraordinary intelligent, so to say are exceptional, some are intelligent. For such students it is very difficult to restrain themselves from expression. If such students are denied expression during the course of teaching in the classroom frustration will prevail over them and their personality development will be hampered. So one of the objective of educational communication should be to provide ample opportunity to such students to speak and express in the classroom while teaching is in progress. The teaching which provides ample opportunities to think and express contributing in the process of knowledge development can only be said true education.

Furthermore, educational communication objectives should also include the following aspects which can only achieved by using audio-visual aids:

(*i*) One of the foremost objectives of educational communication should be to motivate the child to learn by arousing interest in a number of ways. It can be done by providing change from the usual activities of school such as reading, writing and listening. The novelty of the communicative aids can arise interest and motivate the pupils.

(*ii*) The change in the classroom atmosphere should be one of the objectives of educational communication. When the teacher is dominant and pours a lot of information on the students without involving them in the learning process, the students gets bored. But when a film, or a film strip is screened or a transparency is projected on a overhead projector, or some other non-verbal aids are shown in the classroom, children freely talk, question, discuss and comment upon enthusiastically. In such a situation the teachers attitude should also become friendly. This pleasant and natural atmosphere contributes greatly to learning.

(*iii*) The educational communication should comparatively be easy to understand. Usually any description given through verbal communication is difficult to understand and grasp. But when such a communication is supplemented with non-verbal communication, it is easily understood and grasped.

(*iv*) The children learn a lot by acting or doing something. So educational communication give such an opportunity by the use of audio-visual aids. An opportunity to touch a model, press a button and activate the model provides an added appeal to the students.

(*v*) There are certain things which are difficult to explain. Sometimes it becomes difficult for the teacher or instructor to describe certain things in words. Say an animal or plant which children have not yet seen. If the teacher makes them (students) see a photograph or film or film strip on that particular animal or plant. It makes easier to link children's experience to its substitute. They easily describe its texture, colour, posture, body parts and other characteristics. So the educational communication objective should be make the child's experience meaningful.

(*vi*) Educational communication objectives should also be aimed at, that it may enable the students to retain information and contemplation over it. This can only if verbal communication should be suitably substituted by non-verbal graphic media such as pictures, charts, models maps and transparency media such as films and filmstrips etc. For instance if a child is made to read the life of Raja Rammohan Roy or Shivaji. They may learn a lot and may have a good idea of them. But, an average number of children are likely to forget the details or the main events in the long run. Whereas, if the children are provided to view the film based on them, it will have a permanent effect on their memory. It goes with the Chinese adage "what we hear we forget, and what we see we remember".

(*vii*) Educational communication should provide vividness to the learning situations. The Courts of Mughals have been described in various books by the illustrated writings with full descriptions. But no book gives such a grand description as we find it in film vivid experience or on the spot visual experience of Mughal monuments like Tomb of Akbar at Sikandra, Agra Fort, Taj Mahal at Agra, Akbar Palace at Fatehpur Sikri and Red Fort and Jama Masjid at Delhi.

(*viii*) Educational communication should give clarity of the facts. Clarity is not possible through verbal communication. The film on 'A Tale of Two Cities' gives such a clear picture of the French Revolution, its background, its effects in such a way that a hundred volumes on the period of history pertaining to the French Revolution could not do so.

(*ix*) Educational communication through audio-visual aids should present the abstract idea in a concrete form to make the learning really effective.

(*x*) Educational communication should make the learning actively really meaningful when the situation is concrete and interesting it is more meaningful and comprehensive also.

(*xi*) Educational communication should be so designed that various sense organs work jointly. When sense organs of hearing and seeing work jointly learning happens to be more effective.

(*xii*) Generally verbalism dominates the teaching scene in the schools. Also the teachers are over loaded with teaching. Out of eight periods, generally a teacher has to take six periods a day of thirty five minutes. In addition to it most of the teaches have to take up at least one arrangement in schools. As such, on average a teacher has to teach seven periods of 35 minutes a day, which comes about 4 hours and five minutes teaching a day. This impression is gathered from Delhi Schools. Can a teacher speak four hours continuously? It appears unplausable. Therefore, educational communication should aim at the reduction of verbalism.

(*xiii*) It should provide variety. The variety in the classroom procedures can be brought by making the atmosphere life like. The children love variety and a change of atmosphere. Dull and monotonous atmosphere makes the pupil dull, disinterested in studies.

It is, therefore, necessary that educational communication should be planned for educational teaching. It is necessary for proper explaining of the content to the students. The word "Explain" is derived from the Latin word "Explanare" meaning to spread out.

2. APPLICATION OF COMMUNICATION SYMBOLS IN EDUCATIONAL TEACHING

The word 'teach' is derivation from the Greek/Latin word 'Taccon' meaning 'to pass on acquired knowledge', 'to instruct', 'to impart'. The teacher is a person who does this work. Education is not teaching, it is much more. It is a recovery from the students what is already with them. The teacher is a regent, a guide and helper in this process of this recovery. He uses two kinds of symbols – verbal and non-verbal for the recovery what we call education. Verbal symbols are often discursive since with the verbal equipment we generally pour information on the students. Often some of the information is retained and rest of it is forgotten. On the other non-verbal symbols which are pictures, charts, models, maps, flash cards etc., etc. when spread out or shown in the class, play a non-discursive role. The students see these non-verbal symbol, try visualise, grasp and understand themselves. Their mental faculties become active. They start thinking, reasoning and comprehending. As such the real learning process starts.

Thus, for a teacher for good explaining threshold be good spread for the visualisation of teaching aids for the benefits of the students. He should bring out in the classroom some visual material that is broadly termed as spread out. These are pictures, charts, maps, graphs models, specimens, still pictures, film strips and motion pictures etc.

Durrel has observed that often there is a lack of association between verbal symbols and environment and life outside the classroom. Unless the listening and reading are associated with or attached to actual sensory and related experiences at the time of teaching we cannot expect good results. The world of the child, particularly in the elementary school, is a sensory motor world; he is interested in things he can see, hear, touch, taste, smell, plan, make, do and try.

We thus see, that Durrel asks for "experiencing" as a method of learning that can only be done by "spreading out" that is by use of Audio-Visual aids. Therefore, in educational communication we should use both discursive and non-discursive symbols that is verbal and non-verbal symbols of communication keeping in view the aims and objectives of education and national social goals.

3. PLANNING FOR EDUCATIONAL COMMUNICATION

Advance planning for any social, political and economic activities is a pre-requisite condition of these days in the age of science and technology. Since education is an important social activity and is an instrument of change. Man can only prosper if he is well educated and fully aware of about the new serenity methods and techniques applicable to various industrial and economic movements. Without material gains man cannot sustain a civic life and survive, so the modern education has to cater the needs of the individual in this regard. It has to equip the person with modern education, has to cater the needs of the individual in this regard. It has to equip the person with modern knowledge. There are lot of differentiations in the society which breed competition and pave the way for social stratification and social order. Change is the rule of nature. Old social values are vanishing and new ones are taking their place. Educational structure of any society has to meet this challenge and prepare the person accordingly. It is a great responsibility of the school teacher.

As such there are so many subjects on the school curricula are specified courses of content which are to be taught to the students during a specified period of study. The students are prepared for particular examination. After passing out examination the process of certification follows which opens the gates of opportunity for employment to the students. The long range specified courses of contents are divided and spread year wise and term wise. The contents to be taught are further stratified and divided for daily teaching for the convenience of the teacher. All this is carefully and deliberately planned by the authorities and the schools are assigned to carry on teaching accordingly.

The teacher proceeds as per planned curriculum for a year broken into units as per school term. The teacher further divides the unit plan of teaching under the guidance of the school principal into small units for day to day teaching. He prepares daily lesson plans for that. The teacher will have to keep in mind that his teaching may be such that the students involvement could be maximally possible. Keeping this aim in mind he proceeds he should try to involve the students in lesson development as much as possible in order to elicit from them as much as possible. Thus, teaching strategy can only make true education possible. If this does not happen and the teacher passes on only information which does not evoke thinking and reasoning in students, the education is not possible. This will be a one-way traffic, that is, one-way communication. In such a situation the teacher is at giving end and the students are at the receiving end. The teacher is active and dominant. The students are passive listeners and acceptors. There is a very little interaction between the teacher and the taughts. As such, such a conflict model of teaching does not evoke thinking in students. With the result there are very little chances of self-learning, and the real purpose of teaching is defeated since such teaching does not lead to education. So, there should be a deliberate planning for educational planning, for educational communication. It has to be too way communication. Such communication is only possible when verbal communication is linked with sensory experiences. That is only possible when we bring non-verbal communication along with verbal communication. This can happen when verbal information is reinforced with sensory experience. All kinds of sensory experience in real form is not possible. Because, if the teacher is teaching Bhakra dam or Madurai temple or Rameshwaram temple, these cannot be brought in the classroom, as they are. Only their pictures or contrived models can be brought, which will give sensory experiences to the students. This will make the teaching as innovative teaching. So advance planning for educational communication is necessary for teaching at school or at university level. As such there should be unit plans or daily plans for use of audio-visual aids in teaching also.

4. PLANNING FOR INNOVATIVE TEACHING

The word 'plan' means – a drawing, a layout for a building or a project, a scheme of project, a device to carry out a scheme. A sketch of some landscape or nightscape or a seascape is a step to be taken, for carrying out some creative activity. Furthermore, a plan be categorised as orthographic plan, a side plan and a x-ray plan. It is also categorised as oblique plan, perspective plan and isometric sketch or plan. So, the planning implies a process or processes of proceeding for the execution or implementation of some work or activity.

Teaching is an activity. Some educationists called it as a creative activity. A creative activity is that which always has novelty, newness and freshness. It is because when a teacher takes up teaching in the class his endeavour is to make it innovative and interesting. If newness, freshness and activity participation is missing in teaching, and it is carried on a monotonous way, the students will get bored. They will not be attentive. So they will not learn rather they will get frustrated. The teacher will also not get respect from the students and will remain dissatisfied with his/her teaching. Such teaching will not be a creative teaching. A creativity activity always attract attention of the people. If an activity is done in a routine manner, it will appear dull and boring. A creative activity is that which has been done for the first time, and it is new and fresh. This is why a creative activity is always termed as an art activity. A creative activity always give satisfaction to the doer. The doer is never inclinative for any material gains. This is why a piece of art is considered art only if it is done for the first time and without any inclination. An art activity always has newness and freshness because it is done for the first time. The artist makes a deliberate planning for making an art work. He conceives new art forms line and colour arrangements, rhythm and balance which produce virtual element through perspective.

Likewise for a creative teaching, a teacher like an artist has to think of balanced communication which makes teaching possible. He has to plan the strategies for effective presentation of content through verbal and non-verbal communication symbols. For creative thinking it is necessary to balance verbal and non-verbal communication, which is a must for educational teaching. This can only possible when words are supplemented and supported by sensory experience of concrete things and in absence of these by their representative republicas or models or pictures. As such during the course of teaching verbal information should always follow a spread out of concrete things for sensory experience at school level. Such a strategy always helps in the knowledge development. It helps the students motivating them to learn themselves. For this kind of innovative educational teaching the teacher must know before hand. What amount of verbal presentation he would require for introduction of the topic? What innovative method and techniques and, teaching aids he is going to use? How he will make use of chalk board? What steps he is going to take to establish rapport with the students? What should be format of questioning which is essential for elicitation reinforcement and recapitulation? All these need prior consideration and planning. What is observed, that usually the teachers do prior planning for content presentation which they do record in teacher's diary. All other educational innovative techniques are never recorded. Even the chalk board work needs prior thinking. So, the application of all educational innovative techniques such as use of chalk board, graphic material, substitute material for concrete things, motivating material for small things needs planning should not be used in haphazard way. As such planning for the use of audio-visual aids is as necessary as the planning for content presentation and lesson development. All this need careful thinking for the use of audio-visual aids and projects and advance working for their preparation. Such a planning should be given suitable weightage in the school curriculum by the authorities. This aspect should be represented or looked after by experienced teachers at the time of curriculum development. The planning for the use of audio-visual aids should appear at the unit planning and lesson planning levels. Besides, it should look into the aspects pertaining to selection preparation, involvement of students and finally assessment of the teaching gains.

Planning for Education

Man when thinks of doing something he always considers – 'what action is good and what is bad'? 'Which action, whether anticipated, or predicted, expected or unexpected, imposed or self-conceived and with what results'. Action planning is not new. The planning or human actions can be traced in times memorial. The man has ever been planning for food gathering, hunting, shelter making for hot and cold seasons which developed in dwellings and house building planning. In India, in the past a complete science, 'Vastu Shastra' which we call now architecture was developed by old seers. Old civilisations like Mohenjo-Daro, Mesopotamia, Greek, Egyptian, Chinese and Indian are testimony of planning. Not only planning for buildings, the man has ever been planning for life security. He has been inventing weapons to combat and fight war with enemies. He has been planning for peace and fraternal relations and for education of the youngers for good living.

Planning is necessary, because hit or miss is never desirable. Trial and error is a costly affairs. Human consciousness always plays a vital role in deciding what to do and what not to do? In comparison to other animals man is a rational animal as he has been gifted with better human organs like – bigger brain, flexible hands, erect posture, capacity to think, rationalise and plan for future. Thus, he has ever been planning for his future activities including education. So planning is not new to man and human society. Planning can be defined as "a well thought strategy for future actions".

As such, planning is done by man in many areas like earning for living, cooking, housing, child bearing and rearing, education and doing some work for future welfare – personal as well as national and international.

Planning for desired specific purposes like economic development was first conceived and started in erstwhile USSR after October Revolution 1917. USSR had devise Five Development Plans. Some developing countries like India had borrowed the concept of planning from USSR. And as such the concept of planning gradually crept into many fields of Government activities. And organisation like Planning Commission at the Centre and Planning Cells at various levels in the sates came into being.

Contemporary Concept of Planning in Education

Now everything is on the round map of planning like family planning, work planning, house planning, so also planning for education and teaching in order to :

(*a*) to catch the attention and interest of the children,
(*b*) to motivate the children for self-learning,
(*c*) so, to create better learning situations in the classroom teaching,
(*d*) to avoid wastage of time and energy of both of the students and of the teacher,
(*e*) to exploit the talents of the students and to elicit information from the students,
(*f*) to establish class control and pedagogic order in order to maintain discipline in the classroom as well as in the school as a whole, and
(g) to establish rapport between the teacher and the taught.

Educational Planning in the Past

Educational planning was done in the past also.

INDIA

Our seers Rishis had thoughtfully laid down certain ritualistic activities for the society for sound education for good individualistic and social living. This was done through initiation ceremonies, for respectful and reverential living with gurus and elders, respect and reverence to the old and women. Education was imparted orally by the elders. For higher education the parents had to send their children to Gurukulas for education for good and sane living. Education was given for preparation for life, inculcating definite specific social axiological values, imparting desirable social roles to be performed in the society. And finally Diksha ceremony was held in order to infuse a social ethics in the individual. Such an education was planned to prepare a person to lead a good social, sane harmonious social living.

West

In West too educational planning was in existence. We find academies, analogous to Gurukulas in India, in Greece like Platonic Academy, Guilds of artisans in Europe. Since the European societies were basically feudalistic, the children of the feudals were to get education at home by the private tutors, the children of the middle class used to get education at Church schools and, the children of the lower class used to learn skills in trades at the Guilds. Thus, there were three categories of citizens – feudals, middle men and workers and education was planned accordingly and the contents to be taught to them was planned accordingly.

As our Aryan society produced a many thinkers in all ages and in every field like – Vyas, Aryabhatta, Vishwakarma, Patanjli and Charak etc. The West also produced many thinkers, like Hippocrates, Thales, Protagoras, Hereclitus, Parmenides, Socrates, Plato, Crito, Aristocratus, Aristotle, Rene' Descartes, Libnieze, Spinoza, John Locke, J.J. Rousseau, Voltaire, Pestalozzi, Froebel, Madam Montessori, Conenius, Sigmund Freud, who contributed in the field of education which ultimately led to educational planning.

Recently in our country we had thinkers like Mahatma Gandhi, Aurobindo, Tagore, Vivekananda and J. Krishnamurthi who contributed a lot for Indian education. The ideas advanced by the thinkers can only be materialised through the medium of good educational communication.

Therefore, planning for good education is not only desirable but is most essential. The aims of good education can only be achieved if there is a suitable communication strategy for teaching which could not only pave the way for covering the entire course but could also instil spontaneity, create general interest in the students and motivate them for learning. So it is necessary to plan for covering the entire course involving the entire body of the students. This can only be done if this planning is done unit wise. Question arises, whether there should be planning in black and white or not. Educationists advise that such planning should be written for the guidance of the teacher.

Unit Plan

A unit is a part of whole. As an inch is a part of a foot. A foot is a part of a yard. A centimetre is a part of a metre. When a work or a deed is to be done during a span of time, it is considered necessary that the what work should be completed during the specified period – within a year. Academic work in schools and colleges is to be completed within an academic year. This work is to be done bit by bit, so it should be divided or bifurcated into small units, so the work could be done easily within allotted time. Our school academic year starts from April and ends on the last day of March each year. In schools we have two long holidays besides summer vacations. First week long holiday falls around Dussehra in October, and the second long holiday falls between Christmas and New Year Day. So it is desirable that the whole course of one academic year should be broken into three units or for three school terms that is from April to October, from October to December and January to March. The syllabus of the course to be taught should be so divided and framed, keeping in view the number of teaching days in each unit, so that the teacher may complete the unit teaching load within the specified term as per pedagogic norms. And it is generally done in schools.

Importance of Unit Plan

Unit teaching plan is important with regard to:

- It leads to future learning,
- It perpetuates systematic learning,
- It helps the teacher to accomplish his job easily within

stipulated period as per pedagogic norms and prepare the students for annual examination and for other term examinations,

- So also it helps the institution to accomplish the academic goals,
- It also helps the students as they also systematically proceeds, and
- And finally it facilitates the day to day planning and paves the way for the preparation of daily lesson planning.

Soul of the Unit Plan is Teaching Method

Methods of teaching to be used during the term are considered soul of the unit plan. After considering the teaching methods for unit teaching plan it should be thought what teaching aids would be required for teaching during term. Few steps should be taken while preparing a unit teaching plan:

- A time chart for covering the unit of teaching should be prepared.
- General purpose and specific aims to be achieved should be briefly mentioned in the unit plan which should later on should be explicitly and clearly mentioned in daily teaching lesson plans.
- A list of teaching aid should be mentioned clearly including use of chalk board should be mentioned,
- A unit plan should be so designed that it should aim at:
  (*a*) the capabilities and potentialities of the students may be fully utilised,
  (*b*) it should cover the content,
  (*c*) the teaching should give clear insight to the students about the subject,
  (*d*) there is a full scope of two-way communication so as to make elicitations possible. This can only be possible if:
    (*i*) there is suitable method of questioning followed by democratic discussions aiming at responses,
    (*ii*) there is appropriate use of audio-visual aids that is graphic aids, three dimensional aids, activity aids like dramatisations, tours and excursions, sensory aids like puppets,

costumes, pantography and use of audio aids as films TV and VCR, etc.

(*iii*) the unit plan should entail:

- Possible aims and objective to be achieved,
- Possible ways of introductions to the topics,
- Possible predictions about the elicitations,
- Possible methods of reinforcement,
- Possible methods of recapitulation and home assignments.
- A unit plan should clearly indicate in how many lessons the unit will be covered. It should also specify evolutionary techniques. A unit plan should also have a format of its own and should indicate the format of daily lesson plan.

FORMAT OF THE UNIT PLAN

TERM: .... April to October Unit No. 1

INSTITUTION.............................. (Name of the School)

Class ....

Subject ....

Content to be covered ....

General and specific aims ....

Methods of Teaching ....

Methods of Introduction ....

List of audio-visual aids to be used including chalk board ....

No. of lessons to be delivered topic-wise ....

Mode of Presentation ....Presentation cum Questions

Modes of reinforcements and recapitulations

Possible Home Assignments

Teacher/Teachers

Fig. 6

How a Unit Plan is to be Prepared?

In case of centralised educational structure, as we have, a team of expert teachers should be selected for the preparation of unit plans. It would be better if it is done at the behest or under the supervision of the central controlling authority like Director of Education, Chairman CBSE or any other competent authority. This would be better if this work is done during vocation so that teaching work may not suffer. Proposals for the unit plans should be widely circulated to the members of the Unit Plan Committee, members institutions in order to elicit their suggestions. If there are some suggestions these should be suitable incorporated in the proposed draft of the unit plan. It should be followed by all concerned sincerely.

Disadvantages of the Unit Planning

- It makes the teaching mechanically oriented. Innovativeness and initiatives of the teachers are marred,
- It restricts prolongation of discussions because it is time bound.
- It limits the scope of any discovery.
- It makes the teacher a job allotted person and restricts initiatives and limits professional attitude.

In spite of all these demerits unit planning is important for formal education.

Lesson Planning

A lesson is part of a unit and, a unit which is a bigger part of a content whole to be taught during an academic year. In other words a lesson is smaller unit of the proposed curriculum prepared or designed to carry out teaching, which could be educative. A lesson plan is considered desirable to carry out teaching through two-way pedagogic communication.

The teacher cannot teach the whole content in one day, so a fraction of the unit which called lesson plan is necessary for instruction. Planning is a concept used for programming or doing something in order to achieve desirable social and economic ends. So planning for daily teaching is necessary.

Lesson planning can be defined as under:

- "Lesson planning is a little given to a topic or statement of achievement to be realised through teaching in parts through specific methods and means by which these are to attained as a result of certain activities done by the teacher and pupils".

  This definition lends to focus the teachers' attention upon:

  (*i*) Results in terms of pupils' learning,

(*ii*) Application of definite methods, processes and procedures with recognition of an activity as the basis of learning,

(*iii*) Pupils are to be kept in foreground and the teacher in the background as a helper, guide and friend,

(*iv*) The teacher cannot teach by a hit or miss or trail and error method,

(*v*) It provides monitoring in teaching, and

(*vi*) Lesson Plan provides a path to the teacher to proceed.

Essentials for Good Lesson Planning

- The teacher should have broad understanding of the subject-matter and the activities that would provide the nucleus for classroom experience and learning.
- The teacher has to be imaginative and creative.
- The lesson planning should be tinged to realising.
- The teacher should have the ultimate knowledge of environmental forces (like greenery, slums and climatic conditions) that play upon the life of the class.
- The teacher should have comprehensive knowledge of the psychology of the mental processes of the population of class. He should have full knowledge of the laws of learning and human behaviour.
- The teacher must know the most approved pedagogic techniques and teaching methods.
- The lesson planning should have a sequence of presentation of the content so as to achieve the major objectives set in the curriculum.
- There should be a provision in the lesson development for the involvement of the students through their active participation through stipulated activities.
- The lesson planning should help in establishing a rapport between the teacher and the taughts.
- The visual communication should have a place to provide sensory experience. This should be done through chalk board, pictures, charts etc. There should be provision for use of these in lesson development.
- The lesson plan should show the progressive trends. It

should discard the traditional one-way conflict model of teaching which promote bookish method promoting rote memory.

Kinds of Lesson Planning

There are two kinds of lesson planning:

1. Memorised Lesson Planning

The characteristics of lesson planning is under:

- Nothing is committed in visible from in it.
- Its visible form is imaginary and not concrete.
- Problems are not merely anticipated by asking questions orally in the classroom.
- It leads tc teaching proceeds in an unorganised manner.
- Through this process only an experienced teacher can be successful.
- It depends on memory, if the teacher forgets something the students suffer.
- Memorised lesson does not have a form, therefore, sequence wise proceeding is not possible.
- Memory is the sole repository of memorised lesson, therefore, it remains always incomplete.

Advantages

- Only advantage is that the teacher does not require to spend time in lesson plan writing.

Disadvantages

- There are ample chances of skipping over facts in content presentation.

2. Written Lesson Planning

- In a written lesson plan everything is committed in visible form.
- It has a format, as it is subtle and well organised.
- It is systematic, sequential. The teacher can develop the lesson with the help of teaching aids and asking questions thereon.

- Under a written plan the whole teaching procedure is logical, systemic and organised.
- A new teacher can also deliver the goods as the plane acts as a guide to the teacher.
- Preparation of lesson plan provides a refreshing for the teacher. He can assimilate new knowledge with his previous knowledge.
- Since written lesson is a written record of content to be presented and activities involved therein, it does not depend on memory. All steps which are to be taken on the record.

Advantages

- Careful writing of lesson plan leads to thinking and reasoning, which give good results. Writing leads to clarification, rethinking and finally to comprehension.
- Writing of facts in lesson plan protects against forgetting.
- It leads to freedom in teaching.
- It leads to innovations in teaching.
- Since everything is on record later improvements are possible.

Disadvantages

- Preparation of a written lesson plan is a time consuming.
- Noise gets its difficult to prepare a lesson on pedagogic principles.

Essential Elements of a Good Lesson Plan

- The lesson planning should be based on the principles that it is a guide to the teacher.
- It should always be aimed that it is helpful to the students in self-learning.
- In reciprocal terms the students should be able to help to the teacher in lesson development.
- The lesson plan should evince a clear understanding of the outcomes to be achieved.
- It should always relate the previous knowledge of the students, or the related lessons taughts in the past, with the current lesson development.

- The lesson should provide an opportunity for the selection, organisation and presentation of the subject-matter.
- It should have an ample provision of sensory experience for the students through audio-visual aids and students involvement in activities.
- The lesson plan should clearly indicate the application of appropriate teaching method or procedure.
- The lesson plan should provide proper ground for teacher–taughts interaction thus, paving the way for self-learning for both.
- The steps which are to be taken during the course of lesson development should be recorded on left side of the lesson plan book and during the course of development these steps should be developed through chalk board.
- The lesson plan should clearly show the evolutionary steps. Also it should also the steps to be taken for reinforcement, recapitulation and home assignments.
- The lesson plan should motivate the students for further study.

So a lesson plan should have:

- a well formulated forms having aim having techniques and teaching method,
- a well designed scheme for the use of teaching aids including black board summary. It should be record on the left side of lesson plan,
- a provision to meet the individual differences of the students,
- It should include pivotal questions,
- It should cover the content material, and
- In addition to these it should exhibit motivational techniques, inspiring the students for further study.

How to Use a Lesson Plan Cautions

- There are dangers for the new teachers,
- While preparing lesson plan the teacher should avoid over completeness, conveying every detail is confusing rather unhelpful, like separating a tree from forest. It

should have main items. The students should draw inferences,

- Too fragmentary lesson plan is also bad,
- Sameness of the lesson plan should also be avoided,
- Reverence or too much stress for the textbooks or written printing should not be given too much importance. But the study of reference books should be encouraged for further study,
- Too much verbalism should be avoided. It should be used for introduction and for explanations where necessary, and
- A too ambitious lesson plan should not be made.

Some Suggestions for a Constructive Teaching Lesson Plan

- A good lesson plan shouid work as a guide, torch bearer and not as a crunch. Sometimes, when the teacher is fully proficient, a good teaching may also require abandoning of the lesson plan. So it is not desirable to become a slave of lesson plan.
- There should be a sort of flexibility in the use of lesson plan for the teacher when the teacher is required to teach many sections of the same class same topic, he should be allowed to use one lesson plan for all sections.
- The teacher should be creative and cooperative while teaching so as to avail co-operation of the students.
- If a topic is to be taught in more than one day there should be provision of extension of lesson plan previously used. In such a case in the beginning detailed plan should be used and later plan should brief having only content and related developmental matter.
- Outcome in the class of the lesson plan cannot be predicted. The teacher should visualise the mood of the students and should proceed accordingly.
- Assessment questions should be planned in advance and should be used during in recapitulation.
- Also the home assignments should so planned as it forces the students for self-study.
- Finally there should be near approximation there.

POSSIBLE FORMAT OF THE LESSON PLAN

Lesson Plan No. Date ....
Name of the School ....
Class ....
Section .... Period ....
.... Time: From............ To..................

Topic to be developed
....
Specific Aim ....
General Aim ....

Method to be used ....
Teaching aid to be used
Chalk board summary (to be given on the left side of the lesson plan)

Introduction: A statement to be given. If it will have to entail some teaching aid, that should be mentioned. Previous knowledge of the students should be assumed while introducing the topic. If needed it should be written in the lesson plan.

Presentation: The presentation of the content should be linked with the elicitation. That can only done by involving the students suitably in the lesson development. That can only be possible if the teacher avoid verbalism and the students speak enthusiastically. So he should first put questions to the students and should elicit information from the students with patience. The teacher should supplement this information if it is incomplete. So the presentation should proceed in the following way:

Method	Matter
1. Question related to content put by the teacher	Answers by the students. If (The real answer on the content should be written by the teacher on chalk board) there are short of information the teacher should complete it verbally or by showing related concrete things.
2. Qn	Matter
3. Qn	Matter

The whole content should be elicited from the students through questioning and answering
Reinforcement should be done by putting questions and by supplementing of answers.

Recapitulation	For finding out whether the students are having a pace with teaching. Questions should be put on the content taughts.
Home Assignment	It should motivate the students for further self-study.

Fig. 7

Two-Way Communication

Two-way communication is a pre-requisite condition for education. Human beings communicate through verbal and non-verbal symbols. Various symbols are used to communicate messages by one person or group to another person or group. Verbal symbols are combinations of words. These symbols bear no physical resemblance to physical objects or ideas for which they stand for. In the beginning man, like other animals, used sounds like hooting, barking, grumbling or crying to communicate, when human language was not there. The man tried to assemble some sounds and used them to communicate the language was developed. Man continuously tried to develop the language by composing certain sounds and a well developed science of linguistics came into being and took a semantic form and, well developed language came into being. Some sounds were composed to symbolise or represent or identify certain things. For example the chair was thought designate a physical wood object which has four legs, a back and an eighteen inch high seat to sit on comfortably. Likewise each and every word was designated to symbolise or represent a particular concrete thing. For example a table symbolises a four legged two and half feet high wooden structured platform which could be used for keeping papers and writing. In this manner so many words symbolises so many particular things or ideas in absentia. It may be said that words stands for physical things or ideas which though exist but not to be seen by the listener when the message is being communicated. Though the words bears no resemblance with physical things or ideas, but this can also cannot be denied that words do not represent or do not stand for some physical objects, ides or for some scientific principles or for some philosophic axioms or for some other human experiences that were and are carried from older generation to younger generation. Man does a lot of communication through words in spite of the fact that the actual things, which are being communicated through words are generally absent to human vision. Though, this fact can also not be denied that it is easier to communicate quickly through words, but this is also a reality that when an encoder communicates through words, the decoder gets very little of it and finds it difficult to understand. This kind of communication is called one-way or one direction communication. It is like an arrow from the bow which hits its target but does come with a reaction or like flow of water which from higher direction to lower direction.

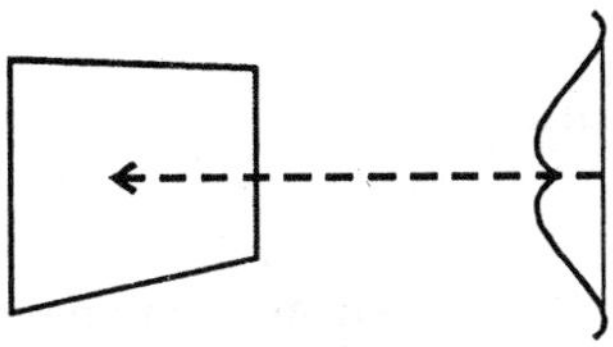

Fig. 8: A Shoot with Bow

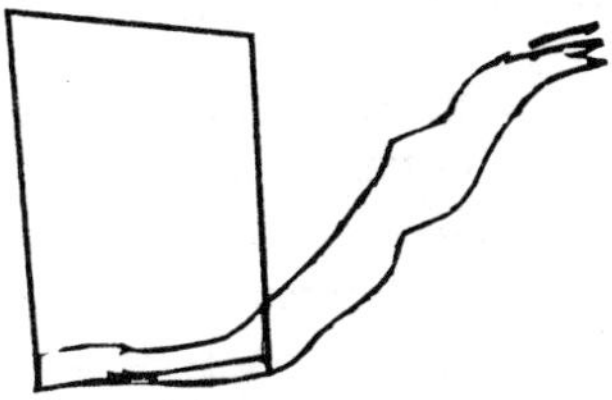

Fig. 9: Flow of Water

One-Way Action

In one-way communication the teacher is always active or it can be said that the encoder is always dominant and, decoder is subordinate. So teaching through one-way communication, breeds conflict model of teaching in which the student is always a listener, absorber and receiver. He has very little chance to speak and express. He hardly gets any chance to think and rationalise. So, he always remains at the receiving end. He never gets chance to contribute, he always remains unsatisfied with the teaching. Since he cannot think and rationalise, he cannot comprehend and learn. He can never contribute. So he can never be a creative thinker and contributor. Thus, such a communication is not good for teaching.

But there is no escape from verbal communication. Verbal symbols are used together with other symbols in teaching. The role of the teacher is to make sure that various terms, ideas, words, principals and other abstractions used should be meaningful the students. The ideas and concepts which can be transmitted through verbal symbols, can be useful if these are supported by concrete experience or experiences given by audio-visual aids. Also verbal symbols give us opportunity to read books, textbooks and written material which add to experience. Thus, verbal and non-verbal symbols are two sides of a pedagogic coin. Both help us in learning.

Non-verbal symbols are those communication symbols which do not speak and tell us or gives us information in nutshell package of words. These symbols are those which can only be seen and visualised. As a matter of fact communication is done through two kinds symbols – non-discursive or verbal symbols and discursive or non-verbal symbols. Non-discursive symbols provide a package of information. Or we can say it is communication which done in words. Discursive symbols provide us only is visual impact on our mind. These symbols do not speak. Every object when it is seen sends back visual symbols to our brain, which in turn gets activated. There is no verbal encoding and decoding. Here the object seen itself encodes and brain decodes.

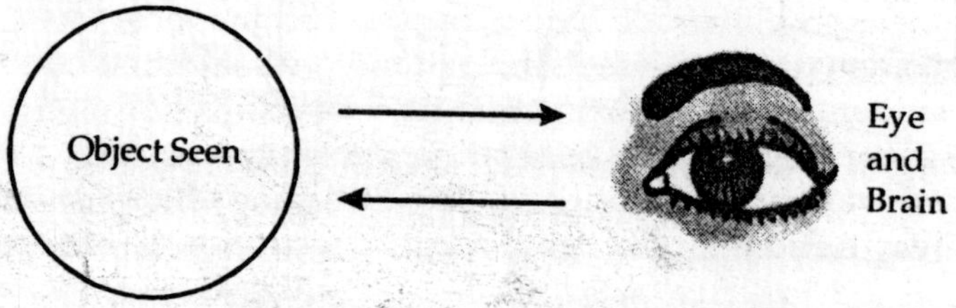

Fig. 10: Non-Verbal Communication

Thinking process starts. The visualiser starts thinking and reasoning which results in understanding. The non-verbal communication can be said a two-way communication because it activates both the encoder and decoder. There is a continuous interaction between the both. And in teaching the two-way communication is most useful. When the teacher spreads or displays concrete objects or their representations before the students in the classroom and, motivates the students to see these, the students see them, their mind gets interacted. These objects emit return signals which make the students to think and reason. As the students become active. They try to comprehend and understand themselves. So the process of self-learning starts which does not happen in one-way or verbal communication. Therefore two-way communication is the boon to self-learning.

Two-way communication is only possible if timely spreading or display of concrete things or of their representative republicas is timely done. This can only be done by proper timely use of audio-visual aids in teaching. These are many. Their use helps the teacher and students both. They also make possible the use of innovative methods and techniques in teaching which make the teaching very interesting and creative. The timely use of audio-visual aids in teaching helps in seeking students attention, developing interest among them and motivating them to learn. Audio-visual aids which make two-way communication reduces verbalism. These supply a concrete basis of conceptual thinking, give rise to meaningful concepts enriched by meaningful associations. These make learning permanent, concretise learning experiences, thus clarification of concepts in leading for better understanding and long lasting learning becomes possible. Two-way communication with the help of audio-visual aids stimulates the students for self-activity. It also develops continuity of thought enabling the range of possible self-experiencing. Above all two-way communication adds the teaching efficiency of the teacher. It also improve the students effectiveness in reducing habits. As such two-way communication is essential for educational teaching and for the all round development of students personality.

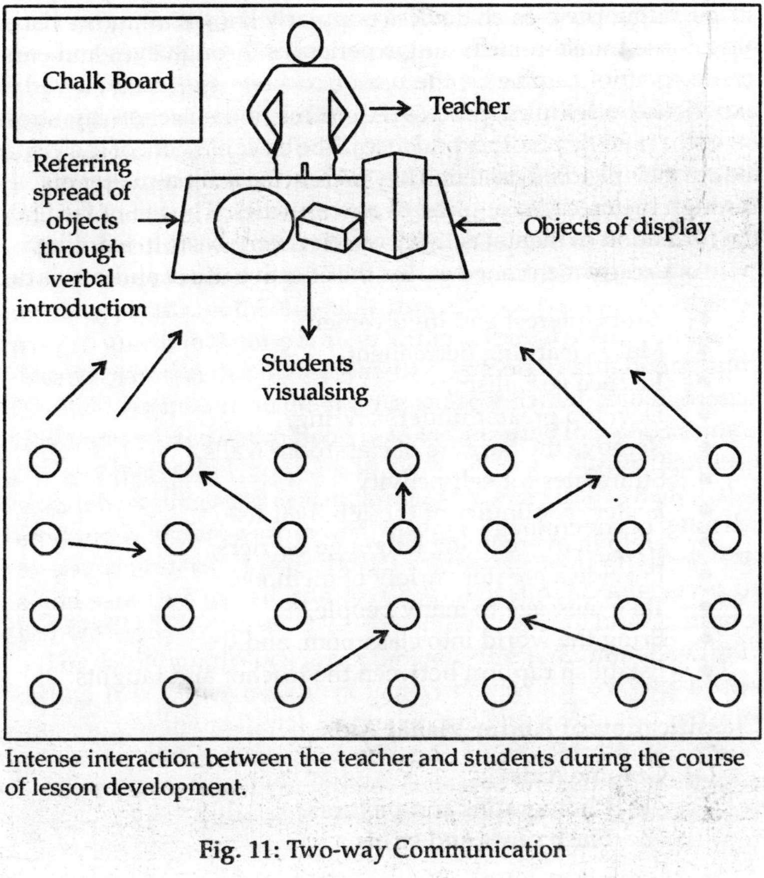

Intense interaction between the teacher and students during the course of lesson development.

Fig. 11: Two-way Communication

8

Audio-Visual Aids — A Classification

Audio-Visual Education involves the use of instructional devices, such as graphic illustrations, like charts and maps, pictures, flash cards, field trips, excursions, demonstration, motion pictures, film strips, puppets etc. Such devices popularly known as audio-visual aids, these transmit ideas and experiences through eyes and ears. The educators emphasise the use of concrete aids for non-verbal experience in learning process. All forms of instruction lay stress on verbal and symbolic experiences. The basic element of the visual aids in their pictorial content. They present the subject-matter mainly through the medium of pictures and sketches. Thus they facilitate the formation of mental activity which is very basic to learning.

As already mentioned earlier the effective use of audio aids do:

- Adds interest and involvement,
- Makes learning permanent,
- Reduce verbalism,
- Develop greater understanding,
- Remove the barriers of classroom walls,
- Stimulates for self-activity,
- Fosters continuity of though their use,
- Help in overcoming language barriers,
- Provide a greater variety of methods,
- Take message to many people,
- Bring the world into classroom, and
- Establish rapport between the teacher and taughts.

Classification of Audio-Visual Aids

(*a*) Graphic Aids:

1. Photographs and pictures,
2. Flash cards and strips,

3. Posters,
4. Charts,
5. Diagrams,
6. Graphs,
7. Maps,
8. Cartoons,
9. Comics, and
10. Illustrations from paper scrap.

(*b*) Display Material:

1. Chalk Board,
2. Flannel Board,
3. Bulleting Board,
4. Magnet Board,
5. Peg Board,
6. Corridor and classroom displays such as corner sculptures, paintings, alpna, etc.
7. Handicraft work display,
8. School museum, and
9. Costumes, and
10. Equipment and tools.

(*c*) Three Dimensional Aids:

1. Models,
2. Objects,
3. Specimens,
4. Tools,
5. Mock ups,
6. Dioramas,
7. Puppets, and
8. Mobiles.

(*d*) Projected Aids:

1. Films,
2. Film strips,
3. Slides,
4. Transparencies,
5. Magic lantern,
6. Epidiascope,
7. Opaque projector, and
8. Microscope.

(*e*) Audio Aids:

1. Radio,

2. Open Circuit TV,
3. Closed Circuit TV,
4. Recordings, Disc Records, and
5. Gramophone.

(*f*) Activity Aids:
1. Field trips and tours,
2. Mock up organisations,
3. Dramatics,
4. Mono and solo acting,
5. Community service,
6. Debates etc.,
7. Role playing, and
8. Group Discussions.

(*g*) Audio-Visual Aids Material.

1. AUDIO MATERIALS

Audio Materials are the sources of audio learning experiences. These are Radio and recordings of Radio, disc recordings, tape recordings of educational programmes. The Television and Film, which are audio-visual materials, too have an effective audio impact.

Value of Audio Materials

Audio materials contribute to useful and far reaching enrichment aids for learning. Audio experiences facilitate concentration, motivate to abstract thinking and imagination for comprehending a theme. They supplement other teaching materials.

Educational radio broadcasts bring current events, happenings and important personalities within the reception area. They develop a feeling of participation on the part of listeners with regard to the actual situation of the content of the broadcast. By providing aural presentations of Dramatic materials, they stimulate imagination.

Recorded audio experiences capture original sound for a later use to develop audio imagery. For learning, apart from having all the advantages of radio broadcasts, recordings have certain added features that make them unique valuable audio materials. They preserve permanently all sounds of aural representations that were once presented as live programmes. These records can be controlled by the teacher, as these can be edited interpreted or used in any way he likes or suitable for education.

Specific Use of Audio Material

Select worthy aid while using audio programmes in education. Use radio and TV programmes when they contribute to the learning process. Good radio programmes and tape records that occur beyond school hours should be re-used. Students should be encouraged to listen good programmes at home. The teachers and parents should guide them in this regard. Tape record is a flexible instrument in the hand of an imaginative teacher. It can be used in language, arts, music and for practices in public speaking.

Use of Audio-Visual Equipment and Material

The Film

As far as visual and aural teaching are concerned in the school, the film is a relative newcomer. Many schools just got silent projects in 1950 in Europe and Africa. In India the position was more or less the same. Today the situation is different. Most of the school have film projectors.

For effective and total utilisation of a wide range of audio-visual experiences, we have to depend upon audio-visual equipment. They provide the major tools for the use of projected audio aids. The basic audio-visual equipment is described as under:

16 mm Film Projector

A motion picture film is one of the most effective audio-visual aids of the three sizes in which films are produced (35 mm, 16 mm and 8 mm). The 16 mm size is standard for educational purposes at present. The 16 mm film project is portable, easy to handle and gives satisfactory film shows for audiences up to 600. For bigger audiences special projectors are required. The 16 mm, projectors are being manufactured by four or five firms in India and are easily available. Useful accessories, which include a screen and projector stand.

Educational films for use with such projectors are easily available from libraries such as Department of Educational Technology, NCERT, State Audio-Visual Departments, Department of Audio-Visual Education, Indian Institute. of Technology,

Roorkee, Uttaranchal. Also in other institutes like Central Institute of Education, University of Delhi have such facilities.

Films may be sound or silent. These are (*a*) black and white (B&W) and Colour (*b*) films. Educational films in addition are (*c*) safety films that is they are not inflammable. In Indian schools 16 mm films alone are widely used. A 16 mm sound film has sprocket holes one on margin and sound track on the other. Therefore in 16 mm sound projector, the sprockets have claws or teeth on one margin only. A 16 mm silent film has sprockets holes on both the margins and the silent projector has sprockets that have teeth on both edges. Therefore, a 16 mm sound film should not be threaded into 16 mm silent projector, as the sprockets with teeth on either margin will totally damage the sound track and the film. In other words only sound projector for 16 mm should be used for sound films.

Some of the advantages of motion pictures (films) are that:

(*a*) they are audio-visual thus appealing to two sense at the same time,

(*b*) they attract attention of illuminated screen in total or semidarkness.

(*c*) they appeal to the emotions of the pupils and very often they identify themselves with the events on the screen, and

(*d*) they enable the pupils to witness the objects, places, and events not ordinarily seen in their day to day lives.

Films are very close to life and motion pictures contributes to realism. But the film and projector are costly and films on suitable relevant topics may not be easily available. Teachers are prone to use them for entertainment and not for instructional purpose. And many teachers do not know how to operate a projector which make them depend on others who are far and few in number. In spite of all these drawbacks and limitations motion pictures are very powerful audio-visual aids media.

The film with its expense of production and elaborate equipment has always tended to attract a good attention and provide a certain indiscriminate use. Films are widely used in general education. Films used for education have been documentaries of conventional kind, of considerable length. Equipped with music they have been liked by children. One question for discussion would be: Does the film perform the function of visual aid or does it take away the teachers authority and establish a rapport with the audience?

What is the Aim of the Film?

The aims of education are factual instruction and influencing the attitude, as well as cultural aspects. Some aspects of education are only worth if they lead to action, but in other cases the aim may be to inform and educate (Burlon 1953). The film can illustrate any or all of these, if the film is made in didactic fashion it can stimulate thought process.

What Skills are Needed by the Teacher?

The film projector can be operated by the teacher. From a consideration of previous questions, it is obvious that the film should be a visual aid, and that is rarely an end in itself, but a stimulation for discussion, although in the imaginatively produced film there may be many opportunities for gaining insight. The teacher must therefore be familiar with the group and participatory methods, which include role playing and the group and buzz discussions.

Without doubt the most successful films are those concerned with human relationships and human emotion, since only the film, an actual situation or role-playing can really involve us in situation. Here, the film is paramount and, Margaret Meads' film 'Bathing Babies' in three culture and Irish Television Theatres' 'Lary' can be suggested in this context. The film 'Bathing Babies' in three cultures has been used successful with secondary modern school girls when discussing the emotional needs of children.

The teacher should have an insight into the content of the film. He should familiarise the students in advance about the film and give direction to clinch notes on important aspects of the film. He should give the students to have an insight. After the film is over there should be a follow-up discussion in the class over the film. He should guide the students to prepare notes after follow-up discussion.

The Cartoon and Suspended Animation Films

The cartoon film is always acceptable especially for small children but, it is expensive to make such films. As other films, there does seem to be a need for the shorter and more economical films which can be made in the locally and produced with local needs in mind. For this purpose the suspended animation film cartoons has been devised, which, though in experimental stage has already had some success. This can be made in the classroom.

It consists of a number of prepared pictures which are photographs in series within Cine camera. Animation effects can be achieved by stopping camera and including a new picture or part of picture, symbol, letter, word or slogan. These can be made as elaborate as required. When the film is required, the different frames will flash on the screen, and the words and actions well 'grow' before eyes.

The Film Flash or Thematic Films

The criticism that film dates quickly and might not be just what the demonstrator needs is often valid. To overcome this, the economical film flash has been produced. This is used by television to illustrate an idea, or a given point to speaker's paper and also in a more advanced way by Cohen Seat (1958), who, with his colleagues at the Film Institute, University of Paris, is using thematic films for training and research in psychology and psychological medicine.

The flash film is a black and white film of one or two minutes duration showing a dramatic human situation for subsequent discussion. Its advantage is that it can be filmed locally, under the direction of the teacher, who can include only that which is necessary for his immediate aim. If the film is well scripted and discussed before hand with the 'actors' little editing is necessary, and the cost of the film be kept to minimum level.

Making 16 mm Cine' Films

Today film making is as simple as the box camera-photography, although certain rules must be followed if reasonable effect and photographic results are to be achieved.

All the rules of good design, production and placing are important as in any visual aid or picture. The essential thing in filming is good camera drill. This is concerned with the correct exposure for film used and light available with the correct focus between the object and the camera and handling of camera, which includes the setting of film speed, the winding of mechanism, the correct filling of the film, and the physical handling of camera on a level and a rigid tripod.

In the script the timing of each shot must be shown, and if planning shots are taken i.e., turning a working camera, these should be slow, steady movements.

An intelligent mixture of long (LS), medium (MS), and close up (CU) shots will give real meaning to the film since all these are used for different purposes; long shot is concerned with the general background scene; the medium shot gesture in detail; the close up shot will show important facial expressions in detail.

Tilting may be done with black board and chalk, stencilled or 'letter set' lettering or a cine tilting outfit. Here we must be sure that we have allowed for 'parallax' i.e., the distance camera and object is under six feet.

If a short film flash is being made, it is well to release the players taking part with cameraman should be again checking his settings on the camera. These film flashes are most economical to make since 100 feet film at silent speed runs for about four minutes.

Making the 'Suspended Animation Film'

In preparing for the 'suspended animation film', a simple card frame is constructed to hold the prepared illustrations, so that they may be placed into the frame one after another in complete alignment. This can be mounted on drawing board held vertically against the wall.

The cine camera, held on a rigid tripod, should be aligned with the centre of the frame and levelled so that the view finder for the lens in use shows slightly less than the frame size. As the distance between camera and the object will be less than six feet, an allowance must be made for parallax. This usually means that the camera must be lifted lightly and turned to right. The distance must be measured carefully.

Each film can now be photographed in its pre-determined order, for pre-determined time and checked on the shooting script The diagrams used should be simple and symbolic as possible and again the best captions are made with 'letter set' lettering. Animation can be added by the substitution of different frames after stopping the camera or by adding symbols or lettering, piece by piece between stops.

Demerits of Films (Motion Pictures) in Teaching

In spite of the fact that motion pictures that is films and also suspended animation films do provide a lot of audio-visual experiences to the children. The world events and happenings can be spread out in the classroom. The children get fascinated and know a lot about so many things in actual form and shape. But two-way communication which is the soul of real education is permanently missing. There is not a chance of interaction. When something new is screened and the student is eager to enquire about it he cannot. The film goes on perennially without stop. As such many points are not grasped. Thus, a film cannot be a replacement of classroom teaching by the teacher. The teacher is always present in the classroom to remove the doubts of the students. He discusses with them. He replies to their queries. As such there is a continuous interaction between the teacher and students which establishes a close rapport between which is necessary in a sound educational process.

However, it cannot be denied that educational films contribute to the desirable educational goals. We can summarise:

Inherent characteristics of films:

1. Understandably visualise the subject.
2. Portray things and processes by employment of motion.
3. Create an illusion of the original environment.
4. Develop adequate narration to direct learners attention.
5. Are based upon the content of the school curriculum.
6. Are an audio-visual synthesis of environmental and interpretative sounds and visual concepts.

Classification of Films

1. Basic Teaching Films
2. Supplementary Teaching Films
   (*a*) documentary films,
   (*b*) sponsored films, and
   (*c*) entertainment films,

Use of Instructional Films

1. Films through the medium of motion catch attention and thus make meaning clear,

2. Films provide the elements for various visual experiences and thus brighten the realities,
3. Films can control the time factor in any operation or series of events,
4. Films can bring distant past and the present into the classroom,
5. The lessons involving films create interest more quickly and sustain it better than the traditional lesson that is so top heavy with verbal instruction,
6. Motion pictures unveil hidden processes thus learning more real,
7. The films can enlarge and reduce the actual size of objects thus create interest and motivate learning.
8. The use of effective and appropriate films results in more learning in less time with better retention of what is learnt, and
9. The films provides a common denominator of experience and thus develop atmosphere for classroom discussion.

Effective Use of Instructional Films

Various possibilities of using a film are listed below:

1. Before starting a topic, show the film with proper preparatory questions and cautions hints that provide a proper mental framework for viewing. Then refer to the film literally as the topics develops in the class.
2. Just use the film without a detailed proper prelude or explanation and let the students fund for themselves the various aspects and related points to the topic. Develop a follow-up discussion after the film and highlight the important salient points. If possible, then show the film again and then expand the topic by teaching.
3. After initiating the topic, revealing some of its preliminary details, the films can be used at a crucial point of developmental difficulty. Thus, the film will review the topic again and prepare and lead the students towards detailed aspects thereof.
4. If the film is shown as a recapitulatory activity, no previous discussion is needed. Let the student discuss at the end some difference of treatment of the topic that arise from the classroom teaching and film viewing.

Some Precautions in the Use of Films

1. Do not use classroom films for mere entertainment,
2. Do not use films when motion is not portrayed,
3. Do not use films that are too long to permit preliminary preparation of the class and subsequent follow-up work or discussion, and
4. To enrich the background knowledge and to reinforce learning.

What Place has a Film Strip in Visual Education?

Audio-Visual aids are sometimes divided into auditory aids and visual aids. These are very artificial divisions as the teacher has many aids at a time. The film strips are aids to be selected at a given movement.

The film strip is too well known, as there are situations when these are very useful in teaching. Suppose a biology teacher wants to make aware his/her students about different kinds of flora and fauna which cannot be brought easily in each section of the class – say different varieties of rose and cacie or some insects. The teacher can have black and white or coloured shots of these and frame these so as to project at film strip projector. The film strips can have single frame or double frame.

The film strip, like other aids, needs careful selection and previewing, since the catalogue and its description may not be at all indicative of the film strip contents in visual form. With modern projectors the room needs little preparations except to place the screen in the darkest corner or to use a back projection screen.

FILM STRIPS

A Rose
Fig. 12

Human Skelton
Fig. 13

Frog
Fig. 14

Cactus
Fig. 15

Many day-to-day experiences can be captured on films and used in education. If they are filmed upon 35 mm. film coloured or black and white, the film can be used in film strip making. What is important is the right picture, that means that the pictures could stimulate thought and interest and, is helpful for discussion. Camera shots should be kept in sequence for film strip making. Many things which generally are out of reach can be brought to the class for sensory experiences through film strips.

Storage of Film Strips

A cabinet should be made for storing the film strips. The holes for keeping film strips should be numbered. And there should be place for keeping an index card in the box.

3. SLIDES (FILM SLIDES)

Many years ago the 'magic lantern' was a force in family entertainment. The slides which years ago were cumbersome, are now small, and their projector can be carried easily in a case. Although the large slides (3¼" x 3¼") are still found, but new standard size is 2" x 2". Usually these slides and transparencies are hold between two sheets of plastics or glass, which protect the slides from heat and dust. Sometimes frames also made of cardboard for holding slides.

Transparencies

Transparencies are very useful in teaching. Transparencies can be made on transparent plastic sheets, easily available. Some illustration can be drawn on transparent pieces of transparent plastic sheets by special pens available for making transparencies. Such transparencies can be projected and used on overhead projector and displayed or taken on screen. Sometimes, the teacher has to teach many sections of one class. Repeating same black board work, diagrams and illustrations in each and every class again and again looks odd and boring to the teacher. Moreover, this cannot be done same in each class. Doing the black board work drawing same drawings, diagrams and illustrations is also time consuming. It is, therefore, desirable that presenting same visual material transparencies be prepared and used on overhead projector.

There should also be cataloguing and safe storage of transparencies. These can be stored in plastic bags and kept in a specially prepared racks.

Epidiascope (Episcope) or Opaque Projector

Epidiascope or Episcope, otherwise known as opaque projector, is used to project flat pictures; graphs, stamps, pictures of coins and other opaque objects also. It is also used to project in enlarged size maps, illustrations and diagrams from books which are used for making charts. Here the light cannot pierce through the object, only the reflected light from a plane mirror is taken by the focusing lenses. Therefore a very bright source of illumination (not less than 1000 W bulb) is required and the auditorium must be totally dark. Generally epidiascopes are used to enlarge figures for maps and other pictures from books and journals. A drawing sheet can be tagged on a bulletin board specially prepared for this purpose out of insulation sheet, the figure projected can be sketched by pencil.

The principles of episcopy and diascopy are combined in Epidiascope that can be used to project opaque as well as transparent materials. A simple level mechanism changes episcope into diascopy and vice versa. There are many reflecting surfaces in an episcope to throw more light on the opaque object. A plan mirror kept at 45° within at top takes light from the opaque object and reflects it through the huge focussing lenses.

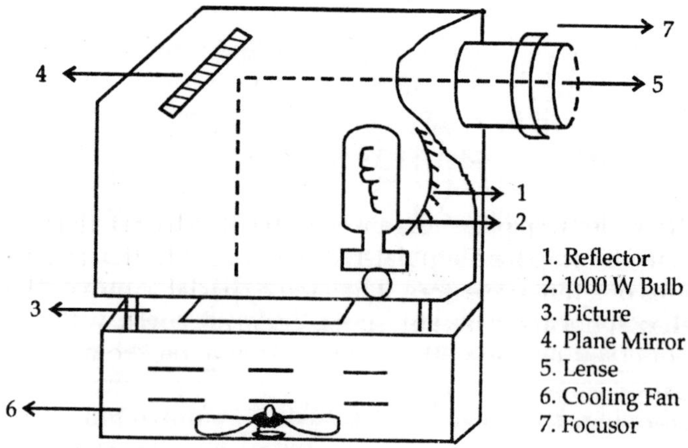

Fig. 16: Episcope

Epidiascope can accommodate medium size book for enlargement of pictures, so picture platform can be adjusted accordingly.

Film Strip Projector

It is a combination of film strip projector and slide projector through which 35 mm film strips and 2" × 2" slides can be projected. There are attachable gates for slides and film strip.

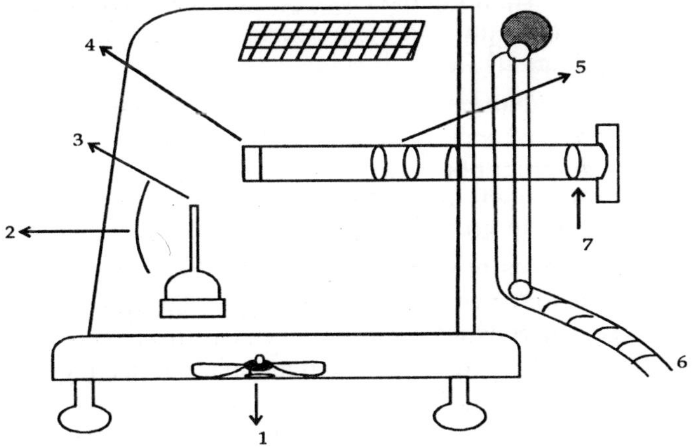

A film strip projector has:

1. Cooler
2. Reflector
3. Bulb 350 W
4. Heat Filter
5. Condenser
6. Feeder Gate
7. Lens

Fig. 17: Film Strip Projector

Now film strip projectors are available which can automatically feed the film strip for a stipulated duration. In addition to common features of a film projectors, it has some special features. There is a feeling spool and a take up spool. There are spects with a single raw of claws or teeth. There are markings on the projector to indicate the apex loop and lower loop. If any of these becomes shorter then the prescribed length gets out while running. Therefore care must be taken to maintain the proper length of the loop. In the sound film projector there is scanning drum with a photo-electric cell in it. This is pretty costly part in the projector. An exciter lamp emits a beam through the sound track into the scanning drum and the photo-electric cell picks up the change in light intensity, which becomes responsible for the production of sound. This is in brief the optical sound system. The scanning drum, the exciter lamp and the other parts of the sound system are absent in the silent 16 mm. projector. The sound film must go round the scanning drum, and it should be neither too tight nor too loose. In addition to the usual precautions to be taken in the use of projectors, the following special precautions to be taken to use projectors (1) Rewinding must be done as soon as the show is over. While rewinding the film close down the sound system, (2) Switch on the sound system a few seconds earlier before switching on the lamp-house system and the running system. The amplifier values require a few seconds to set warmed up, (3) First close down the sound system and then lamp house system at the end of the show.

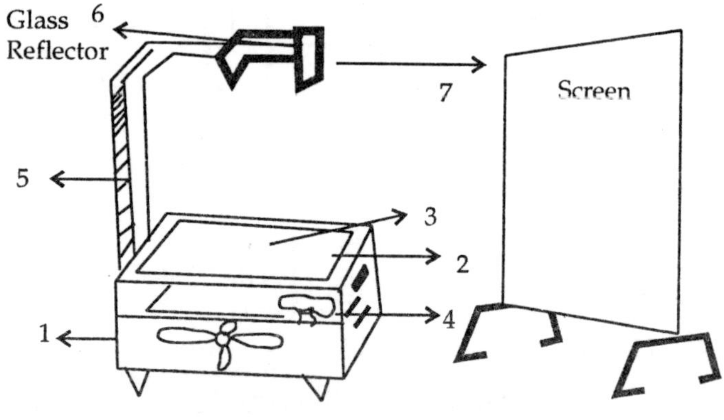

Fig. 18: Over Head Projector

Overhead projector has:

1. Cooling Fan
2. Transparency Platform
3. Covering Opaque Glass
4. Bulb 350 W
5. Beam
6. Reflecting Glass
7. Screen

Now-a-days overhead projector is generally used in schools for transparencies prepared for chalk board work and other illustrations.

MAGIC LANTERN

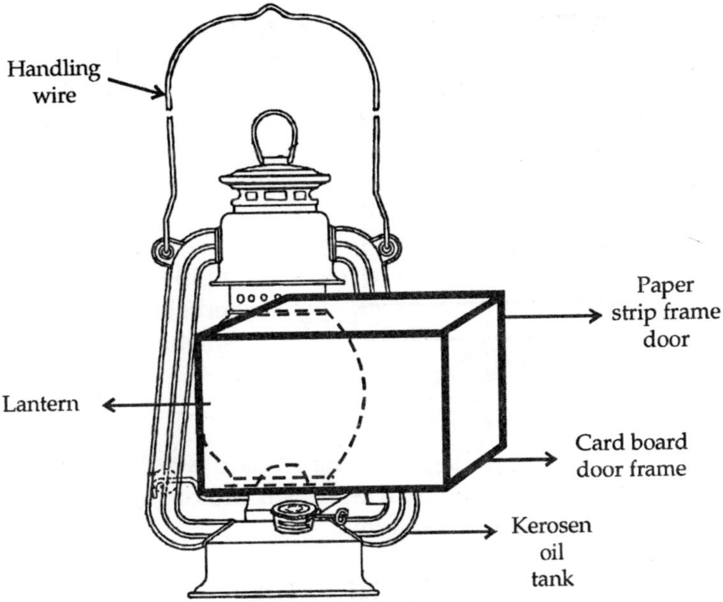

Fig. 19: Magic Lantern

Magic lantern is very useful teaching visual aid specially for small children. A lantern which generally used in houses for light is used. A card board door frame is fixed with the lantern to accommodate a framed picture or a drawing or an illustration made on white paper of medium thickness. When this framed picture is inserted into door frame of the magic lantern and lantern is lit up it gives a good visual impact. It gives a shilly-lite image. This gives a sensory experience to small children and makes the lesson development very interesting and it helps in learning.

Micro Projector

This is used for projecting pictures from microscope slides on the screen so that objects which could only be seen by one student at a time through microscope, can be demonstrated and explained to the whole class.

Screen

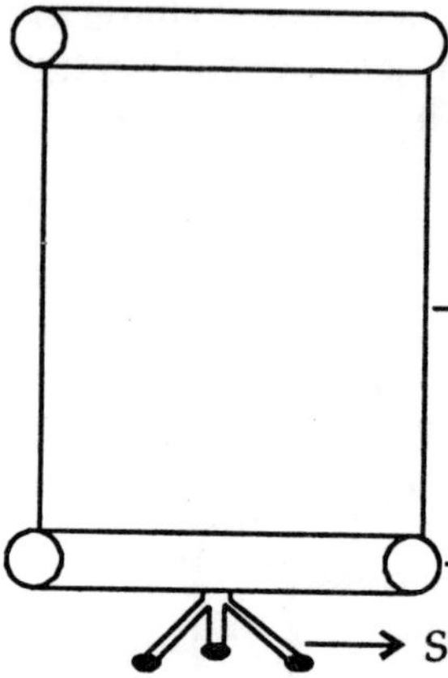

All types pictures, diagrams, chalk board word prepared on transparencies require the clear white surface of good screen on which the picture may be projected.

2. GRAPHIC AIDS

Graphic aids are powerful media for teaching-learning. They visualise and simplify facts and ideas. Conventional graphic symbols are used in them. The word graphic is a derivation from the Greek word 'Graphicus' meaning to represent or depict through illustrations and writing symbols. They represent a judicial blend of drawings, pictures and written words. They are usually two dimensional and a few of them can be projected on episcope. Pictures, illustrations, charts, posters, maps, diagrams, graphs, cartoons, comics, flashcards etc., are some of the important graphic aids.

1. Chart

The word 'Chart' is a derivation from the Greek word 'Charta' meaning 'a prior thought sketch of an action'. Use of chart is very old. Man has been preparing charts before proceeding on an expedition while finding out new lands on the earth. Vasco-da-

Gama had prepared a chart before proceeding on an expedition to find out India but found America. Likewise many persons who had proceeded on voyage for trade and commerce or for finding out new lands prepared charts. Also army generals when thought of capturing rich and fertile lauds prepared charts for launching armed expeditions. Not only army generals and voyagers prepared charts, burglars, dacoits and political marchers had also prepared charts before action.

In the field of education, it was Comenius who first thought of using graphic material in teaching. He observed that the "verbal communication does not ignite thinking in students as it does not emit reactionary signals". He also observed that the real education is only possible, if sensory experience of the concrete things is spread out before the class". Many of the concrete things, being too heavy or too big or being away from the class, cannot be brought in the class. In such a case if their pictures (illustrations, because photography was not there) are shown to students they will quickly learn. Experimenting in the church school he wrote a book "Orbis Pictus" teaching through pictures, which became very popular in European schools. And finally Comenius wrote a book 'Didactics' on teaching. The main purpose of this book was to improve teaching in schools, showing that the teaching should be aimed to deduce information from the students as much as could be possible. In other words the teaching should aim at elicitations as much as possible. He thought it would lead to real education and also would to reduce verbalism. The book on education 'Didactics' written by Comenius became so popular that it was called 'The Great Didactics'. The whole contemporary teaching methodology is based on it. The later educational thinkers, Pestalozzi, Froebel, Madam Montessori, John Locke, Dewey including Indian thinkers, Aurobindo, Swami Vivekananda, M.K. Gandhi, R.N. Tagore, and J. Krishnamurthi were influenced by the theory of Didactics propounded by Comenius.

After Comenius, it was Captain Cook, a British army officer, who gave the concrete shape to the concept of 'Chart'. He was posted in British army in Australia, where he observed the flora and fauna and landscapes of Australia with great interest. He made sketches on Australian life. Later on he visited African continent also. The African animal life, human life flora and fauna impressed him very much. There too, he made a graphic recordings of it.

When he went back to England and started teaching in a grammar school he made use of this material by making charts and showing these charts in the classroom in teaching geography.

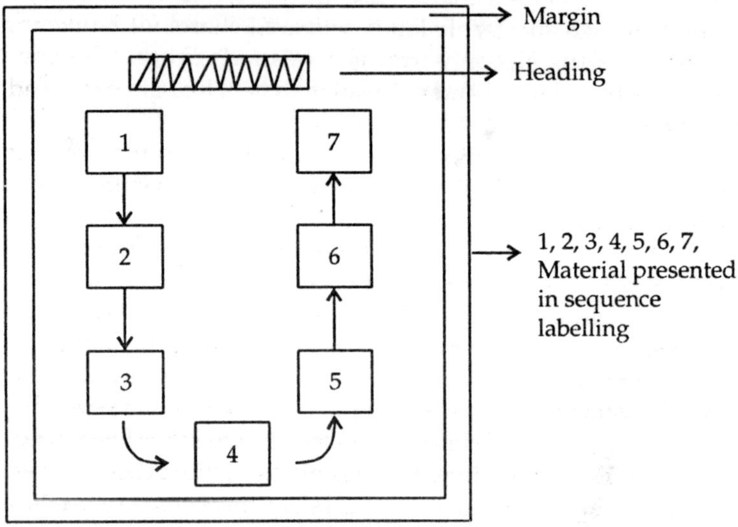

Fig. 20: Chart

The main purpose of using chart in teaching is to deduce as much as possible from the students what they know. It is therefore necessary that chart should be so designed that students start thinking and reasoning. So the chart should have such a graphic composition which is problematic, which compels the students to solve the problem posed before them. Therefore, a chart should have an artistic form – having dominant picture or composition which should be attractive, bold, balanced and rhythmatic. It should have written material only as Heading and Caption as less as possible. If the teacher wants to give some information, which he thinks cannot be elicited from the students, he can prepare back pocket at the back of the chart a teacher keep the material in the pocket. He should use this material at an appropriate time.

For making a chart first of all a topic should be chosen. Out of this topic what is the matter which could serve as didactic, on which questions be spread and elicitation made? Material required will be a while cartridge paper of 28" × 22" size and 072 lb weightage or good chart paper of size not less than 28" × 22". A prior sketch should be made on a rough paper. The graphic material should be well organised or composed. It should have form, rhythm, sequence and good arrangement. After considering all these points, the cartridge paper should be pinned on a middle size drawing board with drawing pins. Thereafter, chart be prepared by pencil and finally it would be prepared in black ink or in colour. The size of the letters of the Heading should be very bold say no less than 2" or 2½" and of labelling no less than 1". When the chart is complete the pencil work should be softly erased. We can fix a hanging strip to it. For protection of the chart an old thin cloth can be pasted with wheat floor copper sulphate added paste. Plastic round bags especially prepared can be used for storing the charts. The charts should be catalogued and should be hanged on especially prepared charts hangers in the school library. Charts once made should not be thrown in dustbin and should be preserved for using them again.

Charts are an important media of teaching since they are didactic. They serve the following important purpose:

- To show relationship by means of facts, figures or statistics,
- To present materials symbolically sequence wise,
- To summarise information,
- To show continuity in process,
- To present abstract ideas in visual form,
- To show the development of structure,
- To create a situation wherein a problematic graphic form could be presented before the students which could stimulate them,
- To present the content sequence wise in parts in order to learn,
- To encourage the students to continue related research,
- The charts helps in maintaining continuity in and development of concept, and
- Abstract and difficult things can be taught through chart.

In view of the above didactic functions of chart it can be defined as under:

"A chart is a combination of graphic material – pictures and a few written words, especially designed for logically and systematic visualisation of key facts".

The teacher should be well versed in chart making. Every teacher is not an artist. He should adopt a technique which could be help fulfil in making a chart. Charts available in the market are not well suited in teaching. Therefore, the teacher should take the following steps for the preparation of chart. For preparing a variety of visual aids, it is necessary to develop some reference file for layouts sketches of your graphic aids. These are called tear sheet file or scrap files. These files may serve as a basic resource for hand made graphic aids including chart. Materials for these files can be assembled form:

- Pictorial, diagrammatic and graphic contents and cuttings from news papers, magazines, comics and other discarded books. Some of the common magazines for the purpose are, Life, Illustrated Weekly, Dharam Yug, Readers Digest etc.
- Pamphlets and pictorial display material from Embassies, Tourist Information Centres, etc.
- Advertisement materials from Industrial concerns and other private agencies.
- Set of pictures, greeting cards and pictorial cut outs produced commercially.
- Tracings of sketches from books, encyclopaedias, and costly picture books.

This material should be categorised and arranged under different sub-heads according to different categories of picture illustrations.

This collection of pictorial material can be used in various ways in making different visual aids including charts. These can even be mounted on bulletin boards and can be used as wall display charts. This material will prove as an asset for chart making as these pictures and diagrams can be enlarged with the help of epidiascope on white paper.

Furthermore the following points should be kept in mind while preparing a chart:

- Concept or theme in various relationships should be clearly analysed which are to be depicted on chart,
- Ideas to be illustrated should be visualised,

- Ideas should be transferred on chart paper artistically with most effective design and layouts, and
- Finally lettering should be neatly done.

Classification of Charts

The charts can be classified as under:

- Genealogical charts
- Chronological charts
- Flow charts
- Progress charts
- Wall charts
- Tabulation charts
- Pictorial charts, etc.

Genealogical Charts

Genealogical charts are used to represent the growth and development of an empire or dynasty or a natural or social phenomena. Such charts have been traditionally used in history to represent blood relationships between the members of the same line with the help of visual symbols. But now charts are frequently used in biology and physical sciences, economics, civics and other sociology sciences. As a chart is combination of graphic and pictorial media designed for orderly and logical visualisation of relationships between key facts and ideas, it is effectively done through visual symbols. Main function of genealogical charts is always to relationships such as comparisons, relative processes regarding development, classification and organisation. Tree charts, developmental charts come under this category.

Chronological Charts

Chronological charts provide a chronological frame within which events and developments may be represented through graphic and visual symbols. They develop a time sense among students, helping them to comprehend and visualise the pageant of time and its relationship. While constructing chronology charts it should be remembered that only important dates should be shown; they should represent only space relation. The scale used should be accurate and uniform. The chronological charts, as other charts are made, should be made aesthetically good and beautiful so as to catch the attention of the students.

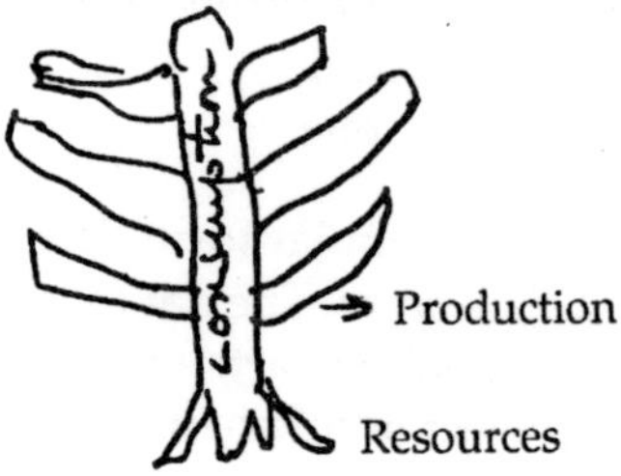

Economic Development

Fig. 21: Tree Chart

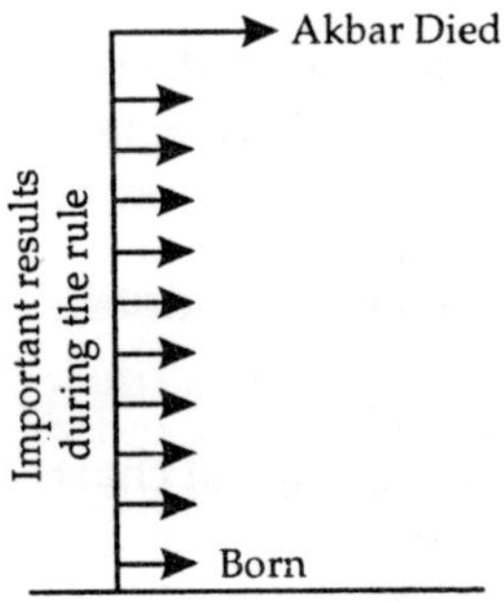

Fig. 22: Chronological Chart

Flow Charts

Flow charts are used to sequence and functional relationship in happenings of any social as well as physical phenomena. It also shows organisational set up and basic tenets of administrative unity. For example, the relationship between the executive, judiciary and legislature, relationships having or showing different checks over each other for their smooth functioning. While designing a flow chart care must be taken to preserve a sense of

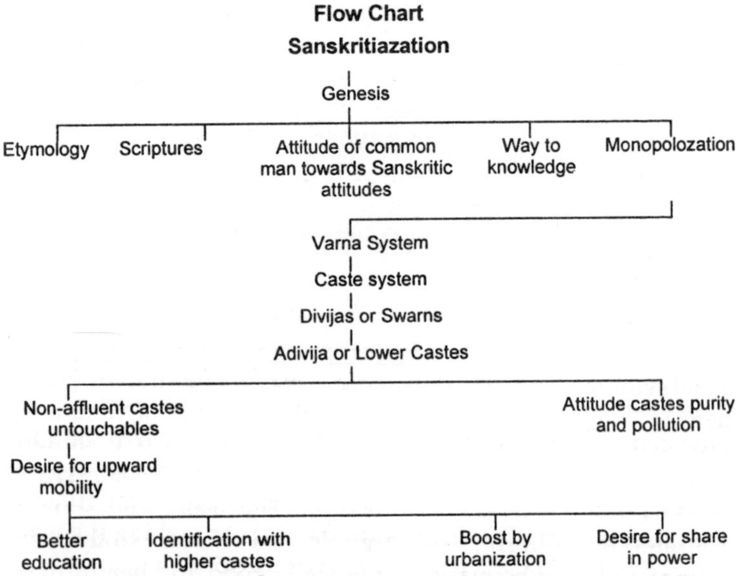

Fig. 23: Flow Chart Sanskritization

order and sequence. Take for example birth of child the presentation of the content should be in order in sequence otherwise everything will go topsy-turvy.

Tabulation Chart

In tabular chart the data is presented in tabular form. It makes to gain comprehensive view of the facts at sight. The data is changed under several heads and sub-heads. Tabular charts are very useful in presenting the progress of any project in nutshell.

Pictorial Chart

Pictorial chart is prepared by mounting or pasting a picture on a chart paper. Such chart is used for eliciting information, and is very useful for small children for teaching language and social studies. A chart is a systematic arrangement of key facts and ideas in graphic or pictorial form. In a pictorial chart a mounted picture is displayed in the classroom and students are asked to visualise the picture and find out themselves what is there in the picture. On being shown and visualised the picture returns or emits return signals to the students which make them think and respond.

Wall Chart

A wall chart can be a useful teaching aid if it is introduced with some discussions and left for sometime on the wall. Such a chart is very useful for teaching skills. For example, teaching joinery in carpentry or teaching developmental processes in tin-smithy, if charts on joints in wood-working or tin-smithy are permanently displayed on the walls in the carpentry or tin-smithy shops, the students will learn a lot themselves and will discuss such technical processes with the teacher. Likewise, in school, such charts can be used to teach good healthy habits in students. Pictures of renowned persons may be helpful in moral education.

There can be variety of charts. A good chart is one which through a systematic arrangement of graphic and pictorial media provides or depicts logical visualisation of relationships by summarising comparing or contrasting in explaining subject-matter and intensely involving the students in the knowledge development. So it can be concluded that the prime function of the chart is didactic which helps the teacher making the teaching educational through two-way communication.

Poster

A poster is a pictorial device that is generally symbolic in nature. A poster is composition with a bold design having a form, colour and theme which conveys a message that attracts attention and communicates just one fact. A poster is a basic graphic interpretation of an issue or topic which leaves greatest possible impact on the visualiser. Because of its dramatic and impressive presentation, it captivates the eyes regardless of the message or pictorial contents. So poster is a pictorial device designed to attract attention and communicate a story, a feet, an idea or an image rapidly and clearly. Posters play a vital role in non-formal education. A poster is very useful to communicate quickly and effectively a single idea and publicise important school of thought and community events and projects. Brevity, simplicity and ability to arrest attention are some of main qualities of poster. Lessons, projects and school projects may be reinforced by using poser with other visual aids. The poster with

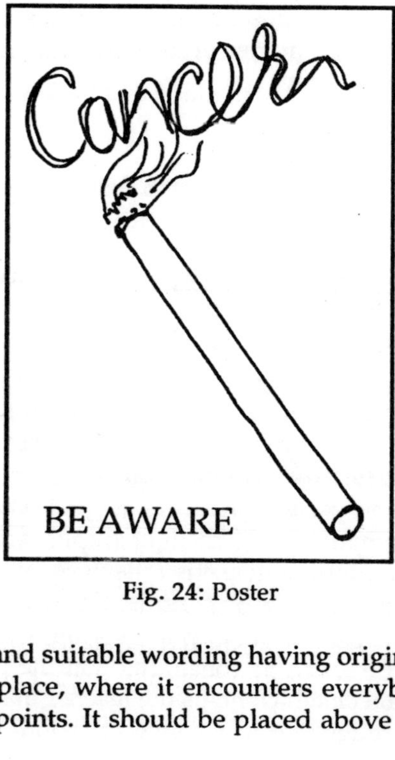

Fig. 24: Poster

a good design and suitable wording having originality should be displaced at a place, where it encounters everybody's attention say at the exit points. It should be placed above eye level of the school children. It should get natural light. Once the attention of the public or class has been caught, the poster should be able to reinforce its message.

Generally posters are used for advertisements. Now-a-days in material rat-race man has no time to see things. Therefore, the business community in order to popularise their products make use of posters. So posters are prepared in enlarged big sizes, which are put at such points from where large member of people pass. We notice such cinema posters. The government and social agencies make use of posters to make the public aware about some dangerous things as drinking drugs addiction and smoking etc. Political parties make use of posters at the time of elections mercilessly.

Diagram

A diagram is an explanatory drawing that explains inter-relationships by using lines, geometrical forms and symbols. Sometimes it is very complex and abstract representation because the pictorial elements are absent and variety of symbols are used. Diagrams as visual summaries of facts that are more condensed than in the form of charts.

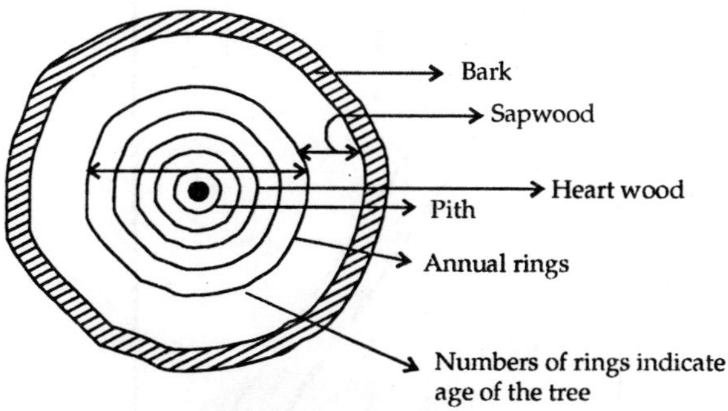

Fig. 25: Diagram of Cross Section of a Tree

Graph

A graph is a representation of quantitative data that present information quickly and effectively. It shows comparisons and relationships of masses of statistical data, clearly and interestingly. Graphs are of many types but basically these have three forms: line, bar and circle.

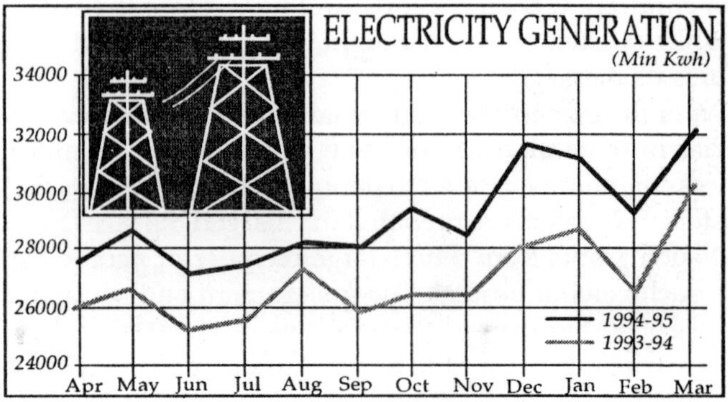

Source: Selected Economic Indicators (April 1995), Ministry of Finance KBK Infographics

Fig. 26: Line Graph

Enrolment of students in colleges for degree courses in India
Note: The figures are illusionary and are not correct

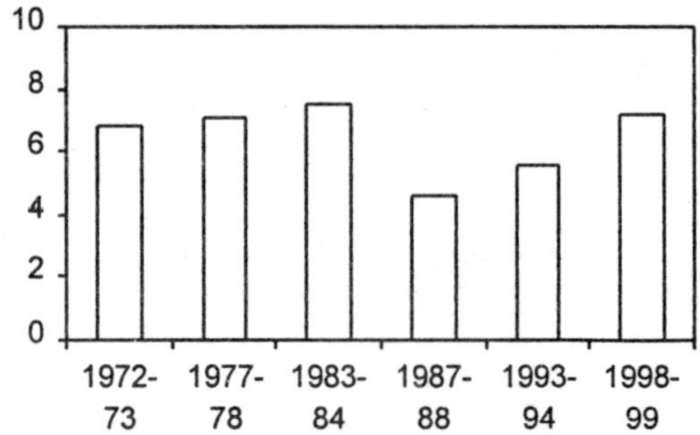

Fig. 27: Bar Graph

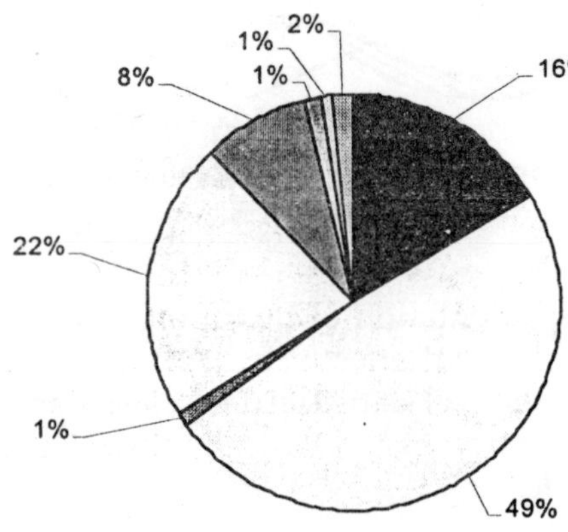

Fig. 28: Circle Graph

Cartoons

A cartoon is a metaphorical presentation in the form of a picture or a sketch. It vigorously presents and dramatises humour, satire, caricature of exaggeration about an idea, a person or a situation. Like the poster, it makes an appeal and conveys a single person. Many artists specialise in making cartoons. Their cartoons are generally published by leading newspapers and journals. Such cartoons make an appeal. In teaching use of cartoons evokes interest in students. They visualise cartoons with keen interest, which in turn emit messages and make the students think contemplate on a particular situation or in specific context. As such, use of cartoons makes elicitations possible during the course of teaching making it a joint venture. Use of cartoons are very useful in teaching language specially at lower level.

Fig. 29: Cartoon

COMICS

A comic strip is a form of cartooning, depicting story in a sequence. In order to catch readers eye they present stories in action. Comics are potential medium of visual education.

Fig. 30: Comic

FLASH CARD

A flash card is potential medium of visual education. It is used for introducing new words or phenomena in the classroom. Suppose a teacher is teaching and is going to tell the children about the word 'city' which they yet do not know. The teacher will take a strip of thick chart paper and will paste a picture of a city on the one side of the strip and two pieces of thick sand paper on the side. For introducing the word city the teacher will use of a flannel board. After doing this he will ask questions about the flash card and will explain to the children what is a city? The flash cards are useful for comparing things also. As a matter of fact flash cards are small compact cards that are flashed before a class to bring home an idea communication of a new idea or new fact requires repetitive methods, drill work and follow-up review of the discussion, talk or lecture. Flash cards usually involve photographs and other types of still pictures.

Flash cards, like flannel graphs are of maximum use in kindergarten and elementary schools. These can also be used for enriching all areas of curriculum. Finally we can say that the main purpose of their use is to provide systematic drill and to teach recognition by sight.

Fig. 31: Flash Card

SCRAP BOOK

Scrap book is a vital visual aid, which can be used in teaching almost all subjects. Scrap book is a book prepared out written scrap. It can be developed bit by bit as a hobby activity.

A scrap is an unserviceable or unfit for use material left out after a manufacturing process. For example when a carpenter manufactures a table, he cuts out wooden pieces of timber according to a cutting out list prepared as per orthographic drawing. In this process he leaves many wooden or timber pieces as waste, which may be called as scrap. In the same way a tailor when stitches a Kurta or Paijama or a Pent, he does the required cutting and leaves behind unserviceable scrap of cloth. Likewise when a tinsmith makes a bucket out of galvanised iron tin sheet he cuts pieces as per patterns. In this process also a lot of scrap occurs.

The scraps are caused in all manufacturing processes. Such scraps are utilised later on. Wood scrap is generally used is fuel. Iron and tin scrap is sent back to iron foundries and is used in manufacturing iron sheets, flats or bars. Cotton scrap is used in paper making.

In the scrap world, the greatest and largest scrap is caused in the field of written material. Many of us generally buy newspapers, magazines and journals. But we hardly get time to utilise or read this written material judiciously. Many of us decorate these in our drawing rooms and finally drag these in our stores for scrap buyers (*ruddiwalas*). Our children also buy books while studying in schools. They hardly read the complete books for the reasons best known to all of us. Reading habit in children in declining day by day. The devices like TV, VCR and VCP contributed to this evil to a large extent. Many chapters of the books go unnoticed. And at the end of academic session the books also meet the same fate as newspapers and journals meet in houses. The books are thrown in the store and when a scrap dealer visits these books are also sold at throw out prices. One reason might be the lack of storage places in modern houses. They sell out old books get a place in the dump of *kabarais* (scrap dealers). They pick up a few of these good looking magazines, journals, books and put them on the road side for casual sale.

All such material contain very useful educative elements which can be used by the teachers for developing the instructional material. This can also be used by the students also. Textbooks, many times have limited material. For the proficiency of the knowledge material the teacher has to depend on other sources. He has to stretch hands on reference books, dictionaries and encyclopaedias in the libraries. If such an effort is done in the last moments the teacher fails to get the desired teaching material. In the nick of time his reading becomes myopic and he misses many things while reading. As such, the teacher should adopt a technique which may help him in developing instructional material in the subjects he is teaching. He had to adapt a "read and catch method". Then he can only become a true teacher. According to Tagore "a true teacher is like burning lamp". The fuel for this burning lamp is his reading habits. If the teacher reads and collects useful material from all sources and arranges it in such a way that it could be used in future when required. Many articles and write-up appears in newspapers and journals which provide a collected useful information to the teacher. Such a collection and arrangement may lead to scrap book making. Such collected material may prove a treasurer house for the teacher.

A teacher teaches at least two teaching subjects in schools. He might be interested in some other special activities in any field – say art and crafts, literary activities or social service. If the teaches perceives the newspaper daily and weekly or monthly journals he can get a lot of material. In addition to these he can find out immense of subject related material in old books. He should carefully read such material and cut at the weekend. The cut material should be pasted in a white sketch book type book, subject wise. This can be used at a later date. Such material should be suitably supplemented by the teacher. Many times, packing material contain very useful information. Very often older generation know many things. If the teachers happens to get some information from old experienced people he should record such information in the scrap book. Such collected material should be documented and increased suitably subject wise. Important things should be underlined. Scrap book should be numbered.

Many teacher training institutes train the B.Ed. students in the preparation of scrap books. Central Institute of Education, Delhi is one of such institutes.

For the preparation of a scrap book the teacher should develop a regular reading habit. He should mark teaching aids of the useful material and cut it regularly at the weekends and keep it in separate files. And when he gets time he should get it pasted in his scrap book. Better would be if he involves the students in this activity. This will motivate the students to read and develop a regular reading habit.

BANNER

Banners when displayed at proper places serve as an effective teaching visual aid. They help in character building and in establishing a healthy social order.

EARLY TO BED, EARLY TO RISE,
MAKES A MAN HEALTHY AND WISE.

Fig. 32: Banner

PICTURES

There is an adage that "one picture is worth one thousand words". What we cannot explain in so many words, we can explain easily through a picture or photograph. And there are occasions when it is quite difficult to explain various natural phenomena in words. For example, a teacher goes to a zoo and visualised there many animals and birds – say he has seen many types of parrots in the zoo. In case he wants to make the students of his class aware about the kinds of parrots it would be difficult for him to explain in words. In case he has a camera and has taken photographs of parrots and show these photographs to the students it would be easier for the teacher and the students to explain and understand. Photographs or pictures are usually pasted on small cards for showing to the students. They are useful in teaching pre-primary and primary school children. They are useful in providing the needed drill or repetition to students. They teach to recognise things by sight pictures and photographs should not be used for prolonged time. Pictures and photographs can be used through a scroll method. A used card board packing base can be used for using picture scrolls. Comenius suggested first to use the pictures.

Fig. 33: Picture Scroll Box

MAP

A map is an accurate representation in the form of a diagram of the surface of the earth or some part of it drawn as per scale. Maps vary in type and form. They are a convenient and universal device that gives various physical, economic and social details. Maps are universally used in teaching.

In the past man used maps extensively. All navigators, wanderers, army generals and sea pirates used maps and charts. In teaching the maps were used at a later stage. Maps are of two types (1) plain paper maps, and (2) relief maps. Plain maps are made either on chart paper or white cartridge papers as per scale. For developing a map the following techniques are used:

(*a*) *Grid Method*: Maps from books are developed by making squares on the paper and on the original map.

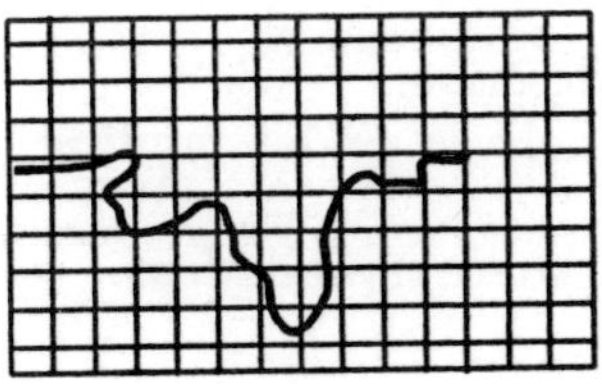

Fig. 34: Small Graph

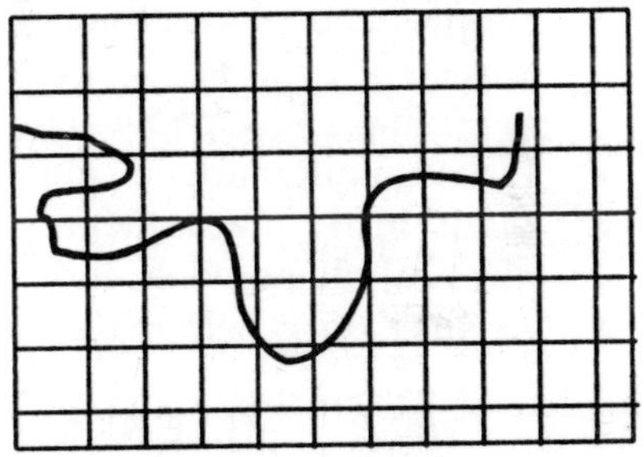

Fig. 35: Bigger Graph

(*b*) *Punch Method*: This method used for draw maps on the chalk board from a master copy. First a map which is big enough developed on a big thick paper. It may be a cover paper or packing paper. For developing the map either a pantograph or grid method or free hand drawing method used. When the map is finally developed its broader lines and punched through a punching nail. And finally the punched maps can be placed against the surface of the chalk board for padding it through the punched holes. These punched holes can be joined together and correct map may be drawn on the chalk board. This is necessary to save time and energy.

Relief maps are generally casted on the moulds by paper pulp. An accurate relief map first prepared on a clay surface out of which a master mould is prepared either of Plaster of Paris or of cast-iron. This master mould is used for casting relief maps. When the casted reliefs are dry they are polished and appropriately coloured. Purposes of Maps are:

- To depict geographic features of the earths surface,
- To show relationship between places,
- To furnish information about distances, shapes, sizes of areas,
- To clarify descriptive materials,
- To stimulate and motivate of people about places,
- To serve as a basic and multipurpose visual aid in the teaching of social studies,
- To create a basis for various experiences while studying peoples and places, maps are universal aids. They lend attractive pictorial symbols and adorn pages of books, magazines, newspapers etc.
- What cannot mapped cannot be describe,
- Maps bring places nearer and help in understanding physical phenomena, and
- As such maps help in developing concepts and ideas.

ILLUSTRATIONS

An illustration is a method of communication through lines. When camera was not invented distant things were taught through illustration and telling. It was Comenius who first thought of use of illustrations in teaching. In his bock 'Orbis Pictus' he has elucidated the benefits of the use of illustrations in teaching. Now an illustration is either a painting, a photograph, an etching, a drawing, an engraving or a graphic production of these or some innovative artistic creation like mosaic or a collage, which tells a more less complete story by itself.

3. THREE DIMENSIONAL AIDS

There is a Chinese adage "we forget what we hear and we remember what we see". Seeing things through pictures and photographs do not provide us complete experience without, analyzing these learning is not possible. There are certain things which cannot be known without seeing these. There are limitation of showing things in the classroom. For example, if we want to make our students aware about distant monuments and religious places or places of national importance, we can neither bring such monuments or places of national importance in the classroom.

Because none of us is Lord Hanuman who had brought the "Sanjeevini" herb from Himalaya to Sri Lanka in order to save Lakshmana, nor the whole class can go to see the monuments. What we can we do, we can show their republicas or a smaller true representations in the classroom. Likewise there are many situations in teaching when showing of republicas things becomes compulsory. So there are many ways of providing such contrived experiences to the students and various three dimensional concrete things are used for that purpose.

Models

"A model is a true representation of a real thing which is either very big like earth or very small like an atom". Models are used for instructional purposes. They provide experiences of things which are either very far of or very big. Models are recognisation of three dimensional things or representation of real things. Models have manageable dimensions. They capture the past and future. They take us to places which are physically inaccessible. Models simplify the reality and demonstrate processes. When involved the students in making of models they generate creativity in them. Models stimulate interest and arouse curiosity in students placing them in natural setting. Models can be classified:

(*a*) Still models,
(*b*) X-ray models, and
(*c*) Working models.

(a) Still Models

Still models are models are for such things which are big like river valley projects like Bhakra Dam, Rihand Dam, Dulhasti Dam, Tehri Dam and other power projects or some monuments of national importance like Sun Temple in Orissa, Ashoka Pillars or some statues of national leaders. Models of such things are made in proportion in scale and are finished in the colour and texture.

Three dimensional models provide an opportunity of seeing and feeling new material. This is real end to the learning process and to interest. It is important however, that the three dimensional still model is strong so that it can be handled by every one, and not reserved for the museum or glass cases. It should not too heavy also. The still models can be termed as reduced model, where a small republica of large object is constructed. Models can be enlarged from original small things like wrist watch or an atom so that important details may studied without further magnification.

If an actual specimen is available to make models of real things should be avoided as possible. Things like micrometer, handsaw, vernier calliper, therm ometer should be shown in real form. Also in many cases making of three dimensional model is not only impossible but also foolish. Suppose if the teacher wants to show muster seeds, their samples should be shown.

Fig. 36: Still Model

Relief Models

Like relief map, a relief model is a recognisable three dimensional representation of a country landscape or part thereof. The vertical development on a flat surface in semi-natural colours brings out orographical features clearly. A relief map of India is of basic importance in teaching social studies in elementary and secondary schools. A relief model of volcano (ज्वालामुखी) is of prime importance in teaching geography at 10+2 level. Likewise relief models are useful for teaching land consolidation, river formation etc.

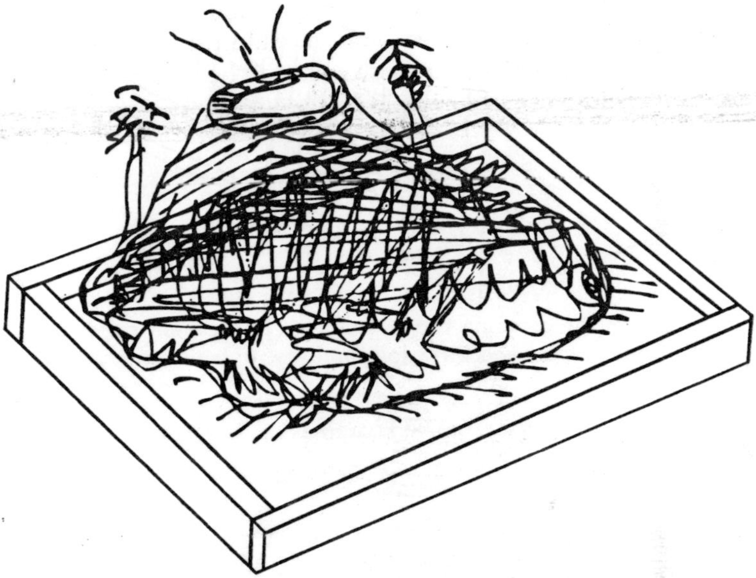

Fig. 37: Relief Models of Volcano

Dioramas

The dioramas are very useful teaching aids. The dioramas depict three dimensional group scenes incorporating miniature objects, like small toys, and background in perspective. A diorama can be compared with a still aquarium wherein small fish are kept. So dioramas are made to depict small group life as a nuclear family, a zoo etc. A diorama depicting a nuclear family will have husband, wife and their two children. It will have a bed room, a drawing room, a kitchen and a combined lavatory cum bathroom. Such a dioramas are useful to give knowledge of things which does not exist in the vicinity, the teacher is teaching, such as a railway station or an airport for hilly areas students.

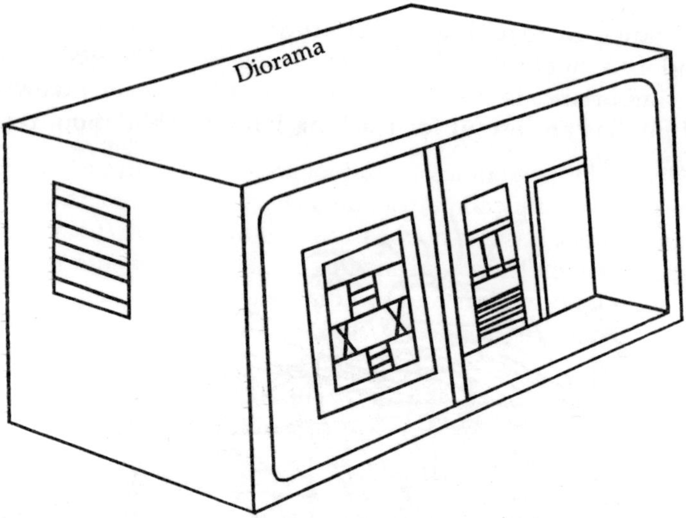

The walls of the diorama can be made of transparent paper or plastic transparency and little dolls and toys of beds etc., may be placed inside the diorama.

Fig. 38: Diorama

Uses

Dioramas are essential aid in learning situations as under:

- The situation which involves third dimension.
- To make experience more concrete, tangible and memorable.
- To depict historical places, periods, scenes from story.
- To show development. In public exhibitions, dioramic displays are effectively used.
- Dioramic displays can be used as teaching aid for many primary concepts in social services, languages and other specific areas of school areas.
- Dioramic displays can be used for mock-up developments.

X-Ray Models

The stills models such as still models of monuments, dams etc., relief models and dioramas generally do not give any inner visualisation of the objects depicted through these still models.

Whereas there are certain things which have inner structures. Without knowledge of such inner structures one cannot know nothing. Say for example, in a biology lesson showing of torso cannot give any knowledge about lungs, human heart, kidneys and liver. Until and unless a student knows about these he cannot understand the functioning of human body as a compact biological organic whole. It is also not possible that human corp (dead body) be brought in the classroom and dissected before the students. Like this, we cannot understand or know many things unless we see their internal structures. As such, instructions many fields cannot proceed. We cannot understand many of human organs like eye brain and stomach and also many machines, like heat and cold engines and structures in wood working. For knowing all such things X-Ray models are necessary. A X-Ray model is a true representation of internal structures. For simple things, like bio-gas plant we have to make a X-Ray model that it can only be understood. In X-Ray model cross section of thing which is truly represented is made visible.

Fig. 39: X-Ray Model Oil Engine

WORKING MODEL

In many cases the working of things is to be shown then only the students can understand the concept things like working of electric motor, functioning of heart, door electric bell can only be known if their working is demonstrated. In disciplines like physics, chemistry, engineering working models not only make the learning easier but stimulate and motivate the students to carry out experiments in the fields of science and technology themselves. Working models make the teachers' job very easy. They generate a spirit of creativity and inventiveness in students.

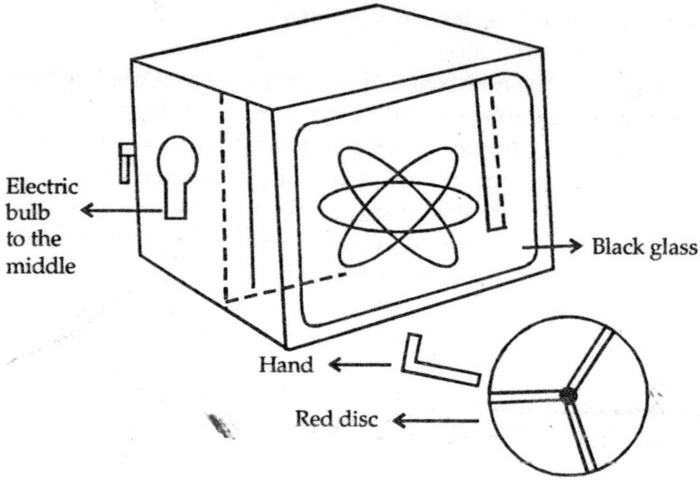

Fig. 40: A Working Model of Rotating Atoms

OBJECTS

Objects which have been removed as units from the natural settings and shown during the course of teaching prove to be good teaching aids. Making of their republicas or models is not advisable. For example if the teacher wants to make the students aware about micrometer, thermometer, vernier calliper, hacksaw, handsaws and other laboratory and workshop equipments making of their models will be a mere waste of time, as their models can never be accurate. The models made of these will not be operative. Whereas if these things in actual shape will be visualised by the teacher before the students in working conditions, the students will know how do these function? They will learn a lot.

SPECIMENS

There are many things which are very small in size like muster seed, wheat seed, bajra etc. These cannot be shown individually being very small in size. So it is desirable that their specimens be shown in small packs. Rapeseed or muster seed or alsi seed (अलसी के बीज) should be packed in empty match boxes and be shown to the students. At the most we can fix, a tracing paper lid on match box's inner box. Such samples should be stored for future showing.

MOBILES

A mobile is a system of correlated teaching materials painted and cut out from card board or consisting of solid models or both, hanging from a single source and balanced with the help of strings attached to comical pattern of wires. Mobiles give a decorative look. These should be hanged above the head level in corridors, halls and big classrooms. These are very very useful visual aid.

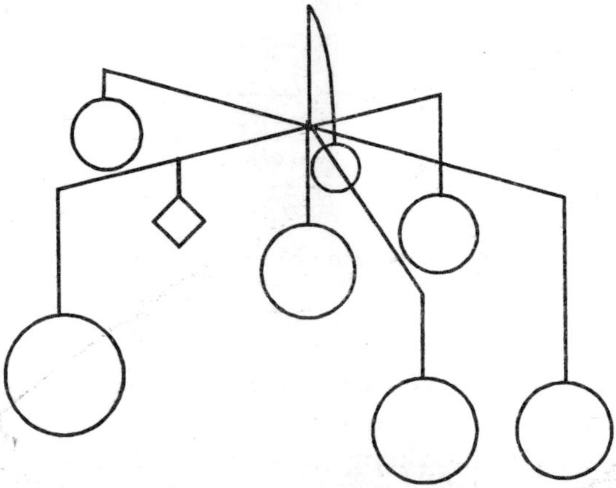

Costumes, Jewellery Coins and Icons-Sculptures

Fig. 41: Mobile

COSTUMES

Costumes are very good visual aids. In teaching literature display of costumes apprises the students about the real social life situations. For example teaching plays, written by Shakespeare, like Macbeth, Julius Caesar, the display of costume of that time could be very useful. Likewise, in social studies showing costumes of the related country would be helpful to students in understanding the cultural patterns of the country.

Fig. 42: Costume

JEWELLERY

Like costumes jewellery is also an attractive visual media. Life styles can be understood by seeing jewellery of particular period.

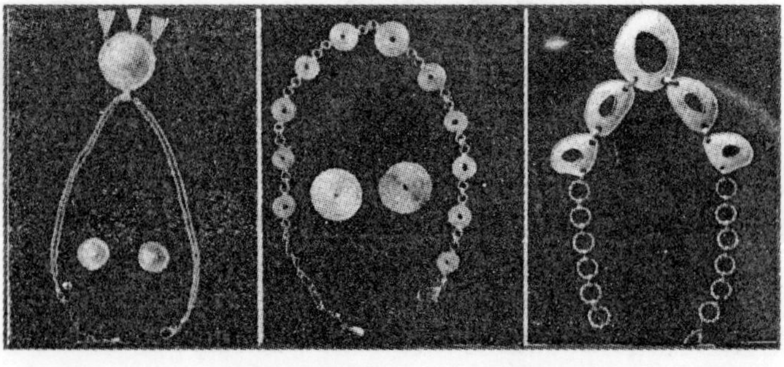

Fig. 43: Modern Jewellery

COINS

In teaching history like jewellery the coins of a particular period, if shown during the course of lesson development prove to be an effective visual aid. The coins can be made out of clay and be painted with pigments.

Fig. 44: An Old Coin

ICONS AND SCULPTURE

Icons and sculptures are vital visual aids. Rulers come and go but leave behind some monuments which speaks about the past. In our Indian temples we find these in abundance which speak about our past culture and social life. For example in Khajuraho temples we find the sculptures on the departure of the girl after marriage ceremony is over. Likewise many social customs of the olden period are seen and ultimately adopted by the new generations. The old miniature icons and sculptures can be had from state museums can be used as teaching aid. These will stimulate and motivate the children to learn.

Fig. 45: Kaniskha

VISUAL DISPLAY AND MATERIAL

Displays

An educational display is a planned arrangement of graphic materials, specimens, handicrafts, dioramas, paintings, banners, posters, etc., correlated around a basic theme.

Purpose of Displays

- To focus attention of the observer on a topic of educational significance.
- To rebuild scattered ideas and undigested bits of information around nucleus for personality development, moralisation, character building, behaviour formation and for national integration.
- To give experience in collecting, making and exhibiting things,
- To encourage for self-expression and build understanding in a concise manner,
- To provide a concrete background to conceptualise abstract ideas,
- To serve as a multipurpose source of education,
- To generate aesthetic temper in students, and
- To create a sense of self-confidence in the students.

Displays and exhibits should be arranged keeping in mind the basic tenets of art such as clear and clean presentation having a form, balance rhythm symmetry. Displays should serve the extra educative purposes which are not covered through formal and informal procedures of education.

Need for Display

Now-a-days, the visual educational displays have become a necessity. In the present machine age, which resulted in industrialisation and consequent urbanisation giving birth to modernisation and ugly consumerism, the job of the school has become tedious. Normally the school is supposed to educate children in 3R's and prepare them for life. For this the school carries on teaching, as per stipulated curriculum prepared by the state, and prepare the students for examinations. Educating the children for good living is not on the agenda of the school. Even though the schools look to this aspect also and tries to enculturate the students and inculcate certain skills in them.

The family is the first agency of education prior to school. The child starts learning at home. He learns speaking, sanitary habits, character building and role playing habits at home. All members of the family, grand parents, parents, siblings and other members of the family contribute in this process. The joint family system in the past and still in the present, where joint family exists, contributed and contributes a lot in educating the children through oral system and through interaction.

Now due to materialistic rate race and consumerism the old pattern of joint family system has broken down and nuclear families have come into existence. The grand parents if they have financial gains and standing in the old age do not want to live with sons and daughter-in-laws or with their own children. They do not want to loose their identity, and sacrifice their independence for the sake of their children. They generally want to enjoy life in old age when there is no office humbug. So generally the grand parents prefer to live separate and independently of son(s) and daughter(s) in laws. The younger married couples, now do not get support from the old people, as the earlier people used to get. With the result they are forced to live at a distance from their parents, with a blame from the parents that their daughter-in-law generally educate her husband to live separately. As a consequence of this they meet their both ends themselves. Both do jobs. And when they have children they rear them up themselves. Due to ugly consumerism the wife cannot leave the job. With the result the children are thrown in crèches and care homes. While their grand parents enjoy their lives seeing VCR, TV, VCPs, visiting tourist spots as newly weds do. As such the educative role of family has gone to nil. This additional educative role of the family has become schools responsibility these days.

How School Displays be Done?

Because our educational structure is purely examination oriented, the fact cannot be denied that school teacher has sufficient work load. He/she has to teach in six out of eight stipulated periods of the school time table. Therefore, it appears a difficult task for the teacher to take this additional responsibility. Moreover, every teacher has no aptitude for this work. On the other hand the society wants the teacher to do the all educative work which was supposed to be done by the family members. If any product of the school prove to be an anti-social element the school is squarely blamed for it and not the family. As such, in the present circumstances there is no way out to this problem except the school do something and educate the children in such a way that they are enculturated. Their behaviour formation should be so that they prove good citizens. This work cannot be done through curricular activities. It can only done through extra-curricular activities. And display is the best means to achieve this end. This is necessary because many parents are uneducated. The social mobility of their children is also necessary.

The principal of the school cannot do it himself/herself. Only he/she can give directions. It is to be done by the teachers. The Principal should tackle this problem democratically. He/she should put this mater before the staff council. Once the staff council is confided the solution would emerge. Surely some teacher would come up and volunteer to do this creative work, and some teachers would volunteer to help him. The in-charge of display should co-opt two or three of his colleagues and some upright students should form a School Display Committee which would carry out school displays smoothly. The Committee should chalk out a display programme for the whole session. The programme may consist display on various occasions such as birthdays of great leaders some religious functions of all faiths. Good ideas may be displayed. Alpna and Rangoli may be arranged. Handwork, like art work may be exhibited. A school museum may be developed. After this areas or places for display may be selected, which should be where there is a maximum passage of students. Display should be arranged above the eye level of students. Maximum students should be involved in the school displays. The area where the parents come and sit should always be properly cleaned and decorated. If possible the school displays should be organised on house wise. The displays should be judged by a judging committee. There should be a permanent display for inculcating spirit of morality and good health habits in students. The art and craft teacher should be involved in displays and creative works permanently. This way the school display can fill in educative gap left by the parents in this material age.

Fig. 46: A Display

Fig. 47

Fig. 48

Fig. 49

सत्य बोलना सदैव अच्छा है।

Fig. 50: Display Materials

Bulletin Boards

Bulletin boards provide the cheapest and multipurpose nucleus for visual education. The bulletin board as it implies is a place for bulletins, news items, announcements, multifarious items and visual displays that are absorbing interest in students. The development of the bulletin boards has also a history. Earlier the bulletin boards were used in government offices. Earliest bulletin boards were made out of soft Balsa and Samel woods. Thereafter, the framed gunny cloth bulletin boards were manufactured and acacia horns (Babul Kante) were used for stitching notifications on these. The latest bulletin boards is made of insulation boards, made of cane beggas. There are many varieties in bulletin boards such as wall bulletin boards, panel bulletin boards, revolving bulletin boards, mounted and unmounted bulletin boards.

Purpose of Bulletin Board

- To motivate and to arouse curiosity in the pupils,
- To display graphic and pictorial materials, possibly linked up with curriculum – both curricular and extra-curricular, attractively and invitingly,
- To introduce and summarise a unit of work or to analyse a topic graphically,
- To display work done by the students,
- To display source material on individual or group projects,
- To display wall magazines prepared by the group of students, and
- To provide basic means of general communication.

Uses

(*a*) First decide a purpose : display may be:

1. Motivational display should pose a problem to the viewers. It should be designed so as to ask questions and excite curiosity.
2. Developmental display should exhibit what should we not be doing, what should we do?
3. Cumulative display should exhibit summutation of a completed study.
4. Didactic display should force the students to find the facts about topic. It should encourage them to read further, and
5. Miscellaneous display can cover such topics as holidays, new events sayings, etc.

(*b*) Illustrations and arrangements should be done.

- Bulletin board may be fixed on a classroom wall or in any prominent place in the school. Pictures, clippings and other material on a variety of topics have to be collected and kept ready for use. If possible, students should be involved in this work. At a time only one essential theme must be conveyed through a bulletin board. The pictures and photographs have to be displayed attractively on appropriate colour background of bulletin boards.
- Lettering has to be done where necessary. It should be large, easy to read from any spot in the room fairly brief, horizontal, colour and contrasting.

- Use either script or block letters. The former can be made on string or wire (electric wire) etc.; the letter of cut-paper, card board wood etc.

Arrangement and Illustration of the Content

- Use illustrative materials that are eye catching, such as photographs, drawings, charts, maps, graphs, posters, pictures and three dimensional paper sculptures.
- Match the arrangement and material against the background. Dull background do not catch the eye. Colour must not be too bright it should go with the arrangement.
- Compose the material artistically keeping in view the basic essentials of the balance and continuity.
- Highlight the main theme by a catchy device. It may be an illustration, caption or text.

Use of Colour

- Colours have functional aspects which heighten the reconstruction of reality and provide strong emotional and psychological effects.
- A jumble of colour splashes are bad. They divide rather than unite.
- Create an accent with pure colours and use shades and hues in the larger areas. Use warm and cool colours together for contrast. In general foreground should be warmer than the backgrounds.

Arranging the Bulletin Board

- Utilise various media of visual appeal involving attention-getting devices,
- Mount the pictures and articles in placing coloured backgrounds in harmony with the rest,
- General informational pictures should be mounted uniformally and arranged together.
- Highlight different areas by labels and titles,
- Questions and short statements arrest attention if placed near pertinent objects or pictures,
- To create a dynamic effect, use coloured strings of ribbons to pictures or statements,

- Use paper arrows in contrasting colours to differentiate different areas,
- For an overall artistic appeal, use flower arrangements and abstract designs, if possible,
- Simplicity and brevity are the keys to good arrangement. In addition, bold lines, variety, form, order, colour dominance and a nice regard for good composition having due spacing, balance are important.

The school offers an ideal situation for display work because there is some convenient display position available in the school building. It can be associated with school subjects covering with enculturation. Bulletin boards play a vital role in the school display because the displays done over the bulletin boards stimulate the pupils' interest and prepare them to perform various useful activities. They are useful in introducing, explaining and reviewing topics to be taught or already taught in the school. Bulletin boards provides ample scope for pupil participation. The ideal size of a board is 6′ × 4′. The bulletin board should be hanged above the eye level of the seers.

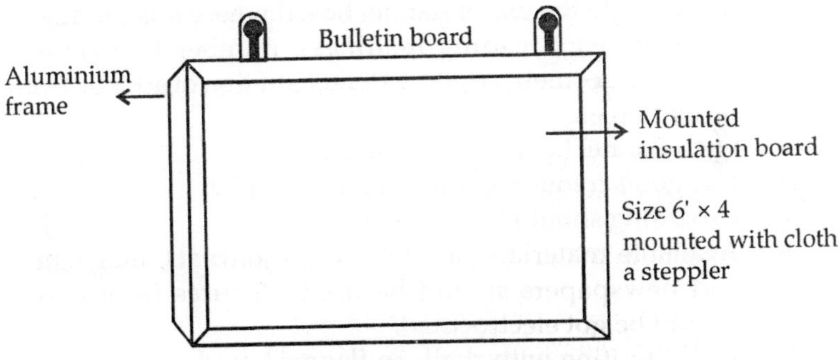

Fig. 51: Bulletin Board

FLANNEL BOARDS

A flannel board is a flannel-covered flat surface. Or we can say it is a flannel covered bulletin board instead of coloured cloth. Sometimes flannel is stretched and then glued to a piece of plywood or masonite board or hard board, but this system is not good. Stitching the flannel cloth to an insulation board with a stapler is good. The flannel can be removed when it is dirty for washing. Likewise a flannel graph which is used on flannel board is called khadi graph. A flannel graph or khadi graph consists a number of separate illustrations prepared on cardboard. Sand strips are glued on the back of these as is done in the case of Flash Cards. When separate pieces of flannel graph are placed on flannel or khadi board they stick to it because of sand paper strips.

Purpose

- To save time during presentation in the class,
- To encourage visualisation of graphic and pictorial material and deduce ideas and concepts out of it,
- To generate a spirit of creativity in students,
- To provide tactual and manipulative experience, and
- To apprise about the cumulative processes.

Proper Use of Flannel Boards

- Incorporate the use of flannel board where it is unique to inculcate e.g., reading readiness, number knowledge, concepts, geometric figures, demonstration of athletic team formation etc.
- Own flannel board should be made.
- Use good colour contrasts flannel graphs.
- Crowding should be avoided.
- Available materials, specially from journals, magazines and newspapers should be used. Pictures from books should be got electrocuted.
- Avoid writing with chalk on flannel board.

The flannel graphs and flannel boards are very useful in teaching small children specially at LKG and UKG levels.

Making the Flannel Graph

Construction of this aid is very simple. The illustration may be drawn on cartridge paper or chart paper. This can be backed with squares of lint at the back along with the strips of thick sand paper. This will hold the illustrations straight on the flannel board.

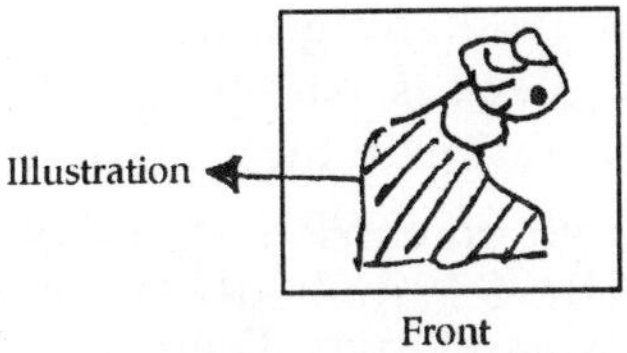

Fig. 52: Flannel Graph

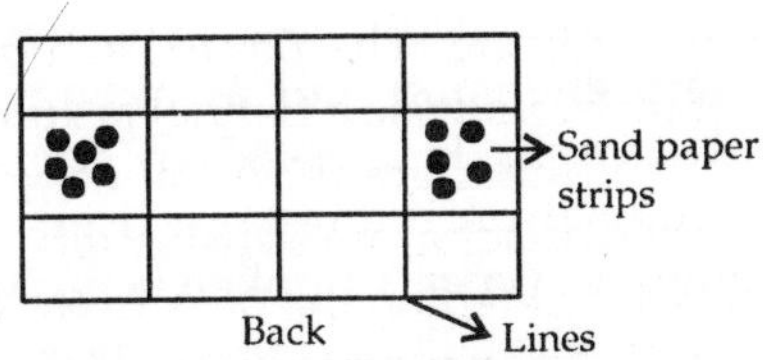

Fig. 53: Flannel Graph

AURAL AIDS

Recordings and Radio programmes constitute the main aural aids. Lingua phone are useful in language teaching, especially in the teaching for foreign languages. Spoken languages require the use of recordings, when it is taught to foreign students. Tape records are very useful in teaching various dialects of a language. They are useful in teaching of Biology, Animal and bird sounds can be recorded and exposed to students in natural History.

TAPE RECORDER

A magnetic tape is used to record sounds. There are too spools – the feeding spool and take up spool. There are separate buttons to be pressed for Recording (R) and Playing (P). There are buttons for forward and backward idle running. In tape recorders having more than one speed, care should be taken to record and play at the same speed. The efficiency in recording can be judged by the quality of reproduction of the recorded sound. There are devices in the recorders like the magic eye or the flickering lamps to regulate the volume while recording.

The tape recorder is now an almost universally accepted aid in teaching, and its uses are considerable in these fields. First, it immediately invites participation. Second, like the camera, it can capture an experience (but in sound not vision). Third, it can be used for recording discussions which can be analysed at leisure or with the class concerned.

RADIO AND TV (ALSO VISUAL)

Radio and Its Use in Education

If we go through the etymological and epistemological perspectives of education we find that its genesis has many facets, that is, verbal communication, non-verbal communication, two-way communication, analysis, aesthetic awakening and finally comprehension and awakening. Language is widely used in education. It is used in social interaction which leads to socialisation. Language used in educating people is spoken language (vocal). Spoken language has wide and varied hues and tones – like talking, gossiping, acting and singing etc. There is also aesthetical language like music. We get it through vocally and instrumentally. We are delighted and entertained by it. We get written communication through books, newspapers magazines and journals. There are also certain books of authority like Vedas, Holy Koran and Bible in which we have blind faith, we believe in what is given in these books. Other books are subject to enquiry. Though we believe we forget what we hear but Radio plays a vital role in education and getting extra information which we do not get in classroom teaching. Several programmes for various levels of students are broadcasted on the radio. The programmes are printed for all educational institutions well in advance.

Radio is an electronic transmission communication media. It is a device of catching voices from air invented by Marconi (Italy) in early twentieth century. The programme are first prepared, thereafter recorded and relayed to the air subsequently with the help of verbal sending components. These voice symbols get amalgamated into the air. This process is called broadcasting. The broadcastings are so relayed that they are distributed in radio channels. These voice symbols' broadcasts are caught by radio components at respective channels. The voice symbols are re-arranged, recomposed and converted into real voice as it was broadcast. This is done simultaneously systematically.

Marconi discovered this novel method when he was experimenting on earphones. He established Marconi Radio first in England. This had a brief life. Thereafter he established Radio in USA on 21.12.1920. The American Radio was successful. And consequently network of Radio-Stations spread throughout the world. Now it is a universal electronic media of instant communication. The BBC, voice of America, Moscow Radio, Radio Ceylon and All India Radio are the strongest radio networks in the world.

Initially, in our country three radio clubs were set-up at Calcutta, Madras and Bombay. They had short life and came to an end for want of finances. It was in 1930 the Govt. of India took over these clubs and named it All India Radio. Before, partition, India had eight All India Radio stations. Three of these went to Pakistan – Lahore, Karachi and Dacca. Now we have so many All India Radio (AIR) Stations. Before the advent of Doordarshan, we basically depended on Radio for communication. Now Doordarshan has put the AIR in the background. Even though it is a unique national communication institution linking the Indian people of far-flung areas together and generating feeling of oneness to the nation as a whole. It highlights the national activities. All important cultural, economical, social and political evens are covered through talks, discussions, cultural activities, musical programmes and news by AIR. It carries these to every home on its eternal wings. Whether these activities are held in far-flung villages or in the major metropolis or on sport fields or on the hills covered with snows, running radio commentaries present these in their colour and hues though aurally. Arrival of a cultural delegation from a foreign country, or a reception of a head of state of a foreign country or any other important national or international event is reported by AIR. Through musical voices of great singers, eloquences, and historians it binds people together. Because of low cost, a poor man can afford to have a radio.

ROLE OF RADIO IN EDUCATION

Education has a wider connotations where considered in its national perspective and wider scope. Education does not only consist of 3R's or mere literacy. Education is essentially a training in art of living. The art of living is richer, better and more fruitful for life. It is deriving the maximum, pleasure out of short span of one's life, to serve one's society, country and people in highest spirits. Schools and universities play an important role in this regard. Radio has a perennial scope to achieve this end in education. It plays an important role in this regard. Special programmes for various levels for students are broadcast on radio.

- Radio can afford to provide all educational facilities at Macro level. Whereas TV still has limited scope in one country.
- Radio is cheaper and easily accessible, so everybody can afford it. It is a poor man's entertainment equipment.

- Radio is useful in Adult education.
- Radio is useful specially in language education.
- Radio has a value as a means of enlightening the general populace – the poor, the labourers, and the peasants. It gives utilitarian information and dissemination of facts and knowledge. In almost all aspects of life right from the science cooking, gardening to great inventions it plays a vital role.
- Radio takes care of all manual work as well as academics,
- Radio, apart from addressing itself to all aspects of life of all sections of the society, its special projects of the school. It does intend to replace the school as short circuit TV does. It rather helps the teachers. It is full conscious tool of teacher's well being.
- Radio is very useful to farmers. It gives them good information about agriculture. They can use it while ploughing their lands,
- Radio is also useful to businessmen, because it informs them about business trends, and it regulates market,
- Radio by giving information about weather trends, improved seeds and manures it helps in boosting the food production,
- Radio provides a great deal of fun and entertainment to children,
- Radio supplements the school education by giving additional information, and
- Even though, the radio cannot meet the shortcomings of formal education which is basically based on traditional methods of teaching.

Some Suggestions Regarding Use of Radio in Education

- The teacher should make out a distinction between radiogenic and non-radiogenic subjects. Radiogenic subjects may be history, geography, sociology, civics and specially languages and dramatics,
- Schedule of educational radio broadcasting in detail should be made known to the students,
- Before making the students listen to a radio broadcast – lesson, teacher have to prepare the students listen to a radio lesson. The students can be stimulated by questioning or by briefly describing what they are gong to listen to,

- During the course of radio-broadcast the teachers must keep quite themselves and allow the students to listen to the programme, when the radio lesson is going on,
- Also the students must be advised not to talk when radio is going on.
- External noise should also be checked,
- Supplementary aids like chalk board, maps charts models should be used along with or after the radio broadcast during the course of follow-up,
- After the radio lesson is over suitable follow-up work should come up. The students may be encouraged to ask questions or discuss about their radio aural experience leading to recapitulation,
- The students should be advised to note down good points emerged out of radio lesson and follow-up discussion, and
- Lastly stimulation should be there for future radio-lessons. Parents should also be involved in it.

Drawback of Radio in Education

- Radio is one-way invisible aural communication,
- Radio does not provide any interaction, and
- Students remain passive listeners throughout, when listening radio programme.

Role of TV in Education

As education is a process of bringing up. The educationists lay too much stress on per. se. and comprehension in the process of learning. Look, see, comprehend and learn is the cry of the day in educational world. As such, modern scientific institutions universities, colleges and even schools have sufficient teaching aids and, have fully augmented human eye. As in ordinary life the human eye is usually augmented with spects when it gets exhausted with age, the teaching-learning process is augmented with certain technological aids. Radio augmented distant communication. When artificial voice is coupled and combined with artificial vision (TV) it becomes more pedagogically useful, as we generally learn by both hearing and seeing.

Definition of TV

TV is an electro-technological device which was devised for converting light patterns or a visual seen into an electrographic image plus voice, giving life like orientations of social happenings. An electro-technologic image-plus voice is sent to space, which is picked up on antenna, translated into a duplicated vocal graphic seen on the surface of a kinescope, generally called picture tube. It is a continuous process. It is called telecast.

Advantages of TV

- TV brings auditory and visual seen simultaneously. It binds distant people together and fosters national as well as international understanding. It makes per. se. (perception) possible of distant things, i.e., various birds, animals, flora-fauna, landscapes and scientific innovations.
- Close circuit TV can revolutionise the classroom teaching and communication system for the crowd, as we daily witness BSE crowds and close circuit network there. At railway stations, inter-state bus terminals, international airports close circuit TV do novels in providing information to commuters.
- TV is a best device of instantaneous distant communication. CNN gave instant news of gulf-war or any other war,
- TV is an active source of enjoyment,
- TV creates better learning situations for the young children, students and adults,
- TV can make aware the people about the past-epics and history as Doordarshan telecast Ramayana, Mahabharata, Chanakya, Krishna and Tipu Sultan. These are seen in other countries like Indonesia, Mauritius and Pakistan.

Working Principles of TV

Working of the TV is analogous to working of the human eye. Light wave reflected from the object strikes the lens of eye ball which focuses the light wave over retina, as the image of the object is seen and impression goes to the brain. TV camera is also analogous to lens of human eye. TV kinescope and antenna can be compared to human nerves and muscles.

How TV Picture is Telecasted?

TV camera, amplifier, transmission tower, antenna and kinescope when energised work together. Sound and pictures are sent over the air simultaneously by means of radio tube records, light patterns are changed into electric (input) impulses. Pictures sent by TV camera are combination of light are darker areas which form the images. Electric mechanism changes the camera plate through which scanning, sweeping telecasting is possible.

TV Programmes

- Quick communication. Recent distant happenings can be seen,
- TV programmes are explicit and open for general public,
- TV is used in political elections and in highlighting national discontent,
- TV can help in enculturation, curbing acculturation, instructional purposes, expert guidance and entertainments, and also extension programmes, and
- In some western countries closed-circuit TV is used as Master Teacher in teaching students of more than one sections of the same class.

TV in Education

TV has made intrusion in every field of life. Harold Hunt of Harvard University, USA said, "TV is our last hope to get rid off the restrictive, unimaginative and one way track education system". Hollis and Caswell said, "TV has little more than the traditional system of education of rope-walking and floor-dusting". Claims and counterclaims have been made about the use of TV in education. Some say TV is useful in education, some say it is not. Some argue that TV is very harmful not only to the school going children but to adults also. We will have to examine all pros and cons in this regard. And we have to examine our educational structure and see whether it is useful and whether TV can be usefully introduced and utilised in classroom teaching situations.

There is a striking difference between a TV lesson, a traditional lesson and a lesson supported by other teaching Audio-visual aids.

- TV teacher cannot interact with the students,

- Neither the students can have chance of any interaction and have pace with the TV teacher,
- TV teacher cannot visualise the individual differences amongst the students, so he neither can instruct, guide and help the students nor he can establish rapport with the students,
- In TV lesson there is no questioning nor clarification – as such no interview and guidance,
- TV lessons are time bound. It looks as it is given in an artificial situation,
- No queries, in case of demonstration, are possible,
- In TV lesson, there is little or no attempt to understand the frame of reference, nor any chance to understand the students ideas. Ideas are presented to students either in colours or in black and white,
- Students imagination remains unexplored and stagnated,
- Because of the lack of two-way communication (encoder-decoder) and absence of students reaction, elicitations which are core to the learning remains an impossibility,
- TV being a system of one-way communication bi-polar learning is not possible in the classroom,
- Students generally remain passive on lookers and not learners,
- TV when employed in teaching prove to be a teacher deserter and unemployment creator, as in many western countries. Close circuit TV employed in teaching has deserted many teachers,
- TV has more harms in store than benefits for the students as well for the teacher, and
- Finally it can be said that because of international jumble of TV transmission, TV is more crime generator, acculturator and time consumer of many budding intelligents. In many cases it damages eyesight also.

Still Televisions are More Effective Than Radio Lessons

- TV has better verbal effects,
- Automation in presentation, effect of verbal impact, visual impact of demonstration have unique results,
- Resource material can be effectively visualised and used later on in teaching, and

- TV gives more information through verbal and visual presentation.

Drawbacks of TV – More Research Needed

- TV cannot cover all areas of learning which are possible in teacher-taught face to face situation,
- There should be well planned mechanism or strategy to visualise and analyse the TV programmes,
- Students should be guided how to take full advantage of TV programmes, and
- A prior appraisal of TV lesson and a follow-up programme should be planned and implemented.

Still TV is Beneficial in Many Areas

- Demonstration in science, technology, scientific functioning (as turning point as UGC programmes) ecological science, information on pollutions, social pre-history, social, political and economic views, religious, teleological programmes and programmes on personalities like 'Galib', 'Dayanand Saraswati', 'Nanak' 'Aurobindo', 'M.K. Gandhi' and 'J. Krishnamurthi' have proved very useful,

How School TV Programme be Planned?

- School TV programme should be planned by exceptionally qualified trained teachers and not by bureaucrats,
- The timings of school TV programmes should be so planned that they may be seen by the children. The TV programmes should not counter with their play as well as sleep,
- The TV programmes should be announced well in advance and schools should also be informed accordingly in advance,
- The school should set up a Committee of experienced teachers to analyse the school TV programmes and guide the students,
- If there is any defect in TV programme, the class-teacher should clear it on the spot and remove the doubts of the students just after the TV lesson is over,

- TV can instil and generate interest in students conveying new ideas, skills in relation to day-to-day curriculum in science, physical education, humanities, civic sensibilities, art and craft and it can enculturate the students, so it should be nicely utilised, and
- TV programme should focus attention on bringing the distant things in the classroom, like dams, river projects and also scientific projects. And the teacher should utilise such a programme to enrich the knowledge of the students.

Telefilms and Close Circuit TV

Every school should have an arrangement for recording events. The teachers training colleges should have this kind of arrangement so the events could be shown to the students on close. Circuit TV at later dates, if required. This kind of recording should be done through kinophotography (continuous photography) for making films, motion-pictures. Classroom use of TV kinophotography can provide audio-visual effects and make per-se (perception) possible.

Difficulties in Utilisation of TV as Aids

- TV cost is prohibitive,
- Timings of telecast are unsuitable and prohibitive to student community. They do not suit them,
- TV in India as an instructional apparatus is recent, and
- Generally TV programmes are loaded with obscenity and loaded with western culture overtones, they generally harm students rather benefit.

Some Suggestions for Using School TV Programmes

- There should be an expert guidance to students to clinch the points from the TV programmes. Also there should be a follow-up discussion with the teacher on ensuing day,
- TV programmes should be, so telecast that they suit the students. Better would be if such school programmes are telecasted during school hours,
- The teacher should be cooperative in the analysis of the TV programmes,

- The students should be made aware about the descriptive foreign TV programme like Zee, Star Plus, CNN and BBC TV. The schools, should counter with such foreign disruptive and acculturative TV programme. The school should arrange nice cultural programmes in schools so as to motivate the students avoid violence and ugly consumerism. In many western countries their governments have been deliberating to create a climate, so that, the youngs could be motivated not to see undesirable TV programmes. It is done in England.

  Lastly it can be said the TV is an enemy to folk arts. It kills the aesthetic instincts of the children and adults. So many western countries are experiencing blatant sex crimes, vulgarity and obscenity because hedonistic TV programmes. In UK a committee has been formed to suggest as to how to delink students from continuous TV watching. Likewise many developing countries including India are facing such problems. For enculturation something should be done in this regard.

ACTIVITY AID

Activity aids are useful to apprise the students of real situations. Excursions (field trips, school journeys), exhibitions, dramatisation, solo and mono acting, mock acting, taking parts in debates, participating in competitions as chalk board writing competition and art competition and also decoration, singing and cleanliness competitions come under activity aids. In addition to these making and displaying of puppets and collages etc., come under this category.

Field Trips

Field trips give students opportunity to see landscapes, industrial installations, monuments, laboratories and places of interest. They learn a lot when they get actual idea of things and learn about these things instantively. Field trips should be chalked out in advance and they should be given in a time table. The teacher in-charge should plan all details regarding the trip. The students should be apprised in advance about the place of visit. The students should also be guided for necessary notings. After the trip a follow-up report about the trip and a discussion should follow.

School Tours

The young students are generally very enthusiastic to go on tours and see new places. Schools and other institutions of higher learning generally take up such tours in autumn or winter breaks when the weather is congenial. School summer breaks are not suitable for taking up such tours because of biting heat. Such school tours should be planned well in advance. The teachers in-charge should first of all have full knowledge about the places they are going to visit. They should enquire about the accommodation and local transport facilities available. After ascertaining all these facilities the teacher intending to go with the proposed tour should find out as how many students, and of what age group, are desirous to go on tour. They should also seek the consent of the parents of the students. The parents should also be informed about the possible expenses on fare, board and lodging and the railway concession they are likely to get. After doing all formalities, the teachers in-charge of the tour should collect money from the students as well as from the school. A senior student be chosen from the group should be asked to handle this money. The teachers should keep a vigil on the expenses. After doing all this railway tickets be purchased and reservation be made. During the course of journey, some students should be vigilant about baggage. Baggage should be counted. In a group generally there are two or three students who are careless, about their belongings, they should also take care of. Students should be asked to follow the team spirit and follow the team orders. They should take some medicines.

After reaching the place of visit first the students should be lodged. They should take bath and get refreshments. After that they should visit the desired spots. The teachers in-charge should monitor the visit and guide the students to take some notes.

Likewise the group should follow the norms while returning back. After returning back, experiences gained through the excursion should be reported in the school morning assembly. A record about the tour should be maintained in school office so that the students may be benefited in future.

Field trips and school tours put the school on wheels. They take the students for an on the spot study of environments, bringing them face to face with reality. Properly organised field trips and tours leave basic impressions on the minds of children, and on these, their future learning experiences grow. Field trips, study tours and excursions are very effective for teaching social sciences and general sciences. Students get first hand experience of handling and organising things, seeing functions, spots and situations which the study in their books. They learn to utilise resources of the environments. They visualise objects and specimens in their natural setting. Field trips, study tours and excursions, relieve the students broaden through understanding and through direct purposeful observation. They add to their interest, variety and involvement to the learning situation. Finally they reduce their boredom of classroom teaching. These should be related curriculum.

EXHIBITIONS

Exhibitions are extension of the simple techniques. An exhibition can be arranged by collecting together all display materials already made and, linking them with some printed captions so that they may illustrate a theme. There should be a preliminary planning for arranging an exhibition. Careful selection of work done by the students may be used for the exhibition. School exhibitions can be organised on special functions like school foundation day, parents day, alumnus day etc. All students should be given opportunity to participate in such exhibitions. Exhibitions can also be arranged on the occasions of school fairs and certificate distribution ceremony.

DRAMATISATION

Different children have different kinds of talent. The school should organise functions to nurture such talent. This can be done by arranging some cultural programmes on the annual day, parent's day and alumni day. This will enable the students to show their talents, as well as give enjoyment to the audience. Dramatisation unfolds many activities such as acting, singing, stage setting make up, dancing and costume preparation. Such programmes enculturate the students.

School Museum

Word Museum is derived from the Greek word 'mouseiom' meaning temple of muses. It is a place of study which specialises in assembling, protecting and showing of objects, specimens and exhibits of great variety. The museums are of various types, like general museums, museum of art history, natural history, applied sciences, children's museums and trailside museums. Dr. Goode distinguishes the following types:

National museums, local museums, provincial or city museums, college or school museums, professional or class museums or exhibits, cabinets for special research

School museums serves a vital source of instructional material readily available for integration into the curriculum. The school museums provide a substitute of field trips on the premises of the school. These can be developed through the imagination and initiatives of the teacher and the active participation of the motivated pupils and of the art teacher. The school management should provide a big room and necessary infrastructure for the museum. The infrastructure should include some show cases, raised and low platforms. The school museum should have natural light and electric light also. Readymade kits, objects, specimens, anatomical pieces, acquries, specimens of eatables, costumes of different periods, toys, coins, ancient relics, pictorial material, raw materials like minerals should be kept in exhibitions.

School museum concentrate attention of the students. It integrates scattered ideas to evolve new concepts. It provides experiences to the pupils in collecting and exhibiting materials. It encourages self-expression and promotes sharing of experiences. It provides opportunities to take up group projects.

Arranging Mock Organisations

Arranging mock things is one of the best activity aids. Many of us do not get chance to enter state assemblies and Parliament. As such, they are quite unaware or immune to the working of these legislative bodies. This is true in case of students, and they fail to know about the actual working of these law-making bodies. In case a mock Parliament is arranged in the school, the pupils will be quite aware about its working. They will understand very much about the different organs and process of law making. And when the student will perform mock functions as that of treasury benches, opposition, their functionaries like Prime Minister, Ministers and Opposition Leader, and also prominent opposition members, they not only understand the functioning of Parliament but also get a chance to express. So arranging mock things are vital visual aids and help in learning.

Debates

Arranging debates in schools is also a very useful activity. Debates build confidence in students and give them chance to express. These promote learning.

Solo and Mono Acting

Solo and mono acting also give chance to the students for self-expression.

Art Competitions

Art promotes aesthetic sense in students. It gives them chance of self-expression. It opens the avenues for sharing cooperation, fellow feeling and tolerance. According to Sigmund Foreud art activities release suppressed emotions and helps in human personality development. Art is that which is new, creative and, has been done for the first time without any inclination. As such inclusion of art activities in school curriculum is a must. It should be an important compulsory activity for all students. When art is a paramount activity there should be avenues for its development. So regular art exhibitions should be held and students should be encouraged and involved.

Puppets

Puppets are a powerful medium of mass communication. They provide a dynamic sources of education for children and create of sense of realism in communication. They also serve as a multipurpose medium of self-expression. The puppets have utility in the field of entertainment, education, self-expression and social action. Since the beginning of modern history, in every country, puppets have been used as an expression of art and as a medium of communication. In European countries the puppet show is more popular with children than the film. And puppet show or theatre is a large business in drama and education. Recently over D.D. telecast 'Potli Baba Ki', a puppet shows on Sundays at 10.00 AM has been educating our children about culture and tradition and has been doing an excellent job in the field of enculturation in addition to entertainment and enjoyment. In health education puppets are being used with great success commercially in South of England. In India, in Rajasthan 'puppet showing' is a vocation. Puppet showers regularly visit adjoining states of Haryana, Delhi, UP, MP and Gujarat and arrange puppet shows in schools and colleges and earn their livelihood. In schools, puppet shows can be integrated with the work of English, history, art and handicrafts. Children love identification, and they may be motivated to produce a figure. Useful previously recorded dialogues when relayed with the puppet show provide a good experience to the children.

Major Types of Puppets

(a) The Glove or Hand Puppets

A glove puppet is worn on hand. The first finger is inserted into the head of puppet, while the middle and third fit into the hand glove. With the movement of fingers the puppet is operated.

(b) The Marionette or String Puppets

These are suspended by strings controlled by puppeteer's hands. A string puppet is a jointed body of limbs and wood strings, stuff cloth and papier-mâché head. Such puppets are action puppets.

(c) The Rode Puppets

The rode puppets have heads or heads with dress of the lower part of the body fixed on a rod which can be manipulated by a hand. Punjabi Bhangra dancers often use such puppets while dancing.

(d) The Shadow Puppets

Shadow puppets consist of flat figures in the form of silhouettes attached to small sticks. These are manipulated in front of a source of light and consequently the shadows thereof fall on small white cloth screen placed in front of the audience.

Making Simple Glove Puppets

- Take a thin cardboard or card paper, approximately 5"x6".

Wrap it loosely around your forefinger, glue the edge firmly and wrap a string around this tube.

- Take a piece of crumbled newspaper and fix it over and around the tube on your finger. Cover this with a plain sheet of paper or with a piece of light cloth.
- Prepare a fine paste papier-mâché, mixed it with glue and china clay.
- Take a wooden stand and fix the trace of the head of the puppet on this. Apply a fine papier-mâché paste all over the base. With our hand or a knife carve the cavities of eyes, ears, nose, mouth, etc.
- Next step is to colour the puppet head. Apply bits of tissue paper or kite paper with glue or paste. Dry and colour it.
- Then make a simple dress for the puppet head which can be worn over head.

Some variations in the techniques of making puppet heads can be done, and the art teacher of the school can guide the teaches who are making puppets.

STATIC VISUAL AIDS

Chalk Boards

Chalk boards are extensively used for instruction. A classroom is incomplete without a chalk board. It is a basic, most widely used and versatile tool of instruction. Even in the modern age of television and teaching machines it remains as most trusted and powerful companion of teacher. In other words chalk board or black board is one of the trusted friend of the teachers. Chalk board or Black boards are cheap readily available visual aid. A lot of information can be put on chalk boards. It can be used both by teaches and students.

If we peep into the history the development of black board, it can be traced to religious Protestant Movement. The followers of Martin Luther were in search of using cheap means of communication for spreading the ideology of Protestants. The printing was in its infancy. They thought to utilise the empty walls of houses in Germany, by painting these walls with black pigments and writing their sermons on these walls with white clay. This experiment proved successful. It was thought why not this be experimented in Church schools. From Germany, this graphic experiment of writing on black with white spread in other European countries. And in due course of time it crossed the British Channel and went to England. Since England had some colonies, wherever they ruled they took black board in the colonial schools. This way the black board became a universal instruction aid. Now the chalk board or black board is basic requirement for each and every class. Actually it is chalk board, since its surface to black it has been nicknamed 'black board'.

There are various types of chalk boards:

- Wooden chalk board with easel,
- Cemented chalk board,
- Glass chalk board,
- Wooden chalk board fixed,
- Hard board chalk board,
- Asbestos sheet chalk board,
- Slate chalk board,
- Curtained chalk board,
- Flexible chalk board,
- Roll-up chalk board,
- Rubber chalk board, and
- Magnetic chalk board

I. Wooden Chalk Board

Wooden Chalk boards are the oldest. These are made by joining wooden planks together. The wooden planks should be seasoned. These should be joined keeping the annual rings of the planks in opposite direction with grooved joints.

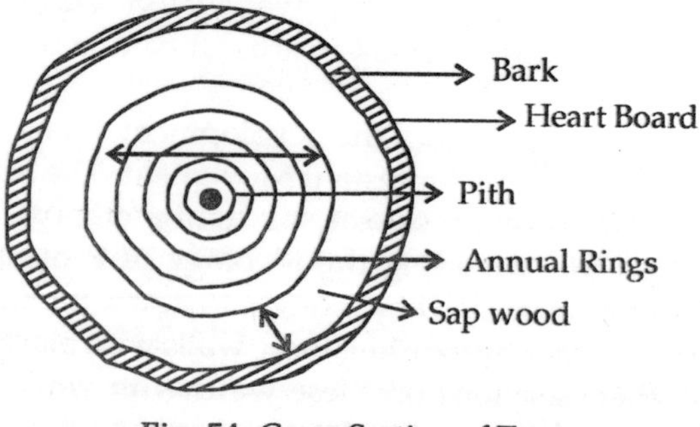

Fig. 54: Cross Section of Tree

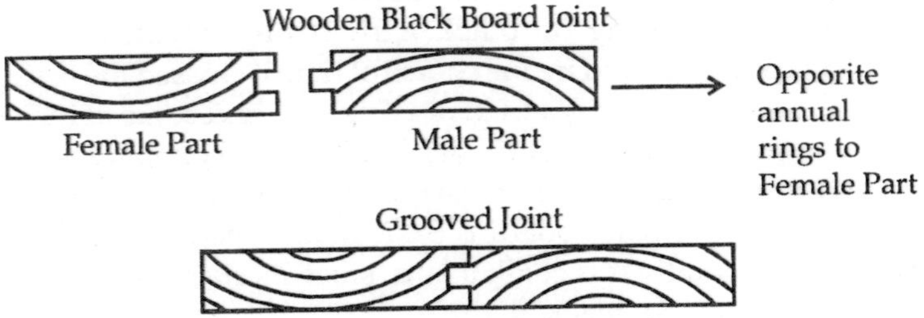

Fig. 55: Grooved Joint

The appropriate size of the wooden black board is 6"x4". It can be fixed on the wall also. It can be put on the easel also. While fixing the black board on wall it should be fixed above the eye level. There should be an allowance for the passage of air so that the black board may not get moistured and get twisted. There should be chalk dust tray.

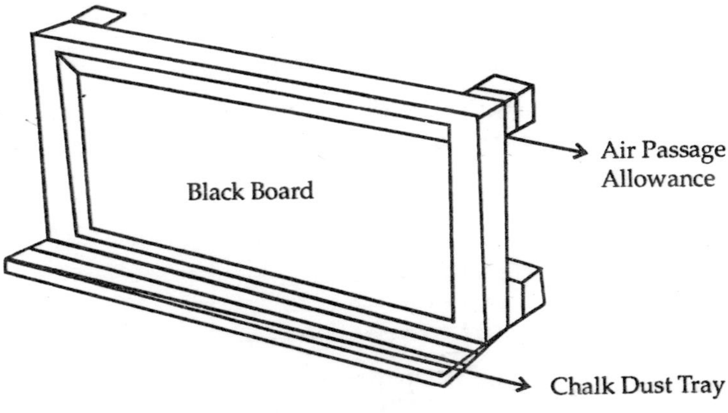

Fig. 56: Black Board

II. Cemented Chalk Boards

There has been an expansion of school education abnormally. Before partition Delhi had only 5 or 6 High Schools. Now the number has gone in thousands. So also the school buildings have been constructed. The same is the case throughout country. There has been a shortage of timber. It became difficult to have wooden black board en masse. So, largely cemented black boards were constructed when the buildings were constructed. These cemented black boards were constructed in a haphazard way as the building contractors were not aware about the quality of black boards. The surfaces of these cemented black boards were largely made smooth, whereas, the surface of the black board should always be rough. These black boards were largely painted with third rate black board paint. The black board paint is basically different from the ready mixed paint. Ready mixed paint is made of three ingredients – (1) pigment, (2) binder and (3) carrier. All these are mixed equal in equal quantity. Whereas, the black board paint has very little quantity of binder that is varnish, and some quality of rough pigment as glass powder is also miseed so that the surface of the black board may remain rough. If the surface of the chalk board is smooth the chalk will not work over it. So the surface of the black board (chalk board) should always be rough. It should be periodically rubbed with sand paper and painted with a light coat of good black board paint. There are companies which manufacture good black board paint. These are – Goodlas Nerolack, Johnson Nicholson, Asian Paints and few others. Locally made black board paints should not be used at all.

III. Wooden Chalk Board with Easel

Wooden chalk board when used with easel is moveable. Suppose the teacher wants to take class in open, he can use this kind of black board.

Fig. 57: Black Board Easel

IV. Glass Chalk Board

Glass chalk board is recent addition. Ground glass (murky) sheets are used in these chalk boards. Such sheets have one rough side and the other smooth side. Smooth side of the glass is painted with desired coloured enamel paint. When the glass sheet is dry it is framed keeping the coloured side inside. These framed glass chalk board is fixed in the classroom where it is free of glare and can be seen by all students. Such glass chalk boards are very useful for higher glasses, because in lower classes such chalk boards are likely to be damaged by the students. Such boards do not require black board paint and painting by it again and again. Glass chalk board can be cleaned with soaked piece of cloth.

V. Hard Board Chalk Boards

Hard boards are used in making such chalk boards. Hardboard sheet is framed and fixed on the wall. There should be air allowance between the wall and the board.

VI. Asbestos Chalk Board

Smooth side of the asbestos is used as chalk board. It is framed and painted with black board painted and fixed against the wall.

VII. Slate Chalk Boards

When slate sheets are used as black board such boards are called slate black boards. Only drawback is that the slate sheets are available in small sizes. These sheets are to be framed together, therefore, such black boards do not provide a continuous flat surface. But there is a definite truth too. These boards do not require black board paint at all.

VIII. Plywood Black Boards

Plywood black boards are easy to make, because plywood sheets are available in big size. Their surface is also not smooth. Only these boards required framing and painting with black board paint. While fixing with the wall space should be left for air passage, otherwise the layers of the plywood would separate due to moisture. Plywood black boards should be saved of glare.

IX. Curtained Black Board

Any type of black boards mentioned above can be curtained. Curtained black boards are useful teaching biology, engineering subjects and mathematics. A lot of visual experience is to be given to the students in these subjects. If all graphic and illustrative information is exposed to the students in one time, the students will be dazzled and confused. Therefore, it is necessary that visual presentation on black board be exposed to students bit by bit. It will give them a chance to learn quickly.

X. Flexible or Moveable Chalk Board

Moveable chalk board is very useful in teaching mathematics. The mathematics teacher has to solve many mathematical theorems and explain many formulae. The students are required to have a pace with the teacher. If the black board is left for sometime the students can follow the teacher. As such the black board wok has to be retained so that the students may cope with it. During the course of their copying, the teacher should not sit or stand ideal. Therefore, the black board should be so designed that both the teacher and students remain busy.

Moveable black board a pair of two equi-weighted black board moveable in two different frames. When the lower black board is thrused upward, the upward one will come down, the teacher work on it.

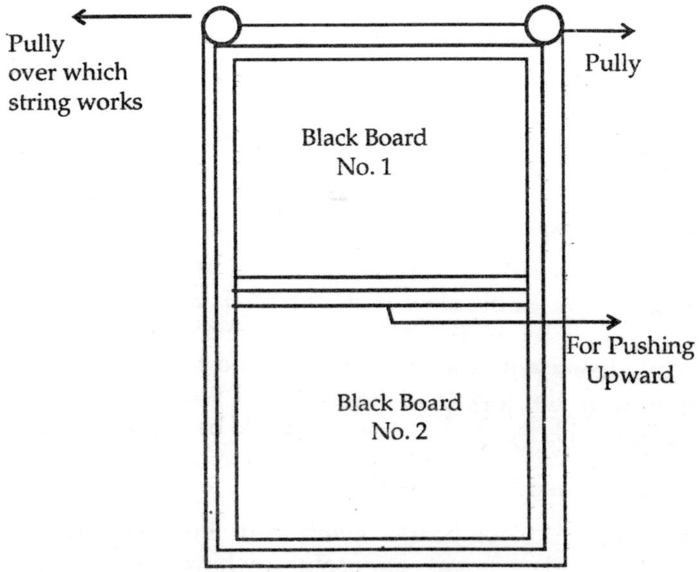

Fig. 58: Moveable Black Board

XI. Roll-up Black Board

The roll-up black board works on the principle of scroll or roll. It is prepared out of either a full size sheet of thick cartridge paper of 28" × 22" size or on a piece of rexine of the same size. The cartridge paper roll black board is always good because it is painted with black board paint. Chalk works well on it. On the other hand, a rexine roll black board, because it is smooth chalk does well. A roller black board is very useful because the teacher can draw diagrams with tables in advance which he cannot drawn well in a period of 35 minutes.

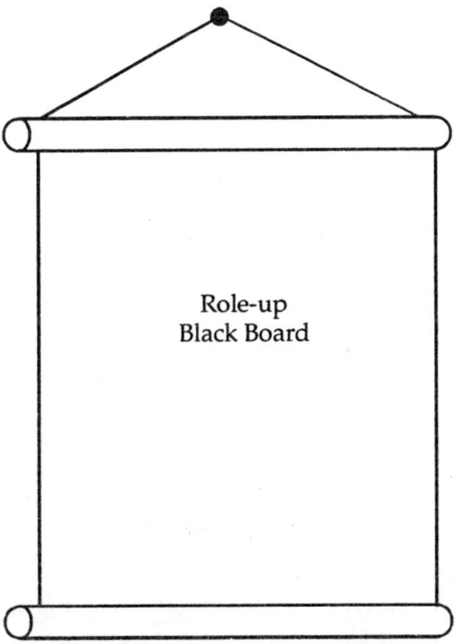

Fig. 59: Roll-up Black Board

XII. Rubber Black Board

To avoid wear and tear, shrinkage and twisting and painting again and again, a new type of black board has been developed. It is a rubber black board. A big sheet of thick rubber sheet, as generally used in electricity transmission centres for insulating purposes is used. The rubber sheet of 8" × 4" or 6" × 4" of ½" thick is generally used. The cost of such rubber black board is prohibitive. Therefore, such boards are generally used by Public Schools which charge high fees from the students.

XIII. Magnetic Black Board

Magnetic black board is very useful in teaching science-physics. A magnetic board is made out of thick iron sheet, say not less than 16 gauge. This sheet is framed keeping an allowance for fixing a magnet at the back of the black board. Suppose the physics teacher is teaching vernier calliper. If he puts the calliper on magnetic black board it will stick with the black board. The students will see the object and will see its drawing also and will have a useful experience.

The following are some of the instructions to be borne in mind while using the black board:

- The low edge of the chalk board should be at the level ot pupils eyes,
- The chalk board should not reflect glaring light to words the viewers,
- There should be minimum distance of 3 metres between chalk board and the first row of students,
- Letters, words, diagrams and drawings should be large enough for the pupils to read without difficulty (e.g. letter size 6 cm. tall can be read from 20 metres, 3 cm. at 10 metres and so on),
- Matter must be written clearly, orderly in straight lines avoiding overcrowding and incomplete writing,
- Writing must be down slowly exerting uniform pressure on the chalk,
- The teacher should not stand in front of black board facing it while writing. This may obstruct the view of pupils, who may like to see what and how you are writing or drawing,
- Do not talk while you are writing or drawing. Avoid dialogues during the course of your black board development,
- Never paste or nail any material on the chalk (black) board, because they may spoil the surface of the chalk board,
- Clean the chalk board gently from top to bottom gently,

allowing the dust to settle down and never struck the duster on the table in the classroom,

- Involve your students in the black board work development. They learn better by doing so, and
- Pink, pale green, light blue, light orange chalks are better than dark red, blue and purple chalks. Otherwise white chalk is best of all. Conventional colours have to be used (light blue to represent oceans, brown for mountains, red for arteries, blue for veins and so on).

Techniques of Using Chalk Board

- Plan before hand how to use the chalk board. This should be recorded in lesson plan book showing sketching, layouts and illustrations to create better learning situation.
- Do not become Picasso, develop skills in black board writing. Constant practice is required. Critical self-examination should also follow.
- The teacher should also learn to adopt correct posture, regular movements of hand.
- Black board work should be free from personal idiosyntaxism which confuses the students.
- Deliberate attempt should be made to draw lines straight.
- Black board materials as chalk duster, templates, and compass etc., should be arranged before hand,
- Overcrowding should be avoided. The black board matter should be brief, simple and concise.
- Glare should be avoided. The window bringing glare should be closed.
- Letters for heading should not less than 2½" (6 cm.).
- A variety of techniques can be employed in chalk board work. Templates are used to draw geometrical figures and science apparatus. Punch technique or pattern method can be used for drawing detailed outlines of diagrams, map drawing. Thus, paper punched is held against the slightly moistured chalk board and dusty eraser is rubbed against the perforated section of the outline. This will make an outline of chalk dots stick to the board. All these dots can be combined to get the figure. The grid technique is used for enlarging diagrams, maps from the textbooks or any source book. This can be done drawing small squares on

tracing paper kept on the original diagrams and by transferring the details according to desired size.

Finally we can say that chalk board is one of most important visual aid, as:

- Chalk board is a point clincher,
- It catches attention, imagination and attention of the students,
- It motivates the students for learning,
- It invites high degree students' participation in knowledge development,
- It supplements verbalism and invokes thinking,
- The average and poor students can have pace with the teacher with the help of systematic black board work. Also, the whole class have a pace with teacher,
- The black board provide maximum contrast background if glare element is eliminated,
- It provide a restful atmosphere in a coloured room,
- It solves the day to day problem,
- Mistakes, if there is any in the process of teaching can be rectified,
- Black board can also be used for display,
- It can be used or rather generally used in conjunction with other aids like models, specimen etc.
- Everything happens before the students which motivate them to express and contribute in elicitations,
- Though black board may have certain limitations, it should be regularly used by the teacher. He should give it a friendly treatment. It should be regularly dusted. Dusting should not be left for the incoming teacher. Periodic treatment like painting colour work should also be regularly given to it.

GLOBE

Globes are of various sizes. The size is usually termed or expressed in terms of the size of its diameter. Common sizes are 8", 12", 16", 20" and 24 inches. The 12" and 16" globes are most frequently used. The various other special globes as air age, celestial relief and climatology globes. Three principal types of globes which are commonly used in schools are: political, physical-political and stated outlines globes. A globe can be made in the classroom itself. The teacher should prepare a clay ball. This ball be used as model and a globe can be casted in two parts, which can be joined with glue. Papier-mâché or small paper strips can be used for casting. Also many fancy and decorative things are available in the market. Hand made globe will be more educative for the students.

STUDY KITS

A study kit is a general teaching-learning device, consisting of a correlated assemblage of audio-visual aids, such as, graphic aids, small models and specimens, film strips, folders, pamphlets and allied literature etc., pertaining to particular subject and theme. These audio-visual materials or instructional aids are carefully selected and arranged in a moveable box, are used to depict various aspects of the main subject. These aids elaborate a topic in details. These artistically arranged boxes with aids are distributed in various institutions for use.

At times, a part of relevant material is fixed in the form of built in displays in the box so that when the box is opened for study a panoramic views of some aspects of the kit engages the viewer and motivates him to unravel and explore other items. In some study kits the elements of display are absent in order to keep it light. The materials are arranged in separate containers to be taken out, displayed and studied as desired. Study kits are a kind of mobile exhibitions for wider use, thus putting dioramas and display-panels around a theme. A study kit is a kind of proto-type exhibition. Study kits provide a solid and fertile background of information to be developed progressively. The study kits involve the learner and motivate him to involve deeper into subject. Specific study kits are prepared for specific subjects such as physics, chemistry, sociology etc. The teacher can also assemble a study kit for his subject with the help of the students. Material like used packing boxes can be used.

PEG BOARDS

Peg boards are also useful aid. A holed plastic sheet is framed with an aluminium angle bar. The holes in the plastic sheet can hold letters and other graphic material so arranged that its loops underneath can go into the holes. Such boards are generally used by business houses etc., also.

COMPUTERS

Computers are also used as a teaching aid in teaching. Some solutions, formulae and important descriptions and many time black board work are fed to the computers floppy, which can be computerised again and again as when required.

9

How Do We Learn?

Etymological and Epistemological Interpretations. It is necessary to know the following words:

- *Learn*: The word learn is a derivation from Anglo-Saxon word 'Learnian' meaning – to know, to be akin with, to learn, to gain, to receive instructions. It is a verb.
- *Learning*: a noun from verb 'to learn' – meaning acquisition of knowledge by study, by experience, by production or by erudition (instruction).
- *Know*: a verb, meaning an act of comprehension or understanding collection. It is a derivation from Anglo-Saxon word 'ennawn' - meaning to know, to perceive with certainty, to be conceived, to be satisfied regarding the truth or reality or any thing, to be aware of, to have experience to understand.
- *Knowledge*: a 'noun' from verb to know, meaning perceived, understood, conceived, or recognised by one himself.
- *Inform*: is a derivation from the French word 'informe' and Latin word also 'informe' meaning to apprise. The French and Latin words have come out the Latin word 'Forme' which means to a shape, to activate, to vitiate or to acquaint with. The word is generally used in art. An artist making a composition gives to it a 'form'. Likewise an acting of informing is tantamount to moulding a person according to the views of the informer. The informed has not his own locus-standi about the information he gets from the informer. That is not his own but of the informer.
- *Information*: a 'noun' from the verb 'inform', which is a derivation from the Latin word 'informe' meaning an act

of informing by communicating news or by words or by writing. So knowledge derived from other sources, excepting one's own is information.

- *Pre-sensory*: is a derivation from Latin word 'prehendre' meaning an act of laying hold of something or an act of seizing something.
- *Prehension*: is from word prehensory meaning – taking hold of or seizing something.
- *Perceive*: a verb, a derivation from Latin word 'perceipie' meaning to visualise, to receive or to comprehend.
- *Perception*: a noun from verb perceive meaning a faculty by which a man by which a man holds or collects communication from the external world or takes cognisance of objects which exist space and time and ideas which exists outside mind.
- *Comprehend*: a verb, derivation from Latin word 'comprehende' meaning to take in, to include within, with certain scope, to include by implication, to take into mind, to grasp an idea or to understand.
- *Comprehension*: a noun from the verb comprehend, meaning knowledge.

LEARNING DEFINED

In education, we generally use these words, and especially these words dominate the teaching-learning process. These are core words on which the edifice of learning is build. The concepts of learning may be defined very briefly through many angles:

(*a*) Behaviourists School

This school is built up on Pavlo's Salio Theory. Behaviourist theories of learning basically focus primarily on change of behaviour. They say learning is the relatively permanent in person's knowledge and behaviour due to 'experience'.

(*i*) the duration of the change is long-term rather than short-term.

(*ii*) the 'locus' of change is the content and structure of knowledge in memory or the behaviour of the learner.

(*iii*) the cause of the change is learner's experience in the environment rather than fatigue, motivation, drugs, physiological intervention or change in physical condition.

For a long time Behaviourists dominated the science. They generally carried out experiments on animals and applied them on man.

(*b*) Cognitive School

E.L. Throndike was the prpounder of this school. Cognitive theories of learning primarily focus on change in content of structure of knowledge in memory. They lay stress on performance which refers to actually behaviour that is learning exhibits on a given occasion.

(*c*) Gestalt Theory of Learning

German Psychologist Guthri believed that learning is not a piecemeal process as theories (*a*) and (*b*) believed, but the learner confronts an object and has overall view of whole and his fund of knowledge increases. But many objects to this view they argue how can a whole give complete knowledge with the knowledge of parts.

(*d*) Initiative Theory of Learning

Initiative learning is a process by which a person observes the behaviour of another. This is a model which display behaviour. An observer observes the display. This generality occurs in informal, non-formal and many times in formal environments. The observer observes any actor doing any action. The process of action emits signals which are grasped by the observer.

The observer is a fresher. He is not an expert. He cannot distinguished and make differentiations. He does not have only history of experiments. He is not experienced to understand multiple aspects of model.

Risley (1968) says that children generally learn through imitation. Only overt behaviour can be initiated. Initiative learning is distinguished from other learning by the fact that the source of movement in the behaviour. There are various forms of initiative learning:

I. Instrumental learning,
II. Incidental learning, and
III. Accidental learning.

Areas of Learning

I. Response learning,
II. Concept learning,
III. Verbal learning, and
IV. Prose learning.

As a matter of fact all learning under non-formal education was initiative. Greek people laid stress initiative learning in learning art and sculpture. And initiative learning is entailed and found in Behaviourist and cognitive forms of learning. It is based on observation. Every type of observation is always followed by cognition, experience and comprehension which lead to learning. Learning cannot be directly observed or tested or measured. It is measured through performance. And all initiative learning is always assessed through performance. It is better than mere information.

Information

Information is that kind of awareness which is heaped on or transferred from one person to another. Information cannot be equated with knowledge or learning because the informer has nothing in it of his own. On the other hand the informer wants to pass on whatever he knows with a view that the informee accepts it. In other words the informer works like an artist who works on a dough of clay and gives it a form. The mounded clay has no reaction at all. Likewise in education mere passing of information not only harmful but undoubtedly dangers for the well being of our future guardians, that is, pupils.

But education, in the sense of term, (modern) that is, education imparted in formal way is not possible without information. In the present age of industrialisation and modernisation, there exists specialisation and differentiation which entails competition and the present learning process is very complex. So all theorists, psychologists and educationists agree that:

- Education is a complex process.
- Perception is the foundation of learning.

Carter V. Good says, "Learning is change in response or behaviour (such as innovation, elimination or modification of responses involving some degree of performance) caused wholly or partly by experience consensus or unconsensus, unorganised or sublimated stimuli including emotional changes in behaviour which entail acquisition of symbolic knowledge or motor skills. Initiative process and information help in learning. Through initiation a person observes the behaviour of another person – a model which displays behaviour. An observer observes this display, and this of observation is really perception which leads to knowledge and learning. In education learning process involves.

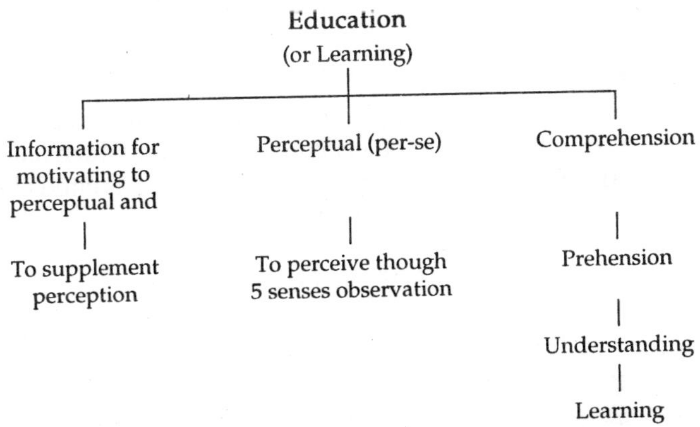

This generally occurs in informal, formal and non-formal learning environments. There is deliberate demonstration which entails reproduction of behaviour of the observer. The observer is not an expert in making differentiations and distinguishing. He does not have history of experiments. He cannot alone understand multiple aspects of the model which is being observed. Therefore, he needs guidance. That guidance is given through information and demonstration.

EPISTEMOLOGY OF LEARNING

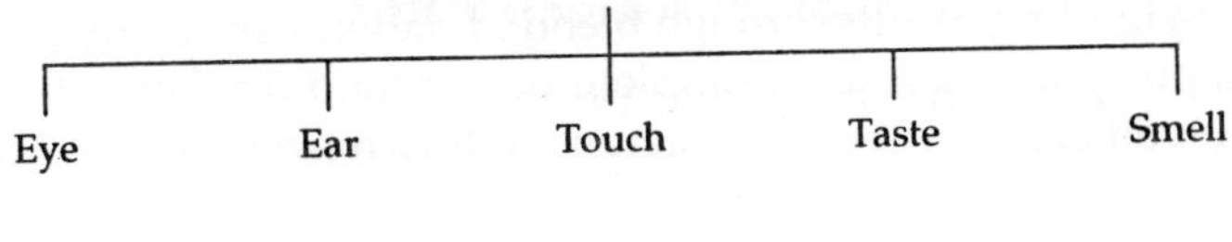

Gaining experience by man is an ontogenogic process. It is the ontogeny of man/women which promotes him/her to gain experience.

The perceptory human sense organs or mechanism as cited above, confronts with:

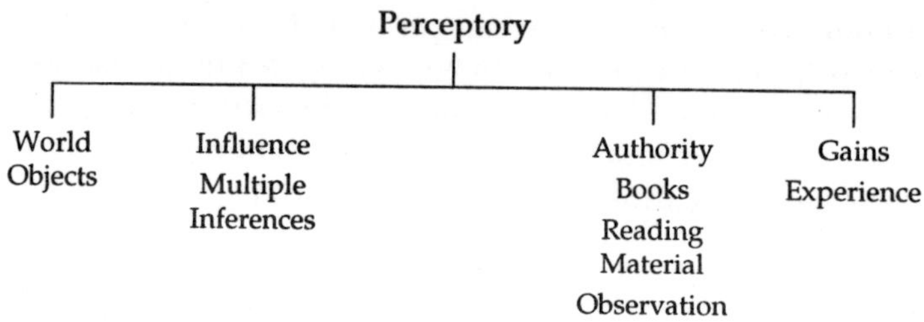

In this process of learning there is one perceiver or learner and other is perceived or an object comprehension which leads to learning and finally to knowledge involves all these as cited above. It occurs through prehensive mechanism.

PREHENSIVE MECHANISM

Prehensory abilities of man and other primates have long been regarded as most significant phenomenon linked with psycho-genetically erect posture, highly refined development of binocular vision, possession of opposable thunder and free moveable hands. Prehension is man's unique quality and capacity given by God enable him to make and utilise tools. Bigger brain is unique ontogeny of man which makes his senonimotor unique than other animals. This is why he is considered to be a rational being. The child is born with diversified reflex repertoire with more muscular growth which is rapid and complex. So the man is capable of learning more quickly than other animals.

How Perceptory Mechanism Works?

The eyes record the multiple impressions when they confront worldly objects. So also happens when one touches or tastes a thing. Understanding results through blended patterns from any or all of perceptory mechanism. Complete understanding depends upon perceived experienced and inferences drawn from them. Vision is the most important of all perceptory organism which gives rise to thinking comprehension, understanding and finally leads to correlative knowledge (Example: Sheep, wool, woollen mill, woollen cloth, etc.) This is why correlation was most important element of Basic Education. It also leads to reactionary knowledge as consumption of sheep as meat, leading to reactionary understanding and knowledge. Man is always in search of information through new perceptions, inferences drawn thereby, reading, observation, interviews, surveys and by examination. One particular perception may result in unique experience which might lead the child to intensive thinking, which finally lead to learning and knowledge.

INSTINCTS OF LEARNING

Common sense view is that the children mostly learn by imitation. Theory of learning by imitation was termed as 'mimics' by Plato. This theory mimicry advocated by Plato was suggested to learn Art and Craft in these days.

In the present times, in general, the theories of imitation recognise a close temporal relationship between a certain environmental stimuli and of a given response. When response is for learning by observation, the environmental stimuli are activities of the model. Learning is evident when responses become regularly associated with presence of stimuli.

Tendency to learn is termed as 'Learning Instincts' by psychologists (from the beginning of 20th Century). E.L. Throndike (1913) took the position of John Locke, who believed in 'Tabula Rasa' about child's mind. He advanced the theory of 'Hardening' regarding the education of the child. He said "there is no general disposition to reproduce behaviour by observing and imitating sense perception (per. se.) is the only source of knowledge. Right experience should be rewarded and wrong experience should be discouraged through punishment. But some psychologists argue and, led support and weight that imitation is instrumental to learning as anger provokes anger. Classical Pavlovian conditioning theory based on theory of employing contiguity Allport (1924) and Holt (1931) argued and reasoned that adults are mimic. Mimicry elicits socially significant random behaviour of children and adults and, it is further developed through imitation and observation as the children continuously try to adopt and follow the adults.

Conclusion

We may conclude from the foregone etymological and epistemological conclusions that:

Sense perception, which always entails experience, is the basis of our learning which builds store house of knowledge. A thinking teacher will have to sense the childs' need and help him providing avenues of sense perception and experience. Whenever tangible and concrete things are not possible to be shown be should provide per. se. and experiences to the child through contrived experiences. This can be done through the use of audio-visual aids. Wittéch Shillar says:

- Perceptions are foundation of all learning.
- There should be thoughtful selection, arranging and shuttling of experience patterns through audio-visual aids.
- Perceptions lead to experience. And experience always generates thinking which makes education possible,
- Perception followed by experience leads to attitude formation. Gorden W. Allport says, "an attitude is mental and neutral state of readiness to learn".
- Interpreted process is necessary for learning. This is not a new idea. Right from Plato up to the present empiricist philosophers experience plus comprehension are the basis of learning and true knowledge.
- Edger Dale says:
  I. The aim of good teaching is to be good education that is, "teach pupils to learn themselves".
  II. Analysing pupils' learning,
  III. Learning is the result of needs. In other words it goes with the adage that 'Necessity is the mother of invention',
  IV. Permanent learning leads to reminiscence and rote learning is always forgettable,
  V. Verbalism can never lead to effective learning, and
  VI. Questioning should be followed after use of audio-visual aids, execution of projects which yield experience. Experience always leads to permanent learning.

Therefore, the school should provide facilities of added perceptions like activities, visits, tours and cultural programmes. Also experimentation should be followed by reading. One of the bad effect of modern TV telecast is that they do not get time to read. They see TV programme late in the night. So they go late to the bed and rise late. Something should be done to check this evil. The children should be motivated to read not only textbooks but some reference and source books in the library.

So, it is true to argue and reason that experience is a must for educational process. And use of audio-visual aids facilitates and perpetuates learning. It is economical for the teacher and taughts both.

10

Sensory Experiences

The concept of experience is wherein the essence of Audio-Visual Education lies. The greatest contribution to our knowledge of the world comes through our eyes, for this reason the term visual education is used. But due to lack of a better term, such as 'sensory', perhaps we must take the word visual to include in certain context, the other for sensous aid as the eye to understand the world. This is all of our experiences are sensory experiences. Sensory experiences form the basis of knowledge. There are five senses – Visual (eyes), Aural (ears), Olfactory (nose), Gustatory (tongue) and Tactile (skin)-and they are called the gateway of knowledge. To begin with, thinking is restricted to concrete experiences, which form the basis of abstract learning. Sensory experiences are concrete experiences. Learning experiences appealing to the senses are far more effective than abstract learning experiences. Thus, there is a strong case for using audio-visual aids in teaching for providing experiences.

Though all the senses are important, stress is placed on the aural and the visual because they are widely involved in classroom teaching situations.

Normally we get experience of a thing only in three ways: First by direct perception of an object or an event, Second by perception of its image or photograph or an illustration, Third by constructing the object or event in our imaginations from symbols such as spoken words, the letters of the alphabet, mathematical signs or by pictographic writing. In this third sort of experiences, minimises the use words, plays a dominant role in our present day education, and without which advanced system of abstract thought would be impossible. The sense of touch is our earliest education. When the mother touches the child for sucking her breast milk and thereafter keeping the child in her lap for love, affection and sleep, it is first sensory experience of touch for the child and his first education. Thereafter he starts gazing things recognising family members, his visual sensory impressions get accumulated, which go to his memory. As such, all five sensory faculties start working and sensory experiences get accumulated, which help the child to understand worldly things.

As such, sensory experiences are very important. They play a dominant action or role in our present day education, and without which advanced system of abstract thought would be impossible. John Locke has rightly said that the child writes himself with his sense perception on the Tabula Rasa (slate) and gathers his fund of knowledge with his own efforts. As the child grows and goes to be adult, he gathers a vast body of senses which result in experience, new sensation will be there and the old ones' will be checked against old ones which will entail appropriate action. This is a kind of continuous process—a circle of experiences. The more varied and vivid the experiences are, which a child encounters the quicker he learns. J.J. Rousseau said if a child wants to know fire and learn about the fire let him touch the fire and get his fingers burnt. It is merely feared that he will burn his fingers if he put them on fire but it will lead him to knowledge though touch.

Hearing and touching or testing are the next two senses by which a child learns of his surroundings. Likewise all senses play a vital role in experiencing worldly things and knowing them. Therefore, the five senses are five gateway to knowledge. Through these five senses child learns first a particular existence; thereafter he learns to generalise. The child is interested what he can see, hear, touch, smell and taste. He is very keen to do. His curiosity and interest should not be checked and hampered. He should be motivated and encouraged to use his senses and get useful desired experiences. He should be guided, directed and helped. The teacher should find out his interests and plan a strategy to exploit his hidden energy. This will provide avenues of experiences to the child. Child is eager to do things himself. He gets self-satisfaction by doing so. Boys and girls have to play different roles in their lives. So their interests also vary. They should be provide different sensual experiences.

Much of our early education is obtained by direct sensual perception by handling things, looking at them, listening to elders and so on. This is how most animals learn to deal with different situations and face them. some lower animals, beast animals and birds teach their youngs. Some birds demonstrate, for example art of flying. Cats trains their kittens to hunt, demonstrating how to hunt. All this is done by a sort of pantomimic activity, like illustrative function. We illustrate books in order to bring more transparency in reading.

Experience is the essence of education. We experience so many things right from our birth to death. These experiences are our continuous education. Life should be an arena of continuous education. Telling and informing is not education. Sending a child to school from the age 4 to 17 will not automatically made him educated. He will be educated if he gets a chance to perceive things and gain experience. The chief need of the childs' education is to protect and nurture the child's curiosity for experimentation, which build the edifice of his interests and desires. Experience unfolds the child's hidden talents, capacities and capabilities to know things around him. This can be done by the full use of all child's five senses from early years.

Visual education should aim at the full use of five senses. The use of audio-visual aids must be graded in order to accord with the physical as well as mental growth of the child. The mental development of child can only be possible, if the experimentation involves all of the five senses resulting in thinking and reasoning. There are some children who are visually handicapped, special arrangement should be made for their visualisation. Some special aids should be designed for them to feel the physical things, so that their 4 other senses may be coordinated for experimentation.

There is one principle common to all forms of audio-visual education; and that is: from of concrete to abstract, from particular to general. A child begins with particular experience and later on learns to classify, generalise and analyse.

But experiencing all things in life appears impossible. What can be done for real experience. Only visual aids can give such experiences. Suppose the students have not seen an elephant, a toy elephant of wood, plaster of paris or doth or picture of an elephant; and in addition to the natural history, talkie films on elephants in which children and see and hear will be useful in giving experience about elephant to the children.

This is a sort of way through which experiences of the physical things mentioned in written books or through spoken words, which necessarily forms the basis of teaching can be given. As a matter of fact the verbalism should be supplemented through concrete things and in absence of the concrete things, these should be supplemented by their republicas or pictures.

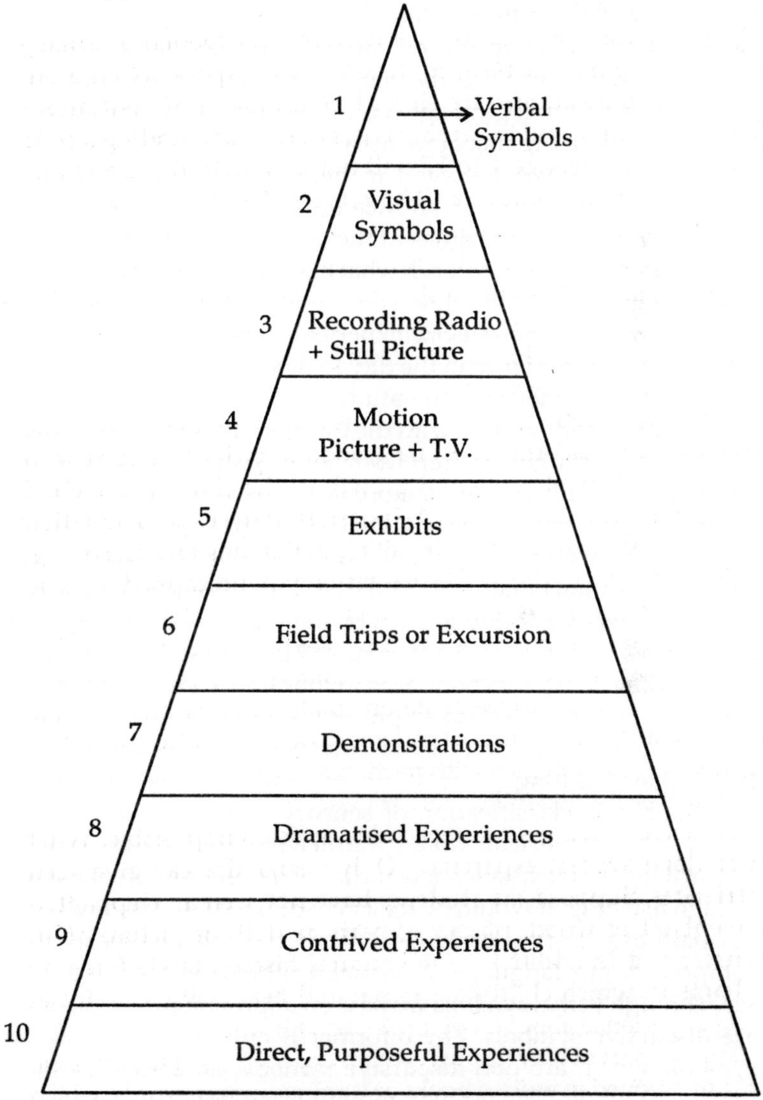

Fig. 60: Dale's Cone of Experiences

The whole field of human knowledge could be possible because many worldly things and, physical environment has been seen, and mapped out and comprehended by different eyes. Man has been continuously searching new things, and has been trying to pass on his accumulated stored knowledge to younger generation religiously. Still the man is busy in search of new things. The modern technological age has made man a fly in the universe like a screw in a big machine, because he has totally renounced, what his forefathers believed in the ontological and religious pursuits. As the store of knowledge of the material world is increasing the responsibilities of the school is increasing, because the teacher is supposed to teach what has been searched and known in this empirical world. How can the teacher do this alone? He can only provide the sensory experience with the help of visual aids. Such an experience in the day to day teaching is most useful for both the teacher and the students. The students should be initiated in experimenting with the things right from the early age. This experimentation can start from home. Today homes have only kitchens. Work places are no more as old occupation are meeting a slow death. In a kitchen a variety of great many chemical experiments may be carried out. And, because of sanskritisation and politicisation of father a child does not do the hand work his/her forefathers were doing. So carrying out sensory experiments by the boys with their father seems difficult now. And their roles of providing sensory experiences to the children has been shifted to school. So the school has to provide sensory experiences along with other curricular and extra-curricular activities in order to enrich their teaching.

The above classification of sensory experience is given by Edger Dale, American noted audio-visual aids educationist. According to this classification audio-visual aids are prepared and used in teaching. It would be logical to divide this classification in five pairs of sensory experiences. 1. Verbal symbols are those which compose of our language. 2. Visual symbols are those what we see. Through verbal symbols we pass on information. Such symbols are discursive symbols. The informer is only active. The verbal symbols which are non-discursive symbols do emit very bleak reactive symbols. The listener, though listen but does not react as he should. On the other hand visual symbols when shown, and only introductory verbal message is given and much is told, the visualiser sees the visual symbols and tries to understand what they are? Or we can say the visual symbols always emit communicative signals which make the seer to think and react. Therefore, visual symbols are always better in teaching. These are called Discursive symbols. In recordings, radio and still pictures, the earlier two fall in the category of discursive symbols, where the still pictures came under the category of non-discursive symbols which forces or motivates a seer to think. The exhibits also come under the category of non-discursive symbols which emit communicative signals and makes a man to think motion pictures which contain discursive as well as non-discursive symbols. But they do not have any interactive mechanism as happens in the classroom teaching. Exhibits and field trips provide a rich experience as the teacher is always with the students to remove their doubts. Lastly the contrived experiences and direct purposeful experience are useful in teaching. Contrived experiences are those which are provided in the form of republicas or models or dioramas in the absence of concrete things.

The sensory experiences are essential for learning. The sense of sight is a better avenue for the acquirement of experience than hearing. The learning process involves seeing, hearing and doing on the objective side and thinking and reasoning on the subjective side. The eyes makes the situation distinctly realistic and the speech serves to give it meaning; both result in achieving delightfulness. What we see with our own eyes gives us a real sense of pleasure than what we hear from others. We judge the merit and demerits of the thing what we see. There is an old saying, "to see with one's eyes is always better than to hear others". Often rumour misunderstandings and even quarrels are spread due to this reason that people believe in heard things. Psychological studies consisting of careful experiences comparisons had led to the conclusions that use of audio-visual aids should be a must in education.

The essential contrast is not between the senses of vision and hearing. It is rather the direct experience which consists of the perception of the material objects on the one hand, and indirect experience, which consists of generalised or abstract though on the other hand. Direct perception is gained by means of various senses – not by vision alone – while thought is gained by mental process which involves thinking, the language gives it a form. But properly regarded, both are not opposed to each other. Rather they are supplementary to each other. Sense perceptions or concrete experiences alone without thought process above have little meaning or significance. Over emphasis on verbalism without concrete experience leads to error and confusion of thought. Doubtful education has tended to, much to verbalism and it needs a closer contact with the world of physical objects and action.

It is, therefore, true that sense of vision is particularly a valuable source of educative experience. First, because it furnishes distinctive qualities of its own. It serves to represent or suggest many qualities which are given directly by other sources, through vision and experience, such as hardness, smoothness and weight. Secondly, it is especially adapted to depict nature.

In the modern pedagogy, it is emphasised that showing things is always better than telling. Audio-visual aids make teaching effective and learning easy. They provide a chance of vision and experience and accelerate the rate of learning easy and increase the span of retention. The teacher who has numerous problems with is students and the multiplicity of duties to perform is largely benefited by the use of audio-visual aids. The prime purpose of his effort is to aid the learner in the acquisition of knowledge, as well as to direct training to words the acquisition of skills. His main problem is, how to convey ideas, to impart knowledge and to pass on information in the shortest possible time in accordance with the principles of learning. This can be done if sensory-experiences are provided to the students. To achieve this end the use of audio-visual aids becomes necessary, which actually does not replace teaching but helps it, and makes the learning easier. According to George Bernard Shaw the number of people who can read is very small, the number who can read to any purpose is much smaller and the number of those who are tired after days of work to read is enormous. But all except the blind and the deaf can see and hear. Seeing and hearing are basically used in teaching. The teacher, therefore, should show as well as tell.

11

Use of Audio-Visual Aids

Edger Dale presents an absolutely new approach when he remarks: "Although we commonly use the term audio-visual, it is merely a short way of describing materials of instruction which are less abstract than words themselves. Even here we exercise care because it would be more accurate to call them audio-visual-verbal materials these relatively more concrete experiences are nearly always with words themselves".

Audio-visual materials assists in methods of instruction and may be used at all stages and levels of schooling. Not only in schooling these are very useful at higher levels. Their use is very appropriate in teaching languages, geography, history, civics, nature study, anatomy, physical sciences, agriculture, astronomy and several other technical subjects. Most of visual as well as audio-aids are also used for educative purposes with social objectives such as family planning, prohibition, national security and for propaganda etc.

As Audio-Visual material reinforces the spoken or written words with concrete images and thus provide rich perceptual experiences which are the basis of learning. These materials make learning less non-verbalistic and remove the boredom of more mere verbalism. These offer a variety of experiences which stimulate self-activity on the part of the pupils. These contribute to the depth and variety of learning and thus make learning more permanent. Due to the additional experiences and techniques offered by these materials or teaching aids a broader curriculum is established and increased meaning is brought to the current experiences. The teacher in order to utilise this broad based curriculum needs a knowledge of unique contribution of different types of audio-visual materials, of fundamental principles and techniques of their utilisation and of reliable methods of evaluation. Only then the teacher can do a good selection of appropriate teaching aid, required for the subject he is teaching.

SELECTION OF AUDIO-VISUAL AIDS

Proper selection of audio-visual aids is one of the most important activity. A properly selected appropriate audio-visual aid can only yield good results. Audio-visual aid should not only be used for namesake or for mere show. A teaching aid should be selected after giving proper thought for the subject requirements and students perception needs and sensory requirements in a given situation for particular lesson developments. The teacher should plan audio-visual aids requirement as per his/her unit plan as well as daily lesson plan. What kind of aid he would require, for the content he is going to teach, and it would help the teacher and students in a particular lesson development on stipulated content? Students' participation in the lesson development and consequent elicitations should focus in the selection of the audio-visual aids in teaching.

There are subjects like physics which outline fundamental understanding of facts, principles and concepts of science and also ushers growth in the use of scientific methods and builds investigative attitudes in the students. The audio-visual aids should help in elucidating all of these. These should also provide a variety of means for analysing the subject. These should also facilitate in the formation of concepts in science. These should also provide a purposeful orientation for learning through observation and experimentation. There are certain basic tools in science such as scales, thermometers, callipers like vernier calliper which are used for measuring. Should these tools be shown to the students as they are of their images or republicas be prepared or shown is a question of proper selection of teaching aids? The teacher should decide all such things being a subject specialist. He should show light handable things during teachings.

The teacher should be in a position to make clear decision what teaching aid is better suited to his as well as students' needs. This is only possible when he is quite aware of the pedagogic functions of all non-projected as well as projected aids. Among the graphic aids like charts, maps, posters, flash cards, bulletin boards and flannel boards, etc., have knowledge about their specific functions.

Charts are very useful for making elicitations as much as possible and presenting the content sequence wise classifying, comparing facts. Whereas posters are used to catch attention highlighting a particular fact. Maps are used for showing geographical landscapes and locations of a country. Whereas three dimensional aids such as models, dioramas, x-ray models are necessary to apprise the students about the things which existed or exist in time and space. Likewise there are many other aids like specimens, costumes and also activities like staging mock things mock Parliament, dramatisation, demonstration, competitions like art competitions. All these have specific purposes. The teacher should decide and select the aid best suited in teaching, helping the students and in getting desirable sensory experiences. He should choose accordingly.

Like physics and other science subjects, the humanities require audio-visual aids. Though these aids would be or may be a bit different than the aids required for science subjects. A history teacher teaching culture aspects of any given period may be required to use model of monuments, costumes, charts, photography and banners highlighting the *Sahi Firmans* (official declarations). In some situation of cultural renaissance in particular, the teacher may require to display so many things depicting cultural patterns of a particular period. So the teacher will have to select best things of art and artefacts, weaponry etc.

It is the teacher, who is a subject specialist, keeping his requirement he should select the appropriate teaching aids. He is the best judge. Teachers of all subjects should decide what aids would better suit to their needs as well as the needs of the pupils. They should make the selection of audio-visual aids with great care.

Other considerations, while selecting the audio-aids, should be kept in mind:

- The audio-visual should be good looking and representative of the real things. As such, as far as possible charts should be neatly made and if possible should be colourful.
- Maps should not give wrong signals.
- The aids should be light and manageable.
- As far as possible the aids should be self-prepared out of the cheap material or unserviceable stuff found in homes.

- The aids should be storable.
- The art-room should help in preparation of the teaching aids.
- Many teachers generally depend on cheap aids available in the market. When such aids are used by the students do not get a chance to work their own hands.
- The school should allot certain amount in their budget for preparation of the teaching aids.
- When there are some regional exhibition, the principals of the schools try to have some aids for contributing to these exhibitions. At the last moment they ask the teachers to have some novel aids at any cost. With result the teachers are allowed to contact some professional aid makers who are not subject experts. These teaching aid makers, who are rare and are few, charge a lot which the schools pay. This practice neither benefits the teacher nor the students. So the teachings aids for such shows should be prepared in school itself.
- The educational authorities should organise some extension service seminars and all teaches, though by turn, should be asked to attend such seminars and workshops.
- The school should provide some facilities of audio-aids class wise.
- These schools which have workshops should utilise such workshops for helping the teacher in the preparation of teaching aids. Usually such workshops are generally kept engaged in furniture repairs. These should be utilised for this creative job too.

12

Some Hints for the Preparation of Visual Aids

Some basic skills, such as knowledge of graphic material and simple graphic techniques, knowledge of art material, also knowledge of display material, raw materials used in the preparation of visual aids like, charts, maps, posters, three dimension models, x-ray models, dioramas are necessary for the preparation of visual aids. In addition to an imagination and creative attitude for using cheap material and most important. One who believes that small is beautiful, unserviceable and scrap is also useful can be successful in the preparation of visual aids. Above all an urge to work and to innovate the students in the visual aids preparation are necessary.

BASIC SKILLS

Basic skills which are necessary are:

- Lines – the knowledge of lines is necessary. Vertical lines depict up rightness. Oblique lines show action. Wavery lines show stillness. Chain lines are used for connecting.

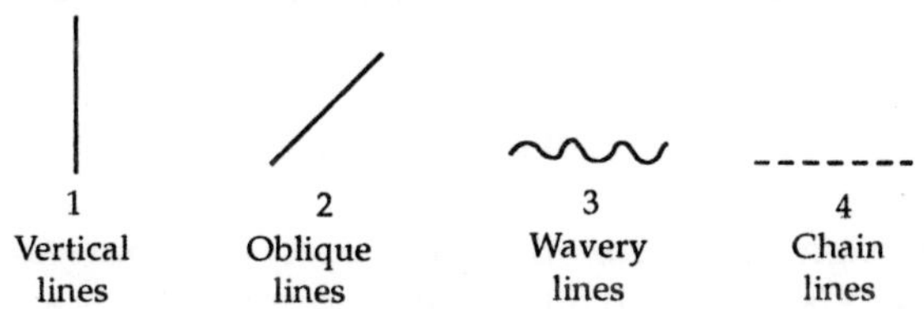

Fig. 61

- How to draw lines? Lines can be drawn either with the help of a scale or with free hand. Generally free hand drawn lines are better, because they show movement and force. On the other hand lines drawn with the help of a scale always look mechanical. Therefore, the teacher should practice in sketching.

- Sketching can never be done mechanically. It is always done with the free movement of hand according to sensory observation, and with a sense of perspectiveness.
- Pencil ! A pencil is used for sketching. There are many varieties of pencils.

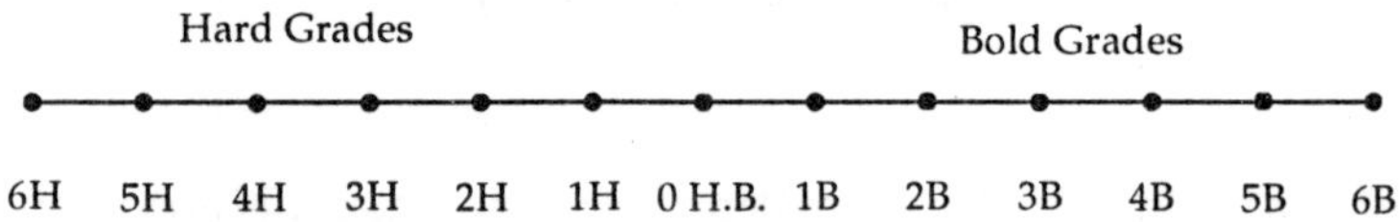

Fig. 62

Bold pencils are soft. These are used by the art students for sketching. 1B pencil is soft, and 6B is softest pencil like charcoal. 1H pencil is hard and 6H is hardest pencil. H category pencils are used for making orthographic drawings and are used by draftsmen, architects and engineers. H.B. Pencil is a common/ middle category which is used for general purpose. Students and teacher while making visual aids should use H.B. Pencil.

PENCIL ERASER

A good pencil eraser should be used while making charts. A good pencil erasers are Venues and Parado brands. After erasing the chart paper with pencil eraser, the paper should be dusted with clean dry cloth. For giving the brightest look a piece of bread (double roti) can also be used. It will remove the dust from the paper.

SIGN PENS

These days sign pens are available in variety of colours and variety of thickness. Camel brand and Atlas brands are easily available in the market. After doing the rough work with pencil the visual aids can be finished with sign pens too.

POSTER COLOURS

Poster colours are available in various shades and sizes. Minimum weight size is 15 gram and maximum weight size is 500 gram. It is advisable that the student should buy a 30 gram weight packs of 10 shades including white. Water colour and oil colours are suitable for the preparation of visual aids.

Colours are hot colours and cool colours. Hot are yellow and red. Cool colours are green and blue. By mixing the hot and cool colours we get secondary colours as orange and maple etc. While using colours care should be taken that there is a dominant colour. Too many colours, when used, create confusion. There is a gradation of colour which is called colour hues. There are three grades of hues – light, middle and dark. On category of colour should have dominance in colour composition. If the composition has much of hot colour, there should be light colour equal to hot colour.

PERSPECTIVE

Perspective, linear as well as colour plays a vital role in a composition. Therefore, the knowledge of linear as well as colour perspective is very necessary.

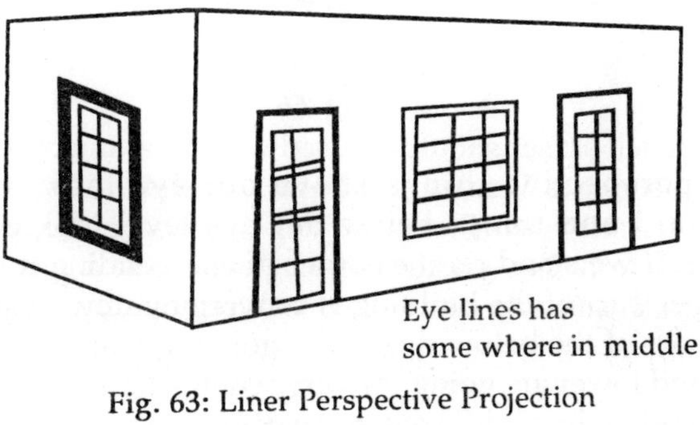

Fig. 63: Liner Perspective Projection

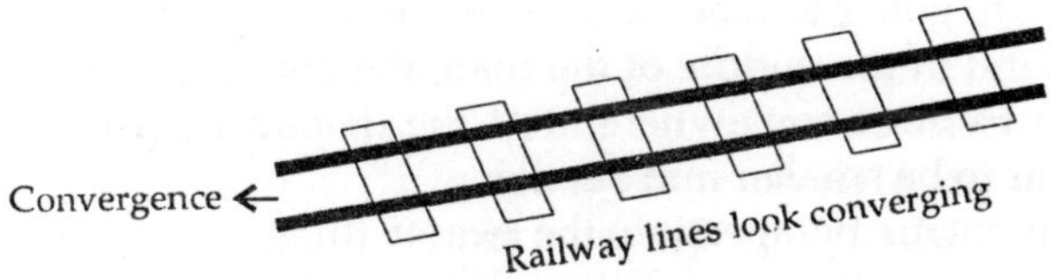

Fig. 64: Railway Line

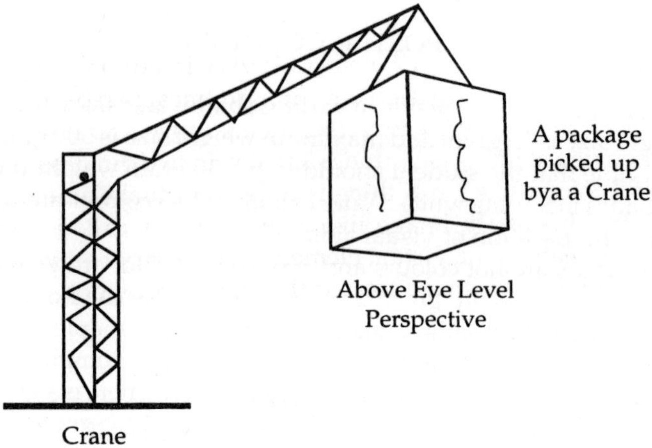

Fig. 65

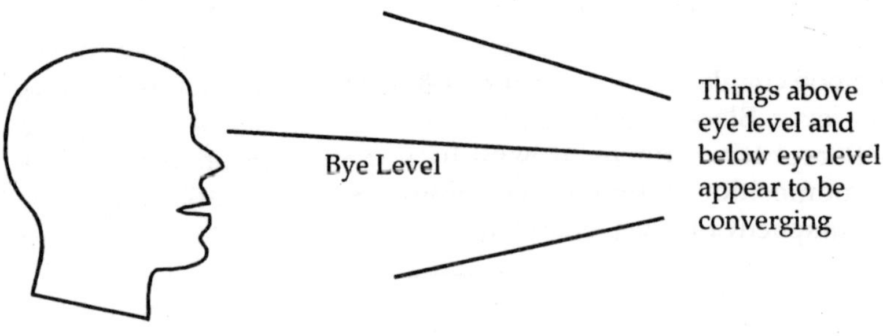

Fig. 66

In perspective things above our eye look converging downward and things below our eye level look converging upward. If we stand on the corner of one building it will look if the upper part of the building is converging downward and the lower part of the below our eye is going upward. And the lines upper and lower are going converge somewhere in long distance. If we stand in the middle of a railway line track it will appear as if these are going to meet somewhere in long distance. Likewise, if we stand in the middle of the road, the both sides of the road are going to meet somewhere, and the distant trees on both sides appear to be smaller and smaller.

In colour perspective, the nearer things always emit darker hues of the colour, and distant things look light in colour.

VIRTUAL ELEMENT

In art the creation of virtual element is very important. What the artist does, he creates an element through lines, perspective and hues which makes his creation like a real thing in an illusionary form. Looking at illusionary things, created in two dimension with lines and colour, like a real thing is called a virtual element. This makes an illusionary image like a real. This is called 'virtual element'. Creation of a virtual element is necessary to give a true representation to an image created through an art work.

COMPOSITION

The concept of composition is very important for a graphic art work. An artistic composition is like an organic whole. It is not an aggregation. In an organic whole all parts are united and placed at their respective places. In case one part is removed the composition is disturbed. In an organic whole, though all parts do their respective functions still they are united by a dominant force – it may be blood or blood circulation by heart or blood purification by lungs, kidneys and lever. Blood is the dominant force which keeps the all parts alive and functioning. Likewise in an art composition any of its elements – be it line arrangement or colour dominance or arrangement of lines, colour and texture – one element should always be dominant. A good competition should have this.

FORM

A form is a stipulated shape. An artist gives a shape to an art composition by arrangement of lines, colour and texture. All this have balance, perspective and unity. If these are scattered and have no unity these will not make a good form. The word 'form' has come out of the Latin word 'informe' meaning to give a shape. Therefore, for a good form lines, colour and texture should be so arranged that they should have a unity. While making a chart or poster the graphic arrangement should have a good form. Then only it give a representative image.

PLANNING FOR GRAPHIC AND PICTORIAL COMPOSITION

"A chart is combination of graphic material and pictorial media systematically and logically so arranged, so as to illicit some ideas". Therefore, for making a chart there should be a systematic planning. The graphic material and pictorial media should be so arranged that it could appeal to the eyes. There should be a space division of the cartridge paper, i.e., space for margin, space for capital lettering or heading, space for labelling and pictorial media. All this cannot be done in a haphazard way. For this, initially trail sketches should be prepared. Out of these sketches, the good looking sketch should be selected. Trail colouring should be done over it. And if it appeals to eyes, finally making of chart should be taken up. Likewise these steps are necessary for the preparation of visual aids including models of big things.

SKETCHING

All hand made graphic aids require some understanding of sketching simple techniques. It is not necessary for a teacher to learn these simple sketching techniques as an artist dos for his professional carrier. An art student in an Art school has to undergo a special training in sketching in different phases. This is not possible for a teacher. Any teacher can draw simple sketches, with the help of some techniques as:

Sketching with Grid or Graph Lines

A picture or an illustration can be reproduced in smaller or larger size by drawing grids or graph lines or squares on the sketch. Make a comparative grid of size into which the final drawing is to be fitted. Follow the block and lines from the original sketch to the final one and copy square to square. For greater accuracy rule-divide the square near the outline of sketch in both the grids. Thus picture and sketches can be reproduced fairly accurately to any size.

Sketching with the Help of Pantograph

A pantograph is a convenient tool for enlarging or reducing a sketch. The instrument can be fixed to a table or drawing board at one of its extremities, set aside for this purpose. As one moves the pointer located at a middle corner, over the outlines of original drawing, the pencil located at other extremity reproduces the original sketch. The Pantography can be adjusted either to enlarge or to reduce the original drawing to different proportion.

Enlarging with Epidiascope or an Opaque Projector

An epidiascope or an opaque projector is probably the most useful equipment of preparing graphic aids. By projecting the original design or illustration from the book to a paper fixed to a vertical bulletin board we can conveniently enlarge in a dark room. Art room in the school should have an epidiascope or projector in a dark room. The teachers required to make charts, posters and maps can make use of it.

Enlarging with a Transparent Glass

Prepare a wooden stand with a frame that can hold a piece of transparent glass. Prepare another wooden stand of approximately half the height as compared to the glass stand. Fix a small wooden piece with a pin-hole for viewing at the top. Place the objects or person in a setting to be sketched in front of the glass opposite to the viewing piece. Draw on the glass with the glass pencil or even with ordinary speed ball pen or sketch pen. This drawing apparatus is useful in providing proper perspective to your sketches.

Techniques of Picture Manipulation

Pictorial elements or details from two or more pictures or sketches can be so arranged to develop or assemble a new picture or sketch. With this technique one can eliminate the unwanted details from sketch and can add the desired elements from other pictures or sketches to create new sketches. This technique is commonly adopted by artists to develop new sketches.

Hand Sketching

Out of all these sketching techniques the hand sketching is the best technique. For this, one needs patience and practice. Hand sketching is usually done from natural objects. A learner should start doing sketching from simple plants and ordinary objects. The knowledge of perspective and proportion is necessary for learning hand sketching. One should sit or stand at six feet far from the object of sketching. As far as possible flow and rhythm should be maintained while sketching. A sketching viewer, which can be made out of a use post card, should be used for viewing the object and its relative proportion to its parts.

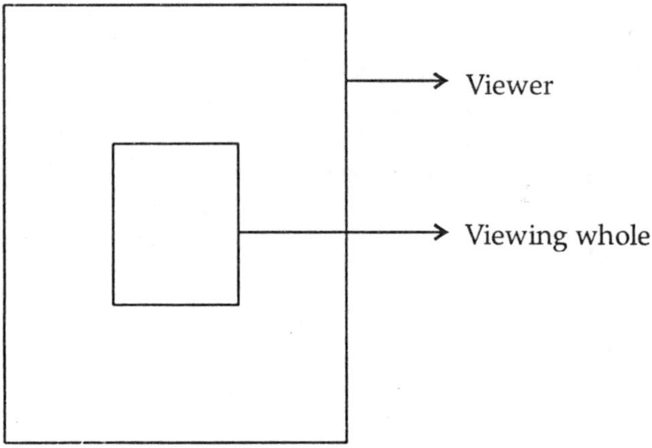

Fig. 67: Sketch Viewer

Skills in Chalk Board Writing and Sketching

Development of skills in black board writing are like any other skills for the preparation of graphic visual aids, needs patience, hard work and a lot of practice.

- First look at things for observing them and see them as they are,
- Black board is a practical subject, therefore, needs practical exercise,
- Rules to be followed for good black board writing:
  - (*i*) always use firm and clean lines,
  - (*ii*) draw your lines reasonably quickly,
  - (*iii*) use the maximum black space, and
  - (*iv*) keep your black board writing and sketching simple.
- Stand towards the left side while writing or drawing sketches on the black board to make the students see black board easily.
- Holding half of the chalk, while writing on sketching on black board will produce good result,
- Learning to draw lines:
  - I. First learn to draw horizontal lines across the black board. Put your hand quite close the black board (chalk board). Keep your elbow quite close to the black board.
  - II. Allow your body to move with hand elbow.

III. Allow your elbow to have movement.
IV. Do practice to draw lines with force,
V. Vertical lines are easier to draw,
VI. Stand in front of empty space only when you are drawing lines, and
VII. Diagonal lines needs little practice.

Always remember that clear and bold lines drawn with quick speed will produce better results.

Drawing of Diagrams, Curves and Circles

First learn to drawn squares, then triangles and their properties. Thereafter learn to draw curves. In drawing curves your wrist and arm must be quite flexible. A curved line cannot be drawn with a stiff arm. With chalk in your hand, but away from the black board practice drawing a curved line in the air. It should be done as if you are doing a physical exercise.

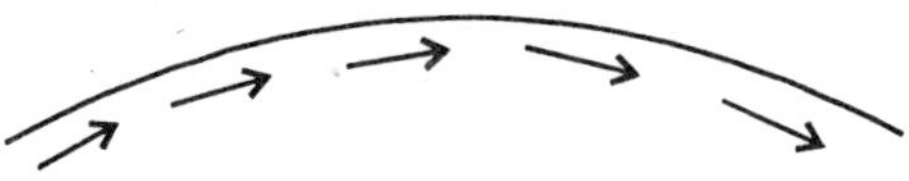

Fig. 68: Curved Line

A circle is a perfect curve. Hold a chalk in your hand, go the black board, place your right elbow on the centre of the black board and draw a circle from the left to right.

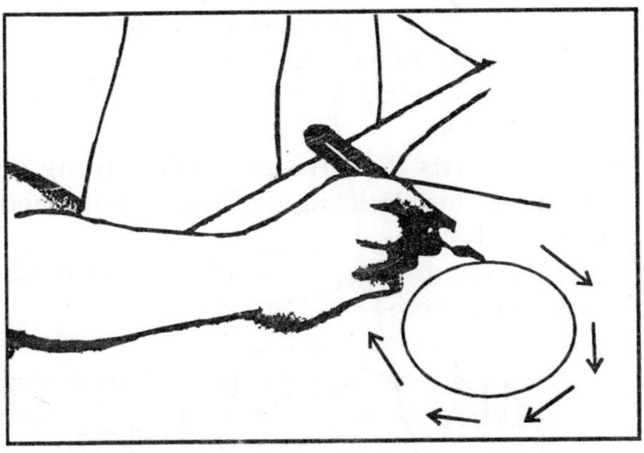

Fig. 69: Circle

AN ECLIPSE

An eclipse is like a faltered circle. It should be drawn on the principles of drawn curves and circle.

Essential Lines (Tree, Grass, etc.)

Essential lines are those which are used as parts of the shape of a thing or a creature. These are as:

I. Grass

Fig. 70

II. A Palm Tree

Fig. 71

III. A Mango Tree

Fig. 72

Sketching with the Help of Templates

A certain cases where accuracy is needed templates should be used. These templates can be made out of cardboard sheets. If possible used packing things, sari packing card board boxes etc., should be used for making a template.

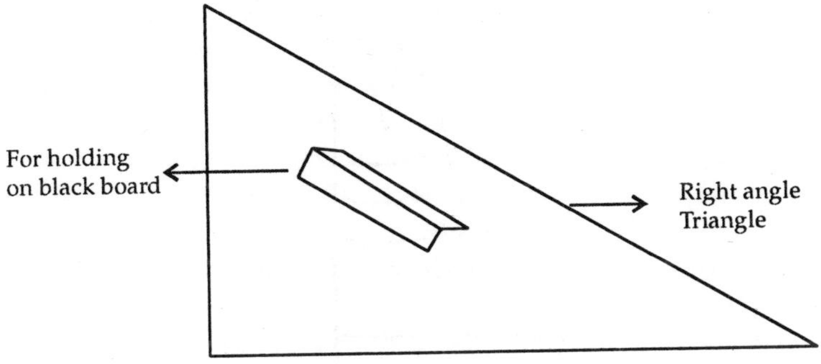

Fig. 73: A Template of a Triangle

Preparation of Chalk Sheets or Roll-up Black Boards for Teaching

Roll-up black boards or chalk sheets of paper painted black with black board paint and joined together at one end with two thin round wooden strips. A single sheet if joined with round strip gives a good result. The sheets can be made of cartridge paper or thick wrapping paper or craft paper of good quality.

Preparation

Take even pieces of cartridge paper or good quality wrapping or chart paper. Generally a size of 28"x22" is quite convenient for use. Paper weight standard should be 72 lbs.

Select a fine variety of black board paint of good make – 'Goodlas Nerolack' or 'Asian' or 'Rajdoot' brand. Paint the rough side of the paper evenly with two inches or three inches brush. Give second coating. Let it dry overnight, thereafter it will be ready for use.

Methods of Using

It is a handy tool for teaching. You can always pre-plan at what movement it can be used. Black board work can be done before hand.

Preparation of Models

Pre-plan what type of model you are going to use? Have a rough sketch from the textbook or any other resource book. Use a scale for reducing or enlarging the original thing. Then start collecting material for its preparation. There are three or four kinds of models. Suppose you are going to make a still model of any personality, say Galib or Buddha. You can make models out of clay. The potters' clay is the most appropriate. For sill models of personalities wooden stands, as given below, to hold the clay will be required.

Cow dung missed clay or bhoosa (wheat threshed dry grass) mixed clay should be used for such still models.

For making models of big national projects like Nangal Dam, Rihand Dam, a wooden base will be required. Appropriate size of the base may be 24"x16½" or 17". Such models should be light so that these may be handled by the students. So the structure should be made of soft material. For making hills we should use broken small twigs of the tree. Old unserviceable cloth like old chunries or old tehmuds should be soaked in rice starch or wheat flour lohi for covering these twigs in a manner that the twigs may give a look of hills. When the hills are dry wet colour should be sprinkled over the hill structure, so that it may look like an earthen and stone mound. The dam structure and attached electricity generating plants should be made either of cardboard or of thermocole. The structuring and joining of all parts that is hills, water reservoir, electricity generating plants should be done at the last stage. Therefore, texturing with Plaster of Paris and colouring with pigments should be done. Trees and jungles should be made of very twigs and kite paper should be arranged at the time of arrangement. When the model is complete labelling should be done.

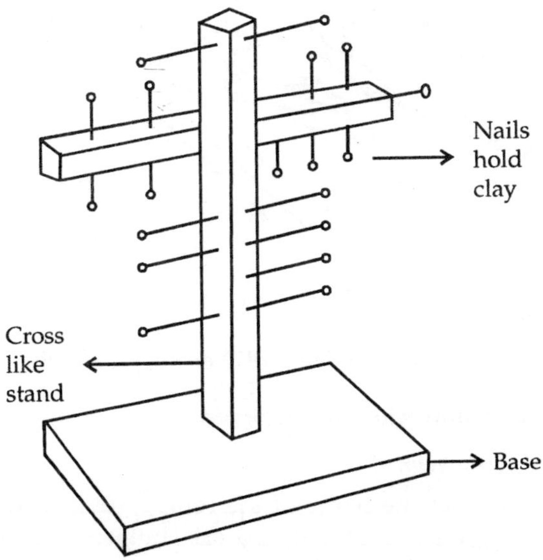

Fig. 74: Stand for Portrait Model

Making of Relief Models

Geographical terrains, agriculture land ceilings and river formation are depicted by relief models. We will need a base for a relief model. It can be made out by plywood or cheap planks used in packing cases. Prior to making a relief model we should know about form of the terrain we are going to depict. We should arrange the material. We can make a relief model out of clay. To make it lighter we put the dried grass or leaves on the base first in the form of the train. After this we should spread wet clay over it. When the clay is half dry we can give the final form by scratching extra clay. When it is fully dried we can give a coat of Plaster of Paris over it. When applying the coat of plaster of Paris we insert artificial greenery planting trees etc. The areas which are to be shown grass, can be shown with coloured wooden saw dust.

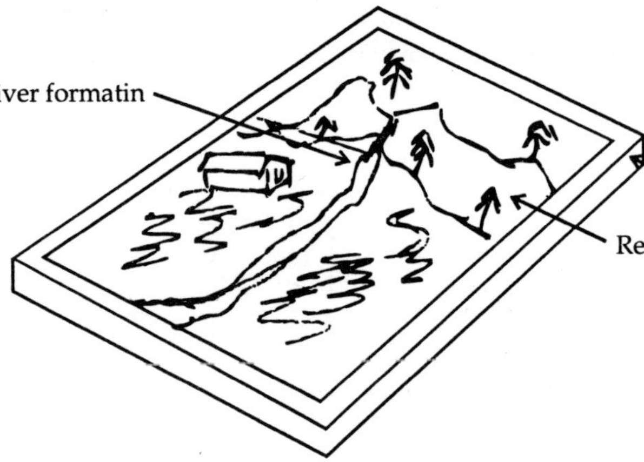

Fig. 75: A Relief Model

Relief models can also made of thermocole sheets.

Preparation Visual Aids out of Scrap

1. Scrapbook Arrangement

As a matter of fact the name of the scrapbook is misnomer. Of course it is prepared out of scrap material but it is an instructional book. Sanjay Baru in his article "packaging is all" in times of India dt. July 10, 1995 says that "India use more paper for packing rather than reading and writing". First step towards the preparation of 'scrap book is' to inculcate reading habits in pupils. It is possible if the teacher himself sets the motto for himself. Important articles from newspapers should be marked, cut and kept in a file. For arranging this cut material a file or sketchbook size 14" x 10", generally is used by art student. First of all sketch pages should be given margin lines on all sides and thereafter numbered. The first page should be kept or index. Index should be made subject wise. On any day when the teacher has time, the teacher should sort out the pictures and articles subject wise. After this, these articles should be cut straight with a used shaving blade. This instructional material should be arranged so artistically that it may give a good look aesthetically.

Likewise, many other three models like dioramas etc., may be made. For making such models the teacher have full knowledge the content he is going to teach. He should have a creative urge to create the memis of the content in actual shape. For all this the teacher should involve the students.

13

Audio-Visual Aids for Important Subjects

AUDIO-VISUAL AIDS FOR SOCIAL STUDIES

The basic function of a course in social studies, in the elementary and secondary classes is the development of certain basic concepts and understandings essential skills and desirable attitudes for improved social living, in every child who studies this subject. An individuals' behaviour is determined by his attitudes, constituting a stage of mental and emotional readiness to react social situations. Audio-visual instructions contributes vitally towards the development of attitudes, since it provides non-verbal experiences and various learning experiences nearer to the reality. By adding interest and involvement through innovation and motivation the visual aids reduce verbalism and make the textbook centred subject, like social studies, lively and interesting. By providing a variety of techniques, these aids bring the world into the classroom and thus make the learning permanent. They emphasise rich learning experiences through purposeful activities as against the mechanical repetitive and meaningless verbalism.

Education is an active process of socialisation, hence learning no longer remains as an individualised and centralised mental process. A major objective of teaching social studies is to provide the young learners with numerous opportunities for group work as a part of their learning process. Hence, it is advocated that the self-made visual aids developed by the teacher and pupils mutual participation, be used. As the basic learning unit in social studies are progressively evolved, related visual aids can be developed as class projects.

Visual Aids for Social Studies

1. Charts and Graphic Aids

Self-made charts other graphic aids like maps, diagrams, flash cards and flannel graphs serve as basic and universal aids in the domain of social studies.

Charts should be planned, designed, developed and prepared as a teacher-students' common cooperative venture. They are more useful than readymade ones, as they are geared to the actual needs and requirements of the units of teaching. Moreover, the students get a chance to do work with their hands. The teacher should take all available resources like pictorial magazines, encyclopaedias and other illustrated material. As a matter of fact the teaching of social studies should be so designed that it has all these materials.

2. Models, Dioramas and Three Dimensional Materials

Models and other three dimensional materials present an edited version of reality in social studies. They help the teacher to present certain physical and social phenomena in the form that gets the attention of the children.

Relief models help us to study all problems of man in his environments. Relief models of any parts of the earth or any physical phenomena or topographical features can be easily prepared with grass and clay or with the help of cow dung clay mixture. Papier-mache can also used but its availability or preparation in the classroom is a problem.

By combination a series of relief models on physical, economic, social or cultural topics, three dimensional models and atlases can be developed.

3. Maps and Atlases

Maps serve as a dominant and basic teaching material for social studies. Large flat or relief maps and atlases can be easily prepared on standard size (28" x 22") cartridge papers joining them together. The details can be enlarged on epidiascope and can be finished in colours.

4. Globes

Cheap and impressive globes can be prepared out of used clay pitchers, with paper pieces papier-mache. Clay should be used as a mould. In case a global is instantly required the clay picture itself may be used in making by covering its mouth:

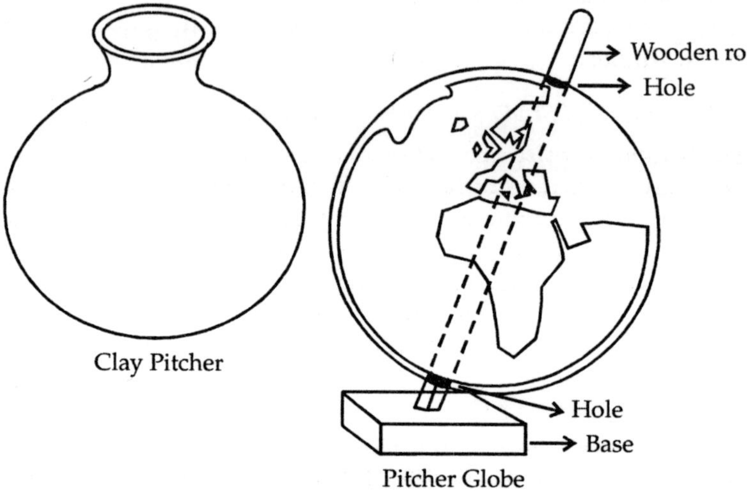

Fig. 76

5. Bulletin Bourds and Display Boards

Bulletin boards serve as windows on the world in social studies room. They provide the cheaper and multipurpose nucleus for visual education.

The display material can be arranged on bulletin boards or display boards and can be fixed in social studies room. These display material can be correlated to the topic in hand. The students should be involved in this work.

6. Developing Museum of Social Studies

A museum of social studies will serve as a vital source of instructional material readily available for integration into syllabus of social studies.

This can be developed through the imagination and initiative of the teacher and active participation of the motivated pupils. Social studies require a wide collection of objects, models and graphic materials which can be progressively developed through the pupil-teacher participation. Out of such materials a museum on social studies can be and should be developed by the students and teachers. This will enrich their experience and execute new interest in them for social studies. They will be motivated to use new reference material in search for answers to their queries about social studies.

7. Preparation of Study Kits for Social Studies

Study kits comprise a collection of audio-visual materials that can be easily seen, read or handled. These materials are assembled and correlated around one theme or topic. Such study kits are used for providing sensory experiences for learning. By encouraging students to help in the preparation of study kits in social studies, the students will be motivated to know more. All such materials can be assembled in small cardboard boxes.

8. Films for Social Studies

All motion pictures are shot against the backdrop of physical or social environments. Motion pictures are vital efficacious in developing social attitudes and conveying factual data. They are the most powerful media of supplying audio-visualised information about man and society. By overcoming the limitations of time and space, they present the social information in a scholarly and scientific fashion. Motion pictures make the past real and present understandable.

Audio-Visual Aids for Teaching Languages

Languages, spoken or written, are the vital source of communication in the human world. There are many diversities and variations in human inhabitant in the world, so the languages and human dialects change after every 10 miles. This has been asserted by linguists. As a communication media, the language do narrate the events of the world. Without narration neither any information nor knowledge is possible. With the knowledge of languages, the man learns and gathers his store house of knowledge. All sciences are taught through language. All audio-visual aids which are used in teaching science and humanities are also used in teaching languages excepting a few exceptional ones as language laboratories. Language laboratories are equipped with recorded gramophones, tape records, VCR, VCP, radio and TV which are used in language teaching.

Audio-Visual Aids for History the Utility of Audio-Visual Aids in Teaching of History may be Summed up as Under

History should be presented in a lively manner in the classroom. Audio-visual aids help to give life to a history lesson and supply a concrete basis for thinking and learning in history. Thus they reduce meaningless verbalism. Use of teaching aids converts the dull subject to a realistic one. Temporal orientation of the learner is basic in the learning of history. Audio-visual aids take us even to the remotest period of history, whereby past comes to life and the present is enlightened. They bridge the gaps in different periods and develop a continuity of thought.

The teaching of history is to be connected with direct purposeful experiences Audio-visual aids provide this. Such experiences cannot be easily obtained through verbalism or other materials. Through Audio-visual teaching aids can do this quite easily. Audio-visual aids develop a high degree of interest in the students and stimulate them for self-activity.

Hence Audio-visual aids by reducing verbalism, adding interest and involvement, stimulating students for self-activity and developing an urge for self-activity, and of thought, they make learning in history permanent.

SPECIFIC AIDS FOR TEACHING HISTORY

Graphic Aids

- Photographs and pictures are very useful in teaching history. Pictures and articles on history should be collected and preserved in a scrapbook. Scrapbook collections is very useful in teaching history.
- Charts as a graphic aid is very useful in teaching history. Pictures of monuments and rulers should be enlarged on epidiascope and a chart be developed. Charts on costumes battlegrounds, chronological charts, art and artefacts and coins may give a good sensory experience to the students and make learning permanent and interesting.
- Maps as a graphic aid are also very useful in teaching history. Maps given in textbooks and atlases can also enlarged on epidiascope and should be developed with H.B. Pencil and sign pens.

- Diagrams and Plans Diagrams on action plans like war operations may be drawn on a paper or chalk board and be used when wars are being discussed in teaching of history.

Display

Displays when arranged on a topic showing to various aspects can serve as vital tools for teaching aids in history. Black boards, flannel boards, bulletin boards and other boards as plywood board can be used for display.

Three Dimensional Aids

Three dimensional aids like models, dioramas, objects, specimens like weaponry, coins, scrolls, puppets and mobiles etc., are useful in teaching history. For making models old used cheap things should be used. For example the Sanchi Stupa can be made out of a used water fashionable waterpot called Surahi.

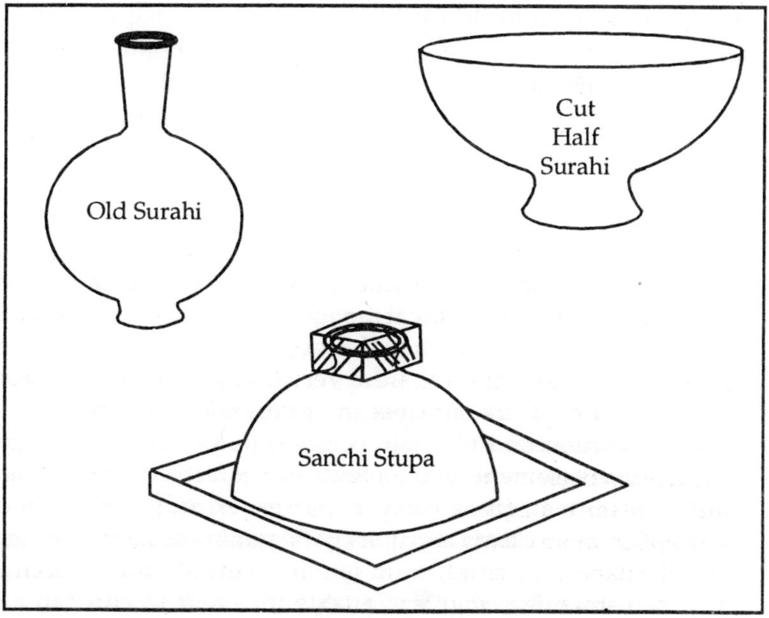

Fig. 77: A Model of Sanchi Stupa made out of a used 'Surahi'

Projected Aids

Films, filmstrips and slides are generally used in teaching history. Films on history can be obtained from film libraries. National Institute of Educational Technology, NCERT, Archives and Modern Gallery of Art, New Delhi have such libraries. Film-strips and slides should be developed by teacher and students themselves in school itself. This will provide a lot of experience to the students.

Activity Aids

Activities like field trips, dramatics, mock durbars if arranged will be very useful in teaching of history.

Miscellaneous Aids

Miscellaneous aids like study kits recordings and radio can be used as aids in teaching history.

Audio-Visual Aid for Teaching Civics and Economics

Teaching aids for teaching civics and economical are identical to teaching aids used in social studies. Only few other things like brochures, statistical information are also used. These subjects have different subject-matters so the graphic aids and dimensional aids will be different. But their method of preparation will be the same as for the social studies.

Visual Aids for Teaching of Mathematics

Teaching aids or audio-visual materials are not new for the development of mathematical thought. Most of the elementary and basic concepts, on which the super structure of modern mathematical theories rest, were evolved by man out of his direct experiences. If we analyse a mathematical problem, its comprehension and ultimate solution hinges around a correct perception of elements of the situation involved. The audio-visual aids present multi-sensory experiences and stimulate our perception more clearly and quickly. By putting something concrete into the hands of a child, or presenting in the form of a visual aid, will be something, that will enable the child to enter into the learning situation and will simultaneously generate auditory, visual, aural, textual and muscular sensations, which when united, lead to better conceptualisation of problem.

Now here are maxims which proceed from concrete to abstract and from known to the unknown, so true in the teaching of mathematics in general and arithmetic in particular. The child's experience of number and the fundamental operations connected with them has to be developed through the sense of sight and hearing.

The traditional approach to teaching arithmetic, whereby abstract concepts are usually presented to pupils in an authoritative manner, under conflict model of teaching, should be discouraged. The availability of audio-visual aids stresses the prior presentation of concrete experiences first. If the abstraction is to be meaningful it should be based upon first hand experience. Numerical abstraction can be developed with series of abstraction with things. Then reverse deductive process can be applied.

Teaching materials or audio-visual aids tend to stimulate reality in the classroom. These help in making the abstraction involved more tangible and concrete. For example the objects and game in teaching arithmetic and geometry represent life like manifestations of quantitative and numerical relationships. It is important that mathematical concepts grow out of direct personal experiences.

Various Categories of Audio-Visual Aids used in Teaching Mathematics

1. The Audio-Visual Apparatus for K.G. Schools

This is a set of scientifically graded wooden blocks, beads, models, etc., whereby the comprehension of the child in the realm of mathematical concepts is gradually developed. This can be seen in most of the nursery schools oriented to Montessorian techniques.

2. Puzzles, Performance Tests and Indoor Games

A vast variety of such items is available now-a-days in the shops dealing with toys and indoor games. Most of these can be profitably harnessed in the classroom to teach arithmetic.

3. Group Projects and Play Way Techniques

The teachers can, with their ingenuity, devise many such techniques and develop or devise activity related thereto, to teach mathematics lesson.

4. Display Material

Mathematical material collected from science magazines can be displayed or bulletin boards. For small children geometrical and mathematical puzzles can be displayed on flannel boards by flannel graphs.

5. Geological and a System of Blocks of Various Sizes and Various Colours

The geo-board can be made of a plywood piece 18" x 8" piece with 2" squares marked on it. Nails of uniform size can be fixed circular rubber bands of various colours to be stretched around the nails making various patterns on the board. We can show 2", 4", 16" etc., squares. By putting them around nails we can develop triangles and so on; most of the geometric figures like polyons etc., can be made. This is helpful in teaching a variety of propositions in demonstrative geometry, arithmetical concepts etc.

The system of blocks can provide a physical and solid basis, for teaching fundamental operations in arithmetic and algebra.

6. The Family of Abaci or Number of Abacus

The abacus is an international and universally known aid. These days, wide variety of these aids are available and they are being used popularly. Abacus is a calculating frame of different colours.

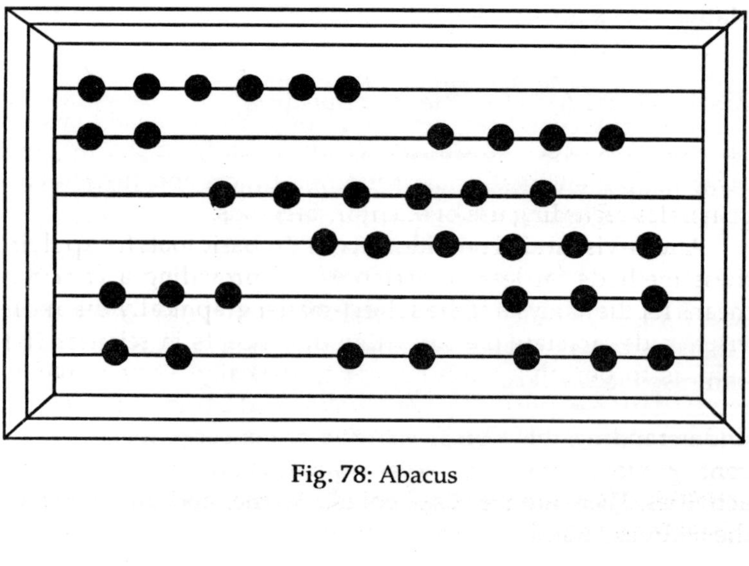

Fig. 78: Abacus

7. Mathematical Instruments

Mathematical instruments such as laboratory instruments applied instruments are useful for measurement. Also applied instruments such scales, callipers, compass and set squares are useful in teaching mathematics. Graphic instruments, slide rules, business machines and calculators are useful in teaching mathematics.

8. Films

Films in teaching mathematics are useful. Their purposes are:

- To create readiness for new concepts,
- To introduce new concepts,
- To provide understanding of social situations and their qualitative aspects,
- To develop computational skills and mathematical understanding,
- To create sensitiveness to a number of social situations.

9. Opaque Projector

Opaque projector is very useful to show recorded black board work for mathematics teaching.

10. Psychological Testing

Many of the mathematical instruments can be used in developing psychological tests for intelligence testing.

Audio-Visual Aids for Science Education

The concepts of science education are basically empirical. These outlines fundamental understanding of facts and their related principles regarding use of scientific methods.

Audio-Visual aids provide some of the basic tools for applying these methods for learning sciences. By providing a variety of means for the analysis of the subject-matter graphically, the audio-visual aids facilitate the formation of concepts in science. They help us to perceive environment empirically. They provide a physical basis, a purposeful orientation and a learning setting for understanding the logical analysis of concepts regarding the content. Observation and experimentation are direct purposeful activities. There are the basic tool of a learner and they constitute the bedrock of audio-visual experiences.

Graphic aids like charts and posters bulletin boards, still and x-ray models and other three dimensional concrete objects, tools, films, film strips, slides, other aids and activities like experimentation and demonstration are some of the basic and simple ways for science education.

The main types of graphic aids for science education are charts, posters, diagrams, graphs, maps, cartoons, comics, illustrations etc. Main characteristics of graphic aids are: vivid clarity, forceful description, effective presentation and emotional impact. Above all their didactic function is supreme which prepares the students for participation, and make elicitations possible.

Bulletin boards display the graphic and pictorial materials possibly linked up with the teaching topics, attractively and invitingly.

Of all the audio materials models and mock-ups are nearer to learning experiences in science. Models and mock-ups are republicas or reconstruction of the real things. They are contrived experiences where reality is presented in simplified contrived form for teaching science.

The role of films in science is to develop an acquaintance with the material world. Good science films depict the basic elements of scientific exploration. They depict the methods or processes that cannot be directly demonstrated or explained with special pictorial or graphic presentation. The depict the action observable vicariously by bring the world in the classroom. They simplify the observable action. They depict the unobservable action through animation. They stimulate reality through recorded sounds. There is a unique technical versatility of this medium by making use of photographic tricks. Film strips and slides being the distant things in the classroom which the students cannot see. For teaching biology x-ray models unveil the secrets of human and other animal organisms. Many things can only be proved through models. This is also true in mathematics teaching.

Some activity aids like demonstration are must in science education. Demonstration reveals clearly how things work and act. They add reality to experiments. In science, chemistry is basically taught better through demonstration. Science study kits play an important role in science education. Students should be encouraged to collect relevant materials connected with the topic. These material should be properly analysed and presented in the form of a study kit which will serve as a general source of motivation for all.

Finally a good of exhibitable materials for teaching science can be evolved. These can be correlated with certain basic themes and developed into an exhibition. A science room should have a bigger museum cabinet which certainly benefit the students.

Audio-Visual Aid for Technical Subjects

No where the preparation and rapport of pupil-teacher for the use of audio-visual aids is so important as in the teaching of technical subjects. By common planning and education in the form of well defined practical projects, the students learn quickly, develop the project progressively. This is only possible, if there is a systemic process of sensory observation and experimentation for the students. In our old system of teaching technical subjects, which was carried on purely in non-formal way, there was a wide and varied spectrum of visual display tools and raw materials followed by occasional instructions. Under such a non-formal system of education the learner was the son and, the teacher was the father.

Now-a-days the technical trades such as carpentry, black smithy, tinsmithy and pattern making are taught in Industrial Training Institutes, where the teachers follow the white collar jobs norms. Many of them are neither experienced nor proficient as compared to those who came up as artisans after getting training and skill acquisition on hereditary lines. If the trainees in Industrial Training Institute do not get sufficient sensory experience and demonstration they come out blank. It is, therefore, necessary that there should be ample provision of audio-visual materials in the institutions such as charts, x-ray models equipments, specimens etc. There should be permanent displays on the shop floors of these institutions. The students should also be given a chance of practical training in some reputed workshops and production units, as their senior counterparts in Engineering Colleges and Technical Universities are required to do as per their curriculum requirements.

14

Methods for Vitalisation of Audio-Visual Experiences

There should be pre and post methods for the vitalisation of gains of sensory experiences given to the students through the use of audio-visual aids:

FOLLOW-UP TALKS

Talking and writing remain the most popular forms of communication, and most effective. In education it is essential to make adequate preparation of the subject, and to use appropriate audio-visual aids entailed follow-up methods for the vitalisations the sensory gains. This will not only act as comprehensive teaching, but will stimulate the pupils and explain difficult concepts.

The most interesting approach towards the subject should be to develop selected bearing in mind the interest and needs of the students and their intelligence, capacities and experiences. These should be well understood and exploited in the classroom for effective elicitations. Once the topic has been chosen, the literature on the subject must be studied and the student must be advised to read it as well.

The talks may be planned for prior introduction of the topic and after completion of the topic. The duration of the talks should not be more than fifteen to twenty minutes. Important points may be explained. Many ideas have to be discarded which may be taken up in subsequent discussion or question time. So the teacher must have some information in reserve.

Any illustration or reference books which are useful for later use of the class, may be shown or referred in the class.

Having decided the main points for the lesson, the script drafting is an invaluable personal preparation, and should include an introduction, which is the main opportunity of arousing interest; the conclusion which may be provocative to stimulate discussion. In composing the script, the teacher should use as much of his own experience as possible, and illustrations of actual cases have an essential appeal.

Selection of audio-visual aids while contemplating introductory talk is necessary. If the talk has been of interest and has stimulated the class, there would be spontaneous questions. Traditionally questions are left to end, but efforts should be that the questions are asked in between and the introductory narration should stimulate for this.

GROUP DISCUSSION

What is Group Discussion?

The talk, is a didactic kind of education, which due to some participation of listeners and the talker is possible. The listeners just sit listen to a number of facts or opinions put before them. Most enjoyment, however, is obtained by exchanging views with other people, and enjoyment in group discussion comes from sharing experiences and participating indecisions with other people. This is a part of Socratic, participatory and permissive education.

Group discussion is not so much instruction, as a method when those faced with problems of every day life may be given new and wonder ideas, helping them to achieve a better understanding of, and support for, their own behaviour.

In didactic talk no 'feedback' is possible between the group and the teacher, and an evaluation of such a session is no easy matter. In free discussion, pupils may share their experiences and show their attitude to other members of the group. In this free discussion each one is helped to clear his/her own ideas and plan for new course of action with the support of group. For vitalisation of the Audio-visual aid a group discussion must always follow.

What Can it Achieve?

When compared with didactic forms of teaching, group discussion inevitably gives an impression of rapport and good feeling amongst the participants, who also enjoy their experience. In a well prepared discussion many facts may be learned, but prime advantage is the sharing of points of view and attitudes never heard before, and the realisation of aspects of the motives behind our actions. Others in the groups may have solved problems successfully, and new actions by the individuals may be more likely if the understanding, sympathy and support of the rest of the group, or if a member can find endorsement for his new attitude within the group.

PREPARATION FOR GROUP DISCUSSION

In practice the preparation for group discussion is a necessary as that for a formal lecture or talk, and the outcome is dependent upon this preparation and the skill and personality of the leader. In a preformed groups, the topic will emerge from the group, the topic will emerge from the group. And after the sensory experiences gained from audio-visual aids there will emerge many points to discuss. As such, the pre and post audio-visual aids' use discussion must be planned aiming at learning and consolidation knowledge. As discussion is an attempt to bring to light all the facets of the topic under development, question must be framed that are stimulating for the group and relevant to the topic which is being taught.

RUNNING DISCUSSION

For a free exchange of ideas between group members, the setting must be informal, a circle and the limited to twelve or fifteen persons. The qualities required by the leader include a sympathetic approach towards the group, and the sympathetic attitude to the subject also, an ability to avoid unnecessary intervention and genuine interest in guiding and listening to other opinions rather than his own.

Occasionally, there is a need to encourage the reserved and tactfully tolerate to verbose, turning questions passed to him back to the group.

The leader should sort out statement by way of introduction, so that the group know directions for the discussion to follow. From time to time he may need to sum up, and think of new direction the discussion should take.

Perhaps the guiding rule for successful group discussion is to remember that one is striving for better understanding of the problem under discussion. And in pre and pro Audio-visual aids discussion's main aim should be to elicit as much as possible from the students.

THE BUZZ GROUP

There is always an opportunity in education for teaching in large groups, although our ultimate aim must be consider the group size as much as possible. In large group it is difficult to achieve any participation unless the buzz is used.

The buzz group is a means of discussion and reporting that gives all an opportunity to express their views and opinions for further discussion by the whole group. This method can ideally be used in the classroom.

Members of the groups, setting either formally or informally are asked to turn so that they face five or six other people, and discuss for a few minutes only the given questions, which has been selected for the topic under consideration. In the case of pre and pro Audio-Visual aids use discussion students should be asked to record the important points emerged during the course of discussion. Buzz group discussion provides opportunity for further discussion.

THE PANEL DISCUSSION

In the panel discussion, a leader and three to six person talk informally before the audience. They have all been prepared in advance, and meet in planning session to define their problems and decide how the discussion will proceed. The function of the leader is to introduce the panel and the topic, and see that members keep the agreed plan of discussion during the meeting.

As a teaching technique, and specially after the use of Audio-visual aids in teaching, the panel discussion can make stimulating impact on students. It can prove to be a worthwhile experience in school teaching programme. In the classroom many pupils may be benefited and the process of reinforcement of teaching can be achieved.

The question selected must be chosen with regard to the capacity of the panel and their experience, and one at least be earmarked for each member. In this way the members are encouraged. The panel should be constituted out of the class students. Time for panel discussion should be fixed and divided among members. Such panel discussions are very useful for educating pupil about social sciences and humanities subjects.

ROLE-PLAY NG AND DRAMATIC METHODS

Most of us can remember the impact of some our teachers had upon us, but have forgotten those others who, for some reason or another never 'reached' us across the desktops. The teacher's role in the development character and personality of students is most important. Many of us must have taken a course of action owing to the influence of the teacher whom we liked and respected or who through insight and careful teaching moulded our lives.

Undoubtedly, understanding human relationship and testing them out is a lifelong long task, but there are general principles which if learned early may help us in our behaviour. These must be taught in the home and school.

Role-playing or 'acting out' different problems in human relationships, through social roles, give us a safe and ready method of testing our attitudes and behaviour, on others in different situations. As a matter of fact role-playing is an activity and for good education. Role-playing can be done prior to the start of lesson as an introduction, it can be done during the course of lesson development and even after the completion of lesson. Lesson in history, civics require mock-dramatisation in many cases. If the students are earnestly prepared for pre and post role-playing and role-playing during the course of teaching by the teacher the teaching may be very much stimulating. Role-playing as an aid builds confidence in students. 'Seeing ourselves as others see us' and seeing others as they would like us to see them are a part of role-playing. In this technique, students may play themselves as other roles. Emotion is an important factor in real life and communication and hence role-playing is significant and conveyed by gesture and other body movements. According to Indian theory of 'Rasas' propounded by Bharata, there should be complete identification between role-playing with the person of which role is being played. As per Indian nomenclature this identification is called 'Tadatmeya'.

SPONTANEOUS ROLE-PLAYING

The most effective role-playing is that which arises spontaneously during discussion and within group and which illustrate with simple example. There is a necessity to initiate the younger ones in role-playing for proper socialisation. Any change of attitude, coupled with new experiences and the resulting motivation of personality is a difficult task to perform; although the experience of life may do this for us. If we can sit back and identify ourselves with the behaviour of good people, we may get some insight into our difficulties and human relationship problems.

Role-playing is a safe substitute for some real life experience. It is, therefore, necessary that people should learn role-playing. It is an aid in itself and supplementary to audio-visual aids in teaching.

15

Audio-Visual Equipments

For effective and totality of a wide range of audio-visual experiences we have to depend upon audio-visual equipments. They provide the major tools for use of projected and audio-visual aids. In addition to these there are some simple equipments like pantograph camera which are hand used. The basic audio-visual equipments are:

16 mm FILM PROJECTOR

A motion picture film is one of the most effective audio-visual aids of the three sizes in which films are produced are – 35 mm., 16 mm. and 8 mm. 16 mm. size films are standard sizes for educational purposes at present. The 16 mm. film projector is portable, easy to handle and gives satisfactory film shows for audience up to about 600. For bigger audiences special arch projectors are required. Such projectors are used in cinema halls. The 16 mm. projectors are being manufactured by four or five firms in India. The prices are also reasonable. In this regard, for further information, the National Institute of Educational Technology, NCERT may be contacted. Useful accessories, which include a screen, a projector stand and a screen stand will cost in addition to cost of film projector. The projectors can be operated by teachers or librarians trained for the purpose, but when the work is heavy, say films are shown to students in many classes a separate projectionist should be employed. The main recurring cost is that of projection lamp used in the projector. A projection lamp lasts 20 to 25 hours of projection. The servicing and repairs of the film projector must be done by a trained experienced technician.

Educational films for use with such projectors are available from libraries such as those maintained by National Institute of

Educational Technology, NCERT, Adhchini, Mehrauli Road, New Delhi-16, State Audio-Visual Education Departments and Embassies and High Commissions. Also 16 mm versions of documentary films are also available from various offices of Films Division and feature films from distributors. Educational institutions can also purchase their own films. If judiciously used, the educational films can be one of the greatest assets to the teacher and beacon lights to the students.

FILM STRIP AND SLIDE PROJECTOR

Film strip-cum-slide projectors are available from number of firms in India. Indian models may cost up to Rs. 1,000/-. The projectors can be operated by a teacher and students. Patronage operated projectors are also available.

This projector can also project pictures from 2" x 2" slides i.e., made from 35 mm photographs. For large size of slides, as are used in Cinema halls for advertisements special projectors or epidiascopes are used.

Films are also available in libraries. These can also made in the classroom. The National Institute of Educational Technology, NCERT, Adhchini, Mehrauli Road, New Delhi-110 016, gives such film strips and slides on loan to schools.

EPIDIASCOPE OR OPAQUE PROJECTOR

This is used when pictures from books and papers and also magazines have to be projected on a screen, in a big size for the benefit of the class lecture audience. Few good Indian models are available in the market. Many makes also incorporate adjustments for projecting slides including those sizes bigger than 2" × 2". Such models are called Epidiascopes.

OVERHEAD PROJECTOR

The overhead projector is comparatively new but a very useful development for classrooms and lecture theatres. The teacher instead of writing on black board writes on a roll of cellophane paper, called transparency. This transparency is placed on the projector's projecting glass and projected on the screen at the back of the teacher. This means that the lecturer or teacher can teach while facing the class. Simple transparencies can be made easily by hand and without having recourse to photographic methods.

Till recently the overhead projectors were not manufactured in India but now these are available in Indian brands in the market.

Materials once prepared for the overhead can be stored and can be utilised again for subsequent lectures. Overhead projectors are very useful for those teachers who do repeat teaching in many sections of one class. One transparency prepared for black board work can be used in all cases. This provide same equals visualisation to all students.

MICRO PROJECTOR

This is used for projecting pictures from microscopic slides on a screen, so that objects which could only be seen by one student at a time through microscope, could be seen and demonstrated and explained to the whole class. Through the microscope the time can be saved. Microscope projector is very very useful in teaching biology and other bio-subjects. Microscope projectors were till recently imported. Now these are manufactured in the country itself, and are available in the market.

8 mm FILM PROJECTOR

Technological progress has now made it possible to provide sound track on 8 mm film. These films can, therefore, be as effective and useful as 16 mm films for audience up to fifty, that is, suitable for all average classes. It is hoped that 8 mm. film projectors and films will be freely available in India very soon.

The 8 mm size of films is especially convenient for short concept films with an average duration of 3 minutes. Such films cover a single concept or ideas and are used by the teacher for illustrating selected points from his introducing talk or lecture in cases where motion picture techniques can be especially useful in providing a clearer explanation or illustration.

SCREEN

All types of projectors require the clear white surface of good screen on which the picture may be projected. A popular arrangement is a 178 cm. × 132 cm. (70" × 52") screen with a tripod stand which can be folded into a compact portable unit when the screen is not in use. Such a screen may cost Rs. 1,000/- a little more. For classrooms a rear projection screen using tracing paper as the projection surface has been developed by the National Institute of Educational Technology, NCERT, New Delhi. This gives a bright picture which can be seen without darkening the room. But this type of screen has a disadvantage. It is not portable. Backwall of the room if brightly white washed, and if the room is darkened, will work as a screen.

TAPE RECORDER

Tape recorder is a very common thing these days. Every tape recorder has two-in radio sets which can play tape recorders also. Through this versatile audio aids, a teacher can record his own talks and lectures. He can also use it for recording the suitable voices of the students. If any student has a command over the English pronunciations, or an other student is good in music or any students has mastery in debate or rheotrics, all such verbal novelties can be recorded and played at later date for the benefit of the students. Recordings may also be obtained from the National Institute of Educational Technology, Mehrauli Road, New Delhi-16. The Tape Recorder is a great asset for teaching correct pronunciation, poetry, recitation, elocution, rhetoric, music and dramatics.

Tape recorders are being made by number of Indian firms, local manufacturers and models suitable for educational institutions are available for Rs. 2,000/- to Rs. 3,000/-. But Japanese made like Sony are still preferred.

RECORD PLAYERS

With the advent of long playing records (each side having a running time of about 25 minutes) talks, features, songs and language lessons were played through these records on gramophone. These were widely used in language teaching prior to Tape recorders. The gramophone and records were kept language laboratories. Such records, together with different types of music recordings can be played back on record player, which in effect an electrical gramophone. Earlier the gramophone were required to wind as wrist watches are wind up. The output of tape recorder and record players can be felt to an amplifier if a larger audience is to be covered.

MICROPHONE – P.A. AMPLIFIER SYSTEM

This would be an asset to any educational system. In educational institutions morning assembly is compulsory in which the whole school population is required to be present, and audience goes in thousands. To control the audience a microphone is a must. The system comprises an amplifier with one or more loudspeakers and microphones. Programmes from a record player, tape recorders, radio or directions from the Principal's office can be fed to the amplifier for a large coverage. Different classrooms in the school or college can be fitted with loudspeakers and programme from the amplifier can also be used or fed to these listening points as and when required. Alternatively the amplifier can also be used to feed loud speakers in a hall or field.

There is a wide variety and range of amplifying equipment available from number of companies in India.

No doubt the material is available, and the school can buy it, but until and unless it is taken care of by the teaching staff and other supporting hands the school the audio-visual equipment cannot prolong and give a good service. So it is necessary that all audio-visual equipment should be carefully handled then only it will remain serviceable.

16

The Teacher

Today audio-visual technology dominates the entire field of teaching and learning process. Audio-visual aids make teaching effective and learning easy. They reduce verbalism and help the students in catching students attention, motivating and stimulating them to learn. They also accelerate the pace of learning and increase the span of retention. They help the teacher to exploit the students potentialities.

Learning experiences appealing to senses are always more effective than abstract learning experiences. They turn the students as active participators and actors, taping their imagination and aesthetic sense. Thus, there is a strong case for using audio-visual aids in teaching-learning process not only in schools but in all other agencies of education like colleges, technical colleges, medical colleges, institutes of higher learning like universities and research centres.

But question arise, can audio-visual aids alone achieve the objectives of congenial teaching and learning? Can these replace the teacher? Answer is no. The audio-visual aids cannot work themselves as they are mechanised. A machine is invented by the man and serves the man. It is the teacher who will use the audio-visual aids for the benefit of the students as well as of his own. If properly used the audio-visual aids will yield good results, and the students will not suffer. Bad use of audio-visual aids will confuse, dishearten, disappoint and will lead the students on wrong track. As such, even the most effective audio-visual aids may become ineffective in the hands of a clumsy teacher. 'Right' use, of the 'Right' material at 'Right' occasion and place, and at 'Right' time constitute the 4 R's of the audio-visual programme.

A teacher who is desirous and keen of utilising audio-visual aids in teaching and make it innovative and interesting must be clear about the answers for the following questions

- **Why do I Teach?**

The teacher must be very clear about the educational objectives. He should have developed a sense and ability to differentiate between information and education.

- **What do I Teach?**

The teacher must be quite aware rather be must have a mastery on the content he is going to teach. Therefore, he must be prepared well before presentation for teaching.

- **How do I Teach?**

The teacher must be very clear about the teaching methodology. Teaching methodology should be so designed that there is maximum involvement of the student in knowledge development. Every student have some innate potentialities and can contribute in the knowledge development. Verbalism should be reduced.

- **Whom do I Teach?**

Human beings are said to be thinking animals, therefore, these are termed as rational beings. The teacher should take these 4Ts' in mind. In the present democratic and socialistic era oppressive rules have no place in any social sphere of human life. In the past oppressive conflict model of teaching was used in teaching. The teacher in the past had authority to suppress the child. He used to communicate information, be it right or wrong, the child did not dare to question it and accept it as it was. As such as, the child was a passive listener and the teacher was an active informer. The result was creation of obedient followers having no imagination and initiative of their own. These are the characteristics traditional non-progressive way of teaching in the past.

Therefore, the teacher should be quite aware about the aims and objectives of teaching, then only he can discharge his duties well. He should be fully aware about the innovative methods of teaching which should be based on democratic models of teaching than conflict model of teaching in which the teacher is always dominant and the pupil is always subordinate. The innovative methods always treat the pupils generally on equal footing. They are given full chance of participation, expression and contribution in the knowledge development. Such teaching require innovative techniques which may stimulate and motivate the pupils. Such innovative techniques and methods require the provision of sensory experience. All concrete or actual sensory experiences cannot be provided during the course of teaching and the use of audio-visual aids in teachings becomes inevitable.

The choice of audio-visual aids is determined by the stipulated aims and objectives of teaching, and the material and content to be presented to the pupils by the teacher keeping in view the techniques and methods to be employed by the teacher and the needs of the learner. Moreover, the actual sequence of teaching in which the aid is to be used also decides the choice of audio-visual aids. And aids may be used mainly in following situations:

- These may be used to motivate, prepare and stimulate the pupils to receive instructions at preparatory stage and prepare them for self-learning,
- These may be used to explain various difficult concepts during teaching for a lesson development. Their use should be at presenting stage,
- These may be used for reviewing and recapitulation of lesson and also for evaluation purposes, and
- In addition to all these instructional purposes the audio-visual aids can be used to generate awareness and for information purposes.

All this can be possible if the teacher is alert and aware about all these facets about the use of audio-visual aids and also, is ready to apply the pedagogic principles with regard to the use of audio-visual aids.

Generally, it is observed that majority of the teachers do not use audio-visual aids during the course of their teaching. Some of them even avoid using the black board. They come, deliver a lecture method and go. It appears that they are not satisfied with their job. This is because the teaching is their last choice in adopting a carrier. They always try to run for a profession which has given them a chance of livelihood. Some of the teachers who want to make teaching profession – a life long profession want to use audio-visual aids but they are not encouraged by the authorities due to many administrative reasons. If a nation-wide survey is carried on about the use of audio-visual aids in school, which is a necessity in national interest, it will be found that there is a dismal and glimzy picture with regard to use of audio-aids in teaching at all levels i.e., primary schools, secondary and senior secondary schools, and also in colleges, universities and in institutions of higher learning. And in this regard we are backward in comparison to other advanced countries.

Why this ugly situation with regard to use of audio-visual aids in our educational institutions still exists in the modern age of science and technology? This because our teacher is still traditional in respect of his/her teaching profession. There may be many reasons for this situation:

- The preparation of the teacher might be defective. There are very few teacher training institutions in the country which are fully equipped for training their pupil-teachers in the use of audio-visual aids. Majority of the teacher training prepare the teachers as nuts and bolts are produced in a factory. These institutions have commercial considerations in mind,
- The lack of attitude towards teaching profession by the talented youths because of low emoluments might be another reason,
- Top-brass in the education bureaucracy usually try to identify themselves with other administrative elite class officers. Once a teacher is appointed as principal he/she will maintain a social distance between him/her and other teacher. As such the teaching skills of the principals go to the background and administrative skills get preference,
- Hardly. there are very few teachers who are completely aware about the boundaries and obligation of the teaching profession. The institutions preparing teachers do not have any item in their syllabus as teaching profession and professional ethics. Many touch the boundary lines of syllabus in namesake. Many institutions do not have provision of teaching audio-visual aids,
- And when the products such ill equipped institutions come in the job market, they outbeat the students of the teachers' training institutions which prepare the students well,

- When these teachers are employed as teachers they fail to use the audio-visual aids effectively. With the result the students suffer, and other teachers also stop using the teaching aids.

As such, in teacher preparation the following items should be given top consideration:

- Only deserving candidates who have an aptitude for teaching should be selected for teacher preparation. And this is job of psychologists to find out suitable candidates,
- There should be a provision in teacher training programme to make the would be future teachers aware about the teaching and professional ethics.

The word 'Teaching' is from the word 'teach'. The word 'teach' is a derivation from the Anglo-Sexon word 'Taccon' meaning to impart, to instruct, to train. So teaching is an act of instructing. The word 'profession' which has roots in the Latin word 'professio'. The word 'professio' has its roots in Greek word 'profitere' meaning to profess, to lay down claim on new knowledge.

If we trace the history of teaching it goes to the antiquity. It is found in all societies of human beings teaching was done. Not only the man, the animals, birds and insects also do teaching to bring up their off-springs. In all human societies, there has ever been an urge to bring up and train them so as to earn their living and to live in society harmoniously.

The teaching starts from the family, community and perpetuates at the school and university. The teachers play an important role in teaching. The teacher is always supposed to have full knowledge of the subject and its methods of teaching and techniques in using audio-visual aids.

Teaching is an attempt to change the behaviour of the pupils by introducing them to new ideas and enlarge their mental faculties. In the past, some experienced persons took up teaching as vocation and trained youth.

- In India the Rishis in Gurukulas, Ashramas, basically dwelt upon ontology, epistemology and axiology. There existed four tier social structure under Varna system. Father trained the son in his vocation and the daughter was trained by the mother to take up family roles.

- In Hellenistic culture the Sophists – the travelling teachers, like Thales, Epicures, Democratics, Protagoras, Anaxagoras, Hippocrates and few others used to teach for their mere subsistence. They used to propitiate but they used to charge for that. On the other hand, there were their counterparts like Permendis, Hereclitus, Socrates, Plato, Crito and Aristotle, who lived for profitiating of new knowledge and promotion of philosophy. They discussed metaphysical, ontological, epistemological and axiological issues like opposites, law, justice, education, good or bad; and justice, truth, beauty and society. They encouraged to think, rationalise and prophitiate.

Guilds in Europe promoted vocational education, Sufis in Islam promoted religious tolerance. Buddhism and Confusism teachers were non-inclinative.

So a teacher is one who passes acquired knowledge to those who does not know. And a professionist teacher is one who tries to acquire more knowledge. Can a teacher be considered a professionist or the teaching is profession in the modern age? Sociologists are sceptic about it. A profession is relationship between an ignorant and an expert, according to T.H. Marshal. A professionist should have specificity in the discipline he is pursuing. He should have sincerity and commitment to his client, as well as to his profession. A professionist should maintain a professional ethics like ethics maintained in medical profession. Hippocratic oath is undertaken by all doctors for maintaining unflinching sincerity for their patients who are their clients. A professionist should have an intense urge to acquire for fresh knowledge for enriching their abilities. He should involve himself in professional bodies for the furtherance of his knowledge. He should not have material craze and should be non-inclinative. Finally a professionist should lead a simple life. Teaching is a process of passing knowledge skills. And teacher motivates and stimulates the students further acquisition of known by one's own efforts and he should be non-inclinative.

Originally the following vocations were considered as professions:

- Clergy (Bishop and priest etc.) because they were considered non-inclinative, committed to their vocations and sincere to their devotees.

- Medical man because he was also non-inclinative and committed to his clients that is patients and used to add to his knowledge was considered professionment.
- Legal man because he too was non-inclinative and sincere to his clients.
- All of the professionists were eager to gain proficiency. They were sincere to their ignorant clients. They had to help the needy.

The teachers' client that is pupil is not an ignorant client like the clients of clergy, medical man and legal man. The teachers' client is an intelligent client and is eager to add to the proficiency of his teacher. Therefore, some sociologists are hesitant to recognise the teaching profession. But the teachers' main role is to elicit knowledge from his students and add to the storehouse of knowledge. In other words it can be said that profiliating is his main aim, so teaching should be considered as a profession. But some say that the present teacher is not non-inclinative. He is a paid servant. He tries to earn money from other sources like doing tuitions. Generally a professionist is one who is expert by his own efforts through carrying out researches, an earns his living for mere subsistence. He is very sincere to his clients and always tries to his specificity. But we look to the so-called recognise professions like clergy, medical profession and legal profession, they are also dwindled with material inclination. The medical man even after taking a Hippocratic oath is after accumulation of money. They are not sincere to their clients. We notice serious cases of negligence on the part of doctors in hospitals. Also the legal man whose main lifes motto to provide justice to the sufferer, now making money. In the past the black apron worn by a lawyer had a pocket on the back. And it was up to the wish of his client to contribute whatever he could. Now the legal man contracts the client. So also the clergy man, under his saintly robes he commits many serious crimes by doing tantras.

Professionals in the past strictly adhered to the professional ethics, some thought process and ideals guided them. Good deeds result in happiness and had deeds bring unhappiness and misery. In ancient India high values and life philosophy was based on Karma theory. Teachers were true professionals. The motto of their life was simple living and high thinking, deep sincerity towards students. Specificity was the motto of their life. They strived throughout their lives to know, metaphysical, ontological, teleological, epistemological and axiological issues. They were non-inclinative at the core of their life. For the good of society, they had to renounce the hedonistic life and live in Ashramas and Gurukulas where were situated in jungles. They had to live on 'bhiksha' for subsistence. The students (Shishyas) were also living in Ashramas and Gurukulas with their teachers (Gurus). This was to inculcate a feeling of renunciation in students. The same was the condition of the teacher in Muslim countries. Madarsas were also run on the pattern of Ashramas.

Old Indian teacher fulfilled all the requirements necessary for a professional. As a matter of fact old Indian teacher was a professional in true sense of the term, as he was:

- expert in the subject he was teaching,
- he was totally non-inclinative – simple living and high thinking was his aim of life,
- he used to maintain the professional ethics,
- he was committed to the cause and perpetuation of social structure by inculcating social values, traditions, customs,
- he used to enculturate the youth, and
- so the Indian teacher was widely respected in the society. His disciples used to treat him as their father,

Kabir said in a couplet:

> *"Guru Govind Dounoo Khare, Kake Lagoon Pawn,*
> *Guru Sheekh Diya Jukhai, Govind Deen Dikhai".*

> "Guru and Govind both are standing before me to whom should I pay respect, Guru gave me knowledge about Govind so I pay him respect".

Todays' teacher does not enjoy as much respect as the old Indian teacher enjoyed. For this the teacher is not to be blamed. The modern materialistic social structure is to be blamed. So the present teacher is a disappointed being. Once a teacher, always a teacher. Even the children from affluent class families consider the teacher as a poor being. Rich class consider the teacher as a straw in the material world. Hedonistic tendencies added much worry to the teacher. He also wants to have luxury gadgets like colour TV, Two in one, VCR, fridge, washing machines and other things of ostentations like sofa-set and double bed which are generally possessed by his businessman neighbours. The society generally blame the teacher if the school products are not good, but do not see the treatment of teacher getting from the society.

Any how, the teacher still holds the key. He is the builder of the nation. He should not forget that if the younger generation are not taught and educated well where the nation will go? The society must know that the present system of education is the gift of western societies which are based on anomie, conflict, exploitation and disharmony. The teacher is the crusader who can bring out the society from the bad evils of western influence on us and bail out our youth to a harmonious social circle as it was before we came into the western influence.

It is, therefore, necessary that the Indian teacher should assume the old Indian teaching professional role. Now, neither the teacher nor the students go to Ashramas and live in jungles. The teacher can make the classroom a pseudo-Ashram by inculcating of friendship, love and affection. This can only be done if he always tries to propitiate by bringing new elements in teaching which could stimulate the students to self-learning. Verbal communication cannot help to attain this aim. There should be some interactive system. Only the use of audio-visual aids in teaching, a positive friendly attitude towards the pupil, sympathy and rapport with the students can achieve this end. The audio-visual aids like any other work needs intelligence, diligence and devotion to work. And all these needs a sacrifice and hard work on the part of the teacher. If the teacher works to rule, he cannot make a profitable use of audio-visual aids in teaching. Use of audio-visual needs – thinking, imagination, planning, preparation, selection and timely use. The teacher alone cannot do all this. He will have to involve the students and seek the blessings and help of the principal, then only he can successfully use the audio-visual aids in teaching which can be a profitable to him and to the students.

17

Evaluation of Audio-Visual Aids Experiences

If etymologically considered, the word evaluation is the derivation of the word value. the word value is a derivation of the Latin word 'valere' meaning worth. The word evaluate means to find out the worth of a thing or action. It can be in the form of numerical validity or an utility appraisal. The word evaluation means an act of find out worth. Likewise the word 'assess' is a derivation of the Latin word 'assideo' meaning to set beside, or to find out value. The word 'examine' is a derivation from the Latin word 'examino' meaning to assess, to bring out, to observe carefully, to look into, to question, to consider all aspects, to question into a judicial enquiry, to question an accused and enquire into the working of any thing.

The genesis of concepts of 'evaluation' and examination centres around all human activities. Every human action is always entailed by a reaction. Most common characteristics, common to all human beings, is to evaluate the results of their action. With various needs and objectives in our mind we always desire to know the outcomes of our activities. So all human activities need evaluation and assessment. If the results are favourable we continue to do the activities otherwise we reformulate them or stop them if the results are unfavourable. Since the dawn of the society and human civilisation the man has ever been basing his activities on this premise. A farmer tills the land saws the seed with a hope the result will be good crop. A civil engineer plans and executes a road bridge hoping that it will facilitate easy road traffic. Likewise all human activities are done hoping good results. These activities are continuously evaluated and examined and if results are not favourable or up to the expected mark these are reformulated and executed. So all human activities entail good or bad results and require continuous evaluation and revaluation. All human enquiries led to the development of sociological, philosophical and scientific thought. And thinkers from time to time, from the times immemorial have been continuously contributing in this regard.

Teaching is, and has ever been, a foremost human activity carried on mass scale with certain stipulated aims and objectives, of which consequent results are always ascertained through evaluation, assessment and examination conducted on certain principles. Firstly, we have certain objectives in mind which motivate us to do certain activities for certain ends. Secondly, the activity is continuously assessed for the degree of success one obtains. Thirdly the pace of improvement occurs in the process of activity as a result of assessment and evaluation.

The process of teaching is a specialised activity. The teaching is an activity which involves the simultaneous performances in respect of three tasks:

- maintaining the classroom environment alive for learning,
- maintaining or providing learning experiences appropriate to the changing needs of the individual pupil,
- Involving the individual students in the process of knowledge development.

For implementing all these task the teacher is an active role player and participant. He plays a vital role in environment maintenance, managing student learning and simultaneously imparting instructions. This he can do if he has some supporting material at his command. He deals with the conscientious material. The students, his clients are not ignorant clients. He moulds them giving a good form to their personality enlightening them in spiritual, mental, physical, technological and other assorted fields by doing himself and make the students doing a lot of activities. As such the activities of the teacher can be compared with an artist or engineer or an artisan or technical man or a doctor.

The aims and objectives of education are many, as:

- mental development of the pupils,
- physical and emotional development of the pupils,
- academic and skill development in pupils,
- and above all social and aesthetic development in pupils.

The teacher is expected to do all these. Can he do it alone without aid? The answer is no. He can do with the help of teaching aids. To see the actual effects of audio-aids in teaching it is necessary to evaluate the use of these aids.

The use of audio-visual aids in teaching is multifaceted – the teacher, the students and physical facilities provided by the school administration are equally involved. If any of three i.e., teaching, the students and administration lacks in involvement the audio-visual aids, whatever might be their quality and standard, will fail to give good results. When looking to the outcome of audio-visual aids, contribution of all three i.e., teacher, the students and the school administration is to be seen and assessed. If any of these does not subscribe to keenness and devotion, there will be an utter failure and use of audio-visual aids will not give any positive results. Following are the expectations from them:

- The teacher should plan in advance about his audio-visual requirements and should apprise the school administration about the needs about audio-visual aids. If the teacher does not anticipate, what audio-visual aids would be needed, he should be evaluated negatively.
- After getting the required assistance from the school, the teacher should plan how to materialise his dreams for using these aids. He should enlist the help of the students in preparation and use of audio-visual aids. As far as possible the aids should be made in school or in the classroom. This aspect should always be kept in mind while evaluating the use of audio-visual aids.
- A lazy and disheartened teacher shall not be able to use the aids. The school administration should locate such teachers and should motivate them to use the teaching aids. This can only be done by the administration. If the administration fails to do it, there should be some mechanism that the administration can also be censored and evaluated, so that there does not remain any lack in the supply and use of audio-visual aids.
- For particular topic specific audio-visual aids should be thought of, therefore, due care should be taken to select appropriate teaching aids. There are situations when graphic aids only will serve the purpose. On the other hand there are topics where three dimensional aids will only

give good sensory experience and will make the things clear.

- On the other hand there will be occasions, when dramatisation will work, it should be arranged.
- Excursions and tours are also important for learning. These should be occasionally arranged.

For the outcome and learning yields, there should be committee of selected senior teaches to monitor all these programmes of use of audio-visual aids in teaching. This Committee should develop a mechanism to evaluate these.

With regard to benefit of the use of audio-visual aids in teaching, learning abilities of the students will show it. Monthly, periodicals and journals, newspapers if read carefully will demonstrate the futility of the use of audio-visual aids. Also the day to day student participation in classroom discussion will also reflect the usefulness of the audio-visual aids in teaching. The teacher should prepare a sort of check-list in this regard and should note and record the gains. If the students are getting motivated and stimulated to learn the use of audio-visual aids appears giving good results. If not, the programme of audio-visual aids should be reformulated and implemented more vigorously.

The organising committee formed for monitoring the use of audio-aids can conduct evaluation survey regarding the gains of the audio-visual aids. A simple questionnaire can be prepared for this evaluation survey and served to the students in the classroom through the respective class-teachers and, views of the students can be ascertained. A survey report be prepared. It should be presented before the Principal and necessary steps be taken to boost the use of audio-visual aids in teaching. This kind of general evaluation on the use of audio-visual aids will definitely yield good results. The individual students will get familiar to audio-visual aids and their use.

The audio-visual aids motivate and stimulate the students for self-learning classroom seminars and discussion should be arranged to find whether the use of audio-visual aids has actually created the habit of self-learning in students. The students if involved in visual aids will make many aids with their own hands. The contribution of the students in this respect should be observed. If the students are learning to do creative things the use of audio-visual aids is beneficial.

The examiner setting papers for the annual examination should also set such question which may be based to locate the use of audio-visual aids. This will encourage the use of audio-visual aids in teaching. And after some time a random checking may be carried on to find out the popularity of audio-visual aids in teaching. For audio-visual aids' evaluation techniques guidance may be sought from the National Institute of Educational Technology, NCERT, New Delhi and from the State Institutes of Education and Central institute of Education, University of Delhi. There are technical institutions like I.I.T., Roorkee, which have full-fledged departments of audio-visual education, guidance may be sought from these institutions of learning regarding evaluation of the use of audio-visual aids in teaching.

And finally the use of audio-visual aids by all school teachers should be assessed by an expert committee and, the teacher or teachers found using teacher aids logically and sincerely should be rewarded.

Bibliography

Ahluwalia S.L., *Audio-Visual Handbook*, NCERT, 1967.

Bhola B.R., *Material and Method of School Display*, NCERT, 1967.

Brow ı J.H. Lewis, *Audio-Visual Instructional Material and Methods*, McGraw Hill, New York, 1959.

Clauder A.C. and Cypher S.C., *Audio-Visual Techniques*, Noble and Noble, New York.

Dale Edger, *The Audio-Visual Methods in Teaching*, Dryden Press, New York, 1957.

Dent E.C., *The Audio-Visual Handbook Society for Visual Education*, Chicago, 1946.

De Kieffer and Cocharn L.W., *A Manual Audio-Visual Techniques*, National Publicity Council, New York, 1956.

East M, *Display for Learning, Making and Using Visual Materials.* Edition by Dale.

Encyclopaedia of Philosophy Vol. 3, pp. 5-38, Collin Macmillan Ltd., London.

Fin J.D., *Audio-Visual Equipment Manual*, Dryden Press, New York, 1967.

Hans B.R. and Pack H.B., *Preparation and Use of Visual Aids*, Parentic Hall, New York.

Jeswani K.K., *Communication and Media Techniques*, Central Institute of Education, Delhi, 1968.

Kleinschmicut H.E., *How to Turn Indian into Pictures*, National Publicity Council, New York, 1950.

Lane J. and Tolleres B.K., *Planning Your Exhibit*, National Publicity Council, New York.

M. Herranya, *Indian Philosophy*, Oxford University Press, London

Mukerjee, *Audio-Visual Education.*

Mcknown H.C. and Roberts A.B., *Audio-Visual Aids to Instruction*, 2nd Edition, McGraw Hills, New York, 1949.

Pierre Denes and A.J. Dalzell, *Health Education,* Social Sciences Paperbacks, Tavi Stock Publications, New Fetter Lane, London EC 4.

Ramshaw H.G., *Skills in Black Board Writing.*

Seton Murie, *The Film as an Education Force in India,* Ministry of Education, New Delhi, 1956.

Weaver G.C. and Bollinger E.W., *Visual-Aids: Their Use and Contribution,* Harper Brothers, New York, 1957.

Wittich W.A. and Schuller C.F., *Audio-Visual Material: Their Picture and Use,* Harper Brothers, New York, 1957.

Index